THE MIKE DONOVAN SAMPLER

This book, a sample from each of my 90 books, serves a triple purpose: 1. It is a fun and informative read at face value, a book I will be happy to offer for sale; 2. **It is the ultimate query letter for publishers**; 3. It helps me keep track of all my books.

This is 'edutainment.'

TABLE OF BOOKS
1. 101 Stories of American History
2. Early American History: From the Vikings to the Stamp Act
3. From Revolution to Constitution: Volume One, From the Stamp Act to Valley Forge
4. From Revolution to Constitution: Volume II, From the French Alliance to Federal Hall
5. The USA in the Time of George Washington: 1789-1797
6. The USA in the Time of John Adams: 1797-1801 [Most of these 'USA' books have also been released, in large font, under the title 'The United States in the Time of' with Michael Edward Donovan the author name. They are two versions of the same book.]
7. The USA in the Time of Thomas Jefferson: 1801-1809
8. The USA in the time of James Madison: 1809-1817
9. The USA in the Time of James Monroe: 1817-1825
10. The USA in the Time of John Quincy Adams: 1825-1829
11. The USA in the Time of Andrew Jackson: 1829-1837
12. The USA in the Time of Martin Van Buren: 18371841
13. The USA in the Month of William H.Harrison: 1841
14. The USA in the Time of John Tyler: 1841-1845
15. The USA in the Time of James Polk: 1845-1849
16. The USA in the Time of Zachary Taylor: 1849-1850
17. The USA in the Time of Millard Fillmore: 1850-1853
18. The USA in the Time of Franklin Pierce: 1853-1857
19. The USA in the Time of James Buchanan: 1857-1861
20. The USA in the Time of the Great Civil War: 1861-1865
21. The USA in the Time of Andrew Johnson: 1865-1869
22. The USA in the Time of Ulysses S. Grant: 1869-1877
23. The USA in the Time of Rutherford B, Hayes: 1877-1881
24. The USA in the Time of James Garfield: 1881
25. The USA in the Time of Chester Alan Arthur: 1881-1885
26. The USA in the Time of Grover Cleveland: 1885-1889, His First Administration
27. The United States in the Time of Benjamin Harrison: 1889-1893

This is from the book, *101 Stories of American History*:

GRANT MEETS KING EDWARD - 1877

Almost as soon as he got out of office, Grant got out of town. With his wife Julia, and his son Jesse, the beleaguered ex-prez left the country for a grand tour of Europe. The Grants departed Philadelphia on May 17, 1877 on the cruise ship Indiana. Thousands were there to give the Grants one spectacular bon-voyage.

The first stop was Liverpool where he was welcomed as if he was Sir Paul McCartney. In London Grant checked into a five star general hotel. He was in his room reading the paper and about to crash when, at about 9:00 p.m., he heard a knock on his door. He opened it up and there before him stood Edward the Fifth, the King of England.

Grant was scheduled to have a formal audience with the King the next day, but Edward decided to first make an informal social call.

The Fifth cracked open a fifth and they had a charming evening together, two giants in the calm eye of the hurricane. To be a fly on the wall for that one. The next day they were grandly introduced to each other at court and pretended to meet for the first time. I wish Americans running for president would do that before debates. Set politics aside and break open a bottle together. Then they wouldn't want to break one over each other's heads the following day.

Grant went on to Paris where the French treated him coldly, because they felt that the United States had sided with the Germans in the Franco-Prussian War of 1870-71.

Grant then went to Berlin where the Germans treated him warmly, because they felt that the United States had sided with the Germans in the Franco-Prussian War of 1870-71.

This is from the book, *Early American History*: From the Vikings to the Stamp Act.

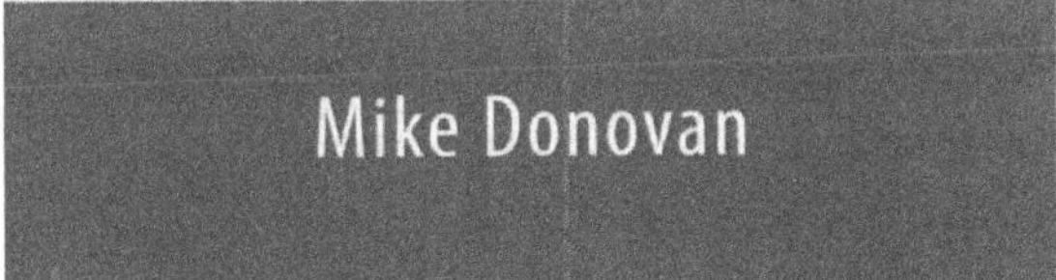

JUAN SOLIS - 1516

Juan Solis was a Portuguese sailor who discovered Uruguay for Spain. His demise provides some food for thought.

Juan Diaz de Solis had sailed with the Pinzon Brothers to Nicaragua in 1508. JDS was an important naval figure in Spain.

Solis set out for South America in October 1515, seeking to find a route to the other side by a careful and prolonged exploration of the coast. The three Spanish caravels had plenty of provisions.

De Solis came to the entrance of the great River de la Plata. His ships entered the wide mouth and de Solis went upriver. His ships had been chosen lightly: they were not very large, so they would be light enough for just such a mission. There was an island in the middle of the wide river, and Solace named it Marty Garcia Island, after a man who died on the voyage over. Solace should have named it after himself. He had hours left to live.

Juan led a landing party of nine, which set down on the north bank of the river. Within 20 minutes, they were under attack by the merciless Charrua Indians. The men on the ships could only watch in horror as the eight Spaniards were killed and then immediately eaten! One guy escaped and made it back to the ship, and it wasn't Solace. There was no solace for Solis. The leader was a burrito. Mission aborted. The Solace quest to find the passage to India was over. The boys sailed home. Watching your shipmates become grilled hot dogs can take the fun out of any expedition.

It's hard to digest this story without siding with the victims, but keep in mind that the only reason Solis had gone ashore was to plant a stupid flag on the soil so he could claim the land for Spain. When you come right down to it, the flagging was more of an act of aggression than the Charrauas eating the eight men for supper. Juan's flag represented 100 ships and 10,000 troops leaning over his shoulder with a menacing glare.

The Indians chanted a slogan at the ships as they sailed away. A friendly Indian on board translated it to roughly mean, "Next time, don't forget the gravy."

This is from the book, *From Revolution to Constitution*

ARNOLD'S MARCH TO QUEBEC - LATE 1775

Arnold's Maine moron march left Newburyport, Massachusetts on September 2, 1775, and arrived near the gates of Quebec in late November. The march was brutal in a hundred ways. There were no roads of any kind across the roughest and most mountainous lands on the eastern half of the continent. And, to use Maine language, it was going to get wicked cold wicked fast.

Washington contracted a boat builder in Kennebec to construct 40 bateaux on short notice. He told Wash that he couldn't do it in the short time allotted. Washington told him you have to. He said he'd try.

If this were a movie you'd have a montage of people working hard, with dreadful music, and making the finest bateaux in the world; and these boats would save the day for the Americans. But this was real life. The 40 boats the AE picked up at Kennebec became, over the long haul, more of a liability than an asset. The work it took to carry them across the land portages did not pay off in benefits because too many of them leaked and broke up. It took major efforts to fix them and most of them in the end were lost. By the time the expedition reached the pivotal Megantic River it had only six bateaux left.

The brave conquistadors assembled on the Cambridge Common on September 13 and marched north to Newburyport.

Scout ships checked to make sure the coast was clear to the mouth of the Kennebec River. When they reported all clear of Royals, the Arnold Expedition sailed out of Newburyport on ten schooners.

The 1,100 men were divided into two battalions, one under Lieutenant Colonel Greene, the other under Lt. Colonel Edward E. Slaughter. There were 13 companies of about 90 men each.

The Expedition picked up their bateaux and started up into the Maineland on October 9, just as there was a chill in the night air. These guys had marched out of Cambridge in the summer estimating the trip to Quebec would be finished in time for Halloween. Instead, they hit the snows of winter and still hadn't reached Quebec Province, let alone the Citadel. When the trip became arduous, the units broke up, covering large distances at will, one surpassing the other, then being surpassed again.

Just getting up the northern route of the Kennebec was rough. They were marching against the flow. Some bateaux were lost even at this early stage.

The first major portage was across 'The 12-Mile Carrying Place.' The 12 was 10 times tougher to cross than anyone had expected. That got them to the Dead River. At this point there had been so much hardship that a meeting was held to decide whether to call the whole thing off and go back to Harvard Square. Four-hundred levelers voted to go back. Arnold and just over 600 decided to drive on.

The intrepid 600 fought against the tide of the Dead River for 20 horrid miles. This was where the weather went nuts and nearly drove them crazy too. Torrential near freezing rain turned the Dead River into a lake. The whole region was a lake. The guys were waist deep in cold water and had to fight their way out of that for miles, while their boats got smashed up, their provisions and food got washed away, and units became so separated that some men got lost and died out there. It was insanely bad, and they were only half way to Quebec, with winter closing in.

At the west end of the Dead River was the next big portage; but the West Branch of the Dead River, which was supposed to be the smooth link in the middle of two tough portages, turned out to be a rougher stretch than either of the two portages, so there was no break in the brutality.

Across the several ponds and portages they came to what is now Arnold Pond and then to the Arnold River. Arnold Pond is on the American side and Arnold River is on the Canadian side. Arnold River empties into Lake Megantic which in turn feeds the Chaudiere River which flows north to the St Lawrence near Quebec City.

Here the men at last saw signs of civilization, yet it was ironically at this stage that starvation became acute. The cold was getting worse. There was a lot of snow and ice. At this stage, across the highlands thresh-hold, some men were actually left behind to die. No one had the strength to carry them and there was no way to help them.

Cold was the monster, not King George. The guys rubbed each other's feet at night to prevent them from falling off. Frostbite was routine. Death here and there. Men were drinking moccasin juice. The oxen had been killed and eaten a long time ago. They hadn't performed well in the clutch anyway. One guy looked at Captain Farrel's Yorkshire terrier and said "I could go for some tasty hot dogs." Then they voted on whether to kill and eat it. I won't tell you what happened next.

The ragged men finally put the last six remaining bateaux in action at the top of the Chaudiere River, the one with all the white rapids. Within ten minutes, all six bateaux had broken into bits against the big rocks in the Chaudiere. A march one mile down river revealed a treacherous waterfall - The boats and the invaders inside them would have been bashed to bits - The destruction of the last six boats had accidentally saved many lives.

Arnold's Patriot lunatics, minus at least 100 dead, now had to march all the way to the St Lawrence River, another 80 miles away. Almost a third of them were sick, many had no shoes or weapons, and all were on the verge of starvation.

Then, like a mirage, there appeared three of their advance party driving cattle back towards them! Everyone raced towards the first beast and slaughtered it on the spot. They ate like burger kings. The rest of the march to the St Lawrence River was a better experience. There was some elation when they got there.

The situation was still precarious, but at least they weren't going to starve to death and didn't have to sleep in three feet of ice water.

This is from the book, *From Revolution to Constitution: Volume II*, From the French Alliance to Federal Hall [the previous book has been divided into two volumes]

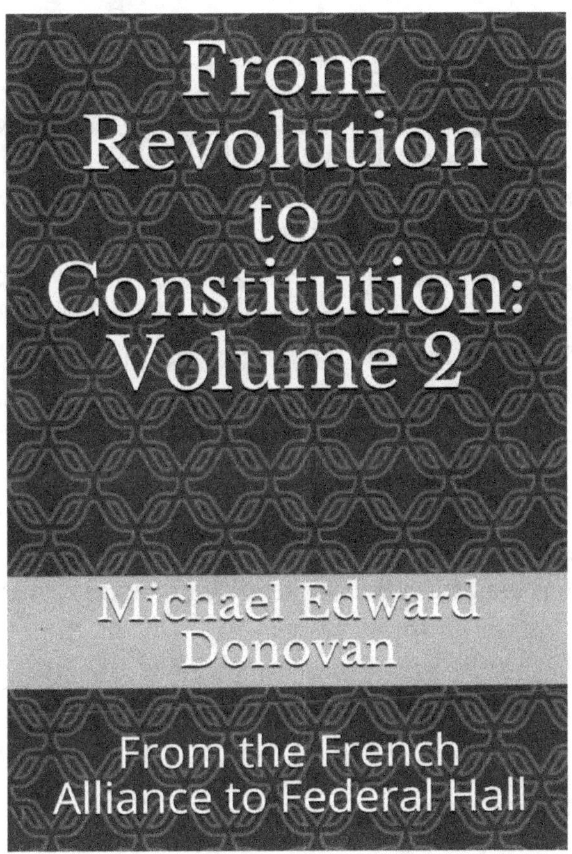

SULLIVAN EXPEDITION TO THE FINGER LAKES - AUGUST 1779

When the British shifted to the Southern theatre, Washington realized he had a few more options with his forces in the north; and he was happy to give them something to do. It wasn't quite a 'use it or lose it' situation, but why have idle troops while Greene and Cornwallis were running around the Carolinas?

So Washington and his brains trust decided on a punitive expedition to the wild west of western New York and northwest Pennsylvania: that is the regions where the year before, the Indians,

Tories and British had combined to massacre Yankee settlers at Cherry Valley, NY, and Wyoming Valley, PA. The mission was to devastate, retaliate, and come back with hostages for future talks.

Many names were suggested to Washington to lead the expedition, but he waved his hand away and said:

"Give me Sully."

George knew that General James Sullivan would teach them a lesson. This would be the mother of all reprisals.

Sullivan soon had more than 4,000 troops of scattered types. 4,000 might not sound like much, but it was quite a lot for the western theater. Bad guy Butler, the Tory commander in western NY, learned via spies, of this Patriot build-up going on in Pennsylvania. It was like Ike gathering divisions for the cross-channel invasion. The Yanks were coming back with vengeance. The Red/Redcoat side knew it was coming, but what could they do? Butler, and his Indians and Tories, added up to only 1,100, and both had show a propensity for breaking out Merlin's magic act when the going got tough. The Americans were more committed.

The Sullivan plan was to avoid the traditional attack routs from the outer edges of Indian country, that is, by way of the Hudson and then the Mohawk. Sully was going to go right up into the central Indian lands by way of the Susquehanna. The minute he makes contact he is in the heart of Indian country, and the fight spreads from there.

It worked.

But it took a while.

The campaign was supposed to commence in early June. On the Fourth of July, Sully still sat still. He was having a pen-pal fight with Washington on what was the fair balance between the need for supplies, and Washington's need to get the offensive moving while it was still baseball season. Sullivan was angry that the locals around him in Pennsylvania had not contributed troops, munitions, or any other supplies.

At one point some towns in Pennsylvania petitioned Sully to spare some troops to defend them from Indian attacks. James wrote back a curt denial:

"I'm sure your state militia is available to help you, since they refuse to help me."

Sullivan finally got the war wagons on the move at the end of July. In spite of the delayed start, his mission was a strategic success. There was only one spot where the enemy stood and fought back like pros. That was at Lake Archer, just south of Tioga, New York. The Arch was a draw, with some 30 total KIA's, but even that one time, it was the enemy who quit the field and fell back towards Niagara. Other than that there was no genuine resistance to Sully's Raiders.

A second American column under Colonel Richard Clinton met up with Sully's 4,000 at Tioga. It was now a monster force, 6,700 soldiers ready to go up into the five Finger Lakes and dish out five-finger slaps.

Sully wrote back to Washington that the Indians and the Tories want to come to some sort of negotiated settlement, and end the fighting.

Washington wrote back, and this is not an exact quote but is absolutely accurate:

"The last thing I want is a negotiated settlement. Great, now that they're about to lose, they want a diplomatic solution.

Look, Sully. We're old friends. Read my lips. Destroy the region. We have to completely eliminate the Indian food supply. We want to drive them out of the region with such righteous cruelty that not only will they never again threaten us, they will never return. Use terror. If you have to kill a lot of people, I will back you up 100%. That is they price they must pay for what happened last year at Cherry Valley and Wyoming. You now have my word in writing that the policy comes directly from me. If they approach you to negotiate, it is a treacherous scheme to buy time and regroup for another massacre at our expense."

Sullivan read the message loud and clear. Get moving, and don't take too many prisoners.

Wow. That's tough stuff. Washington must have just had a fight with Martha when he penned that one off.

Sully's Rangers wasted west New York for a month. It was very ugly. General W. T. Sherman would have said, "Hey, this is a bit much!"

Sully's Bummers would branch off and find new lands to destroy that weren't even on a map. They destroyed all the way from today's Elmira-Corning country, all the way up to the head of the Genesee River. It was a hot dry summer and it was easy to burn crops and Indian dwellings.

After the Revolution, the ex-upstate Indians referred to President Washington as 'Destroyer of Towns,' as his matter of fact name. They did not blame Sully. They knew their history - that the destruction of their lands was Washington's plan and decision.

Most of the red-refugees fled west into Canada.

Sully's Expo isn't as famous as it should be, probably because it makes the USA look murderous.

Sully and Clinton in the summer of 1779 killed a lot of Native-Americans to: 1) help win the war; 2) avenge Cherry Valley; and to, 3) secure the beautiful Finger Lakes for long-term all-white settlement. George Washington literally used the word "terror" to describe what he wanted Jim Sullivan to inflict on the Indians. No one has really estimated the number of Indians massacred, but it's at least 200. The number that starved to death over the next winter was as high as the number killed directly.

The five Iroquois tribes of the Finger Lakes were sent packing forever, but left their names all over the land (Seneca, Cayuga, Oneida, Onondaga, and Mohawk.) The Tiogas were also driven out, although Tiogas aren't Iroquois.

Sullivan's Savages returned east in the fall of 1779 as victors. The New York-PA Indian frontier would no longer trouble the Patriots in their goryous cause.

The news was very good for national morale. The Valley Massacres of 78 had been avenged.

The mission succeeded in devastating the region for Indian residence, but Sully failed to come back with the hostages. The SCOOM Indians were good at not getting taken as hostages.

As a war measure, the Sullivan Expedition was not a total success because the Indians who fled to Canada became fiercely loyal fighters for Britain. The Indians were not exactly eliminated as a fighting force; the Senecas, Cayugas, Onondagas, Oneidas, and

Mohawks were merely expelled from the region. Still, keeping the enemy at bay was part of the mission too, so overall it was a win, and Washington set the region up for All-American development after the war ends.

This is from the book, *The USA in the Time of George Washington: 1789- 1797*

ADVISE AND CONSENT

The new national leaders were feeling-out the new system as they worked it. The Constitution provided that the President could make treaties with foreign powers with "the advice and consent of the Senate." But no one knew exactly what that meant. Legal precedent for the President would have to be established through a delicate trial and error process.

One spring day, Washington and his Secretary of State, Thomas Jefferson, reached agreement on seven foreign policy decision-points. They decided to take them to the Senate for "advice and consent." The Senate didn't know they were coming, and was in active session when Washington arrived and told the doorkeeper that he wanted to address the body.

The guard went inside and announced to a startled Senate that the President had arrived and was going to ask for advice and consent.

Washington made a dramatic entrance and handed his papers to Knox, who passed them on to Vice President Adams, who started to read the first page out loud. Just then, a noisy horse and carriage went by the window and no one heard a word he said. The Senators asked Mr. Adams to repeat it and he did. This happened several times. Every noise pollution nightmare seemed to happen just when Adams tried to read out loud. One time it was a leafblower that made him stop.

Adams finally made it through the reading. Washington then addressed the Senate to expound on some of the points that had just been read, but again, noisy horses and buggies wet roaring by, and no one heard more than a word here and there of Washington's carefully thought out talking points.

After an awkward silence, Senator Morris asked that the full seven points be read again. Adams started all over again and this time the Senate deliberated on each point before the next one was read. Each time, the Senators came to the same decision: They were not sure, needed to study the issues further, and would give Washington the answer some time in the future. When this happened the seventh time, Washington turned rose red and rose from his seat, trembling with rage. Washington exclaimed with burning eyes, "This defeats the whole purpose of my coming here!" One witness later said that Washington managed to make angry eye contact with every single Senator in the room within the time frame of this one short sentence.

This was a defining moment in the American political system. If the Senate had snapped to serious respectful attention and appreciated the moment for what it was - the moment when Congressional influence on foreign policy was in the balance - all Presidential decisions in the future might have had to make their way first through the Senate. By making GW angry that Saturday morning, the apathetic Senate shot itself in the foot. Washington decided that from that moment on he would do as he pleased as President, and enact any measure on foreign affairs he wanted to. GW would consult the Senate for advise and consent only after the policy was decided on and implemented, and he would only do so when absolutely necessary as the Constitution dictated. Essentially this meant that instead of working out the governorship of the nation (especially foreign policy) with the Congress as a team, Washington would lead the nation as a powerful executive and the Congress could then say 'good work,' or, 'hold on a minute.' Congress was there to do second tier work and keep a check on the President's possible excesses through the power of the threat of impeachment. From the moment that Washington's insulted face turned beet red, Congress lost its power to make foreign policy, in part or in whole.

In June, the Senate proposed that the President should require its consent to remove a cabinet member from office. The Senate already enjoyed the right to advise and consent on cabinet appointments. That is, they could reject an appointment they did not approve. The President, however, could reject and sack any cabinet officer whose performance he did not approve.

The Senate was now asking the President to agree to a double-standard in their favor. They could reject someone they did not like, but the President would not have the same right, once the person took office. This would place cabinet officials in a position where they were serving for life (or at least the length of that Presidency) as long as the Senate approved.

The proposal was defeated, thank God/Allah.

This is from the book, *The United States in the Time of John Adams: 1797-1801*

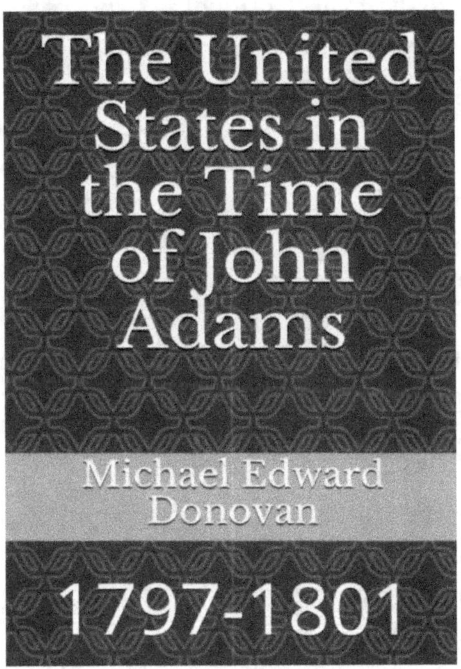

A GRISLY FIGHT WITH PSYCHO LYON - 2.15.98

Matthew Lyon, a former indentured servant, was a Republican Congressman from Vermont. Matt Griswold was a Federalist Congressman from Connecticut. In 1798 the two Matts went to the mat. They had a physical brawl in Congress.

These two had exchanged insults in the press for a while, mostly over Fed Griswold's support of Britain over France. On January 30, 1798, Griswold, in Congress, ridiculed the poor military record of Lyons during the Revolution. Lyons went over to Griswold and spit a mouth full of tobacco juice into his face. It was a grisly moment for Griswold. MG cleaned up his face, and kept his cool.

Congressman Griswold hoped that the House would expel Psycho Lyon for his bad behavior. When they did not, he decided to take matters into his own hands.

One week later, Griswold snuck up behind Lyons, who was sitting at his desk, and began to beat him on the head with a cane. Lyons got up to defend himself, and the two of them had a prolonged schoolyard scrap, wrestling, and punching, and rolling all over the floor of the Congress while the other members cheered, laughed, and applauded. For once, both parties had the floor at the same time. Lyons ended up in front of a fireplace, defending himself with a pair of hot tongs.

Matt vs. Matt was the talk of the country. Half the scandal was over the reaction of the other Congressmen. The idea of a fight on the floor was understandable. A fight can happen anytime anyplace - I saw two elderly librarians duke it out in Southie back in 1968 - but if the fight breaks out in an inappropriate setting, someone usually jumps in and breaks it up. No one broke it up. Europe ridiculed the barbarian Americans in story and cartoon.

The Griswold's attack on Lyons was similar to the Preston Brooks 1856 attack on Sumner. In 1856, Congressman Brooks of South Carolina beat Massachusetts Senator Charlie Sumner with a cane while a Southern gang of Congressmen blocked the doors so no one could break the caning up.

What is it with these guys and their canes? People must have faked a limp, just to keep one handy back then.

For his deeds, the Vermont Congressman won himself the nickname of 'the Spitting Lyon.'

This is from the book, *The USA in the Time of Thomas Jefferson, 1801-1809*

AFTER OFFICE - ANAS

Thomas Jefferson made $25,000 a year as President. Today, any former president makes that at one speaking engagement. Tommy owned tobacco, slaves, and a nail factory, but his generosity, plus the way he loved to pump money into home improvements at Monticello, left him tight for cash when he left office.

When Jefferson left the presidency he went south to help found the University of Virginia. He was rector from 1816 to 1825. Tom died on July 4, 1826, a few hours before John Adams.

Thomas Jefferson's holiday death opened the door for the publication of *Anas*. In this collection of Jefferson writings, he rips Al Hamilton to shreds with facts, fables, innuendos, distortions and arguments, all disguised as facts.

OK, fine. Who hasn't done that to someone on Facebook? Jefferson wrote these attacks under the condition that they be published only after both he and Hamilton were dead. Wow. That is some seriously mean-spirited work. The editor who first published Jefferson's complete works was a big fan, and even he could not bring himself to say a word of praise for anything in the *Anas,* nor could he defend the criticism that work has received. Jefferson's *Anas* was a bad thing to do and inspiration to not do that to others. We should write our praise of others in stone and our condemnations in sand (I'm adopting an aphorism I saw on the wall at an Elks Club.) That's why you should never write anything negative about someone on internet social media. It's totally made of stone.

This is from the book, *The USA in the time James Madison:* 1809-1817)

THE BATTLE OF LAKE CHAMPLAIN - SEPTEMBER 11, 1814

With the defeat of Napoleon, the British were ready to attack America with renewed vigor. The feeling that America had stabbed the British in the back in the middle of their moral crusade against France ran high and the new offensives planned for America seemed more designed to fill emotional needs than strategic ones. The word "chastise" appeared more often than "occupy" or "conquer" in the military plans.

So the British were going to start a three part program to "chastise" America: offensives in the North, in the middle Atlantic, and in the Gulf of Mexico.

Some historians seem to say that the British were trying to win the war and/or at least occupy key areas so that a peace treaty would grant huge new territorial concessions to Britain. Other accounts say that all three operations (Plattsburgh, Chesapeake, New Orleans) were part of a grand chastisement. A friend of mine recently spoke of the Chesapeake plan as an attempt by Britain to "win their old country back."

I would say that the raids in the Chesapeake were clearly only punitive in nature, but the attempt to invade America by way of Lake Champlain clearly was not merely punitive, but was an effort to take upstate New York and part of New England and to keep it. The attack on New Orleans was clearly an attempt to take and keep New Orleans. So there is some truth to both versions. The 3-part plan was: an attempt to win the war per se; a definite moral effort to chastise; and it an attempt to take and keep some important and productive parts of the United States. It was not an attempt to get its old country back and return to status quo pre-1776.

The commander of the Northern British invaders, arriving fresh from wars in Europe, was major General Sir George Prevost. He arrived in America, with Captain Downey and 18,000 men. The first thing Prevost did was dispatch ships and 2,000 troops to occupy eastern Maine.

Prevost then proceeded with an invasion of the upper Hudson Valley that could have been a repeat of Burgoyne in 1777 with better results. - But the route from Montreal to Albany had some obstacles to overcome. There was only one way to do it. Down the Richelieu River, through Lake Champlain, and on to the Hudson. The Prevost pre-game plan was to stop after Champlain and not go too far south, but to slice off a good portion of upstate New York and hold it until the peace negotiations enables the British-Canadians to keep it.

Prevost saw an opportunity near Plattsburgh because most of the American ground force was protecting Lake Erie, not Lake Champlain. Only 3,000 militiamen guarded the Lake Champlain area, and Prevost was going to send far more men than that after the target.

There was one catch: Transportation. The British were going to have to get the troops past the guard shack of Lake Champlain, a bottleneck of geography. If the Americans can't hold Champlain, the British hold the champagne. But if the Americans could cork the British up on Champlain, they pop the cork.

As the word spread about the large force heading down from Montreal, the 'Battle of the Carpenters' began. Both sides began building their little battle fleets along the side of the lake. Hammers sounded all over the lake for weeks as the showdown loomed. It was like two boxing managers building robots for tomorrow's championship fight. Trees near the lake came down and were employed for war.

The British suffered from arrogance and overconfidence. They did not have many experienced sailors: They were a force of land troops trying to improvise.

The American Captain, Thomas Macdonough, had a more experienced group of naval hands, and their boats were better built, and his positions were better chosen.

Tommy played it smart. He knew of the high winds on the lake and kept his little battle fleet tied and anchored, and at a favorable position at the southwest corner of the lake, near Plattsburgh-town. Macdonough also kept his ships close to his shore batteries so that if the British closed in on his fleet he would have double-power counterforce.

Prevost and Downie were supposed to coordinate their lake plan with a land attack north of Plattsburgh

The British fleet (the four main craft being *Confiance, Linnet, Chubb* and *Finch*) arrived off Cumberland Head Point in the morning of September 11, turned southwest, and entered the battle against the American fleet. The four main USA ships were *Saratoga, Eagle, Ticonderoga,* and *Preble.*

The fight was going fairly even, overall, for a while, but the Americans won out with clever maneuvers and exploitation of the wind. The British couldn't get the wind out of their sails and couldn't do what they planned to do. Within sight of the townspeople of Plattsbugh, the lake battle raged. Captain Downie died within the first 10 minutes of the battle, which didn't help the British. Both sides lost more than 100 men.

Three British ships (only one, the *Confiance*, was technically a ship - the *Linnet* was a Brig and the *Chubb* and *Finch* sloops) surrendered, and the *Finch* was chased into the sand on Crab Island. Several little British gunboats were all that was left and they fled back to the North shore of Champlain.

Tommy McDonough won a strategic victory. Prevost and his troops marched back to Montreal in a humiliated position. Upstate New York was to remain American territory. If Prevost had won a total victory and kept on, perhaps the British would have re-thought the Chesapeake plan as upgraded to more than a punitive raid.

Prevost had to face courts martial for his failure on Champlain.

Yes, September 11 is a glorious date in American history. The Battle of Brandywine was fought on 9.11.77.

This is from the book, *The USA in the Time of James Monroe*: 1817-1825

ELECTION OF 1820

There was no 'Battle of 1820.' The Election of 1820 was over before it started.

With defeat in 1816, the Federalist Party dropped out of the painting. So from 1816 to 1826, the United States had only one political party of any consequence: the Democratic-Republican Party of Thomas Jefferson.

Monroe was up for re-election and no one was interested in challenging him from within the party. This was the high tide of the Era of Good Feelings. There was no campaign for the presidency in 1820. There was no "I'm James Monroe and I approve this message," attack ads against some Federalist banker candidate. Monroe didn't have to kiss any ugly babies, answer needlessly nasty questions from bimbo reporters, or talk to stupid people in diners. Those were the days. Monroe ran unopposed and won virtually unanimously.

Monroe won 231 out of a possible 232 electoral votes. One New Hampshire elector voted for John Quincy Adams because (he claimed) he wanted to honor George Washington by insuring that he was the only unanimously elected President.

A few electors however, did vote for a Federalist challenger for Vice President. Richard Stockton, a stout Federalist got eight electoral votes for VP. Most of Dick Stockton's delegates were from Massachusetts. In spite of the Stockton challenge, the sitting VP, DR Daniel Tomkins, won re-election with more than 200 electoral votes.

Monroe was the last candidate to run unopposed for president (unless you count Reagan in 84.)

This is from the book, *The USA in the Time of John Quincy Adams*: 1825-1829

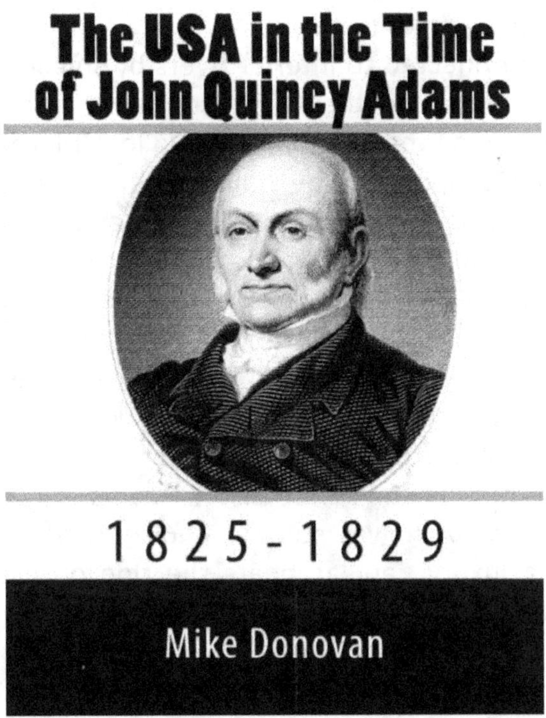

ERIE CANAL OPENS THE APPLE - 10.26.25

Near Schenectady there is a stretch of the Erie Canal where ghost sightings are frequent, and there they spell it the 'Eerie Canal.'

In Adams' time the Erie Canal was finally completed. Work began on the 425 mile canal connecting the Hudson to the American interior, back in 1823.

On October 4, 1825, the Erie Canal opened to water traffic with much deserved fanfare. Governor DeWitt Clinton rode a boat called *Seneca Chief,* from Buffalo to New York City, arriving there on November 4. The Canal had only cut the travel time from New York to Buffalo by around 40%. It used to take about 14 days, now it took about 9. The big difference was that Canal barges could handle much more than stagecoaches, and riverboat boat travel was more enjoyable.

The canal, once derisively called "Clinton's Ditch" connected the Great Lakes to not only New York City, but via New York City to the entire Eastern seaboard. NYC grew at a sudden, fantastic rate and, became the number one city in America, surpassing Philadelphia for the crown and hanging on to this day.

The Great Lakes connected to interior rivers by smaller canals, and thus, the Erie Canal opened the entire continent to a more lively commerce. From now on the east coast would look more to the west than to the east (Europe) for the bulk of its business. Theodore Roosevelt's grandfather worked on the Erie Canal, and so did future President Jimmy Garfield. My great great grandfather fell in to the Erie Canal but that's long story and the charges were dropped.

The Erie Canal facilitated the infiltration of the far west by the wild pioneers. It gave them a starting point much further west. Now the crazy-crackers could jump off from the middle of the continent instead of having to start from their own 1-yard line.

Canals were the rage in the John Quincy Adams era. The railroad was in its infancy, so boat was still the choice in travel whenever possible. Today, a luxury Cadillac beats the ride on a Long Island Sound ferry ride any day, but that dynamic was reversed in 1825.

The success of the Erie Canal inspired many new canal projects, one of which stretched from Plattsburgh New York all the way to Root, Maryland. You know it as the famous Root Canal.

Some canals succeeded, but others failed. Too many others. With the rise of the railroad, and the Panic of 1837, a lot of canal investment money went south. The canal boom sprung a leak. A lot of ex-rich people found themselves hauling barges for a penny an hour, 12 hours a day, in the broiling sun, on the very canal they lost all their money on. That's gotta hurt. That's like me cleaning the floors for six bucks an hour at the comedy club that fired me for telling a heckler to "die in your *&#$^!%* sleep!"

Senator Van Buren, in the ignoble interest of New York State, tried to block the construction of some new canals that might compete with the spectacular new one.

On the day the Canal opened, a salute of cannon marked the event all the way from the Great Lake Erie to New York Harbor. The cannon were placed at intervals all the way from Buffalo to NYC. The sound signal moved from one to the other like Indian smoke signals till the last cannon shot off in New York. Then President Adams took a vial of water that had been transported from Lake Erie via the canal to New York, and dumped it into the bay. The Erie Canal was open.

From this moment on, the rest of the cities of the eastern seaboard would have to look up to New York City. The Erie Canal put the core in the Big Apple.

This is from the book, *The USA in the Time of Andrew Jackson*: 1829-1837

TRAIL OF TEARS

Several Indian tribes (particularly the Choctaws, Creeks, and Seminoles) were victimized by white American aggression in Jackson's time. The Cherokees suffered the most. They migrated involuntarily during a long march from Georgia to Oklahoma

Jackson evicted the Cherokees from their homelands in Georgia and exiled them to the desert, like the Pharaoh in the Ten Commandments. The Native-Americans were given the 'insult to our intelligence' consolation prize: distant dry brown land to the west went to John Red while the green east went to James White.

Georgia for the longest time had no problem with the Cherokees living in the state. Then the whites discovered gold in northern Georgia in 1829. Suddenly, Georgia had a real problem with the Cherokees living in the state. Three thousand white '29ers' invaded Georgian Cherokee lands. In addition to acquiescing in the invasion, the Georgia House of Representatives made it illegal for Indians to mine in the state. The '29ers could mine the gold on Cherokee land but the Cherokees couldn't.

The next offense against the southeast Indians was the Removal Act of 1830. It wasn't so much a bill to decide on the question of removal of the Indians, but rather a bill on whether to appropriate the funds to do this. Removal was a foregone Jacksonian conclusion. The question was whether Congress was going obstruct a presidential foreign policy decision within its borders by not funding it. Congress did not obstruct. With the Removal Act, Jackson expanded the powers of the Presidency, and assisted that cause of racial malice.

Some Cherokees took a collective five million dollar bribe from the US government, and left voluntarily for Oklahoma, but most of them resisted.

A long legal battle took place between the federal government, the Supreme Court, and the state of Georgia on the one hand - and advocates of the rights of the Cherokee and other Indian people on the other. Chief Justice John Marshall of the Supreme Court, in his *Worcester vs. Georgia* 1832 decision, overruled Georgia's decision to force the Cherokees out. President Jackson defied the Supreme Court and said, "Justice Marshall has made his decision. Now let's see him enforce it."

Jackson was in-your-face defying a ruling of the Supreme Court and he did so successfully.

The final outcome was that the entire tribe of 20,000 Cherokees marched at gunpoint a thousand miles on foot with inadequate food, clothing, and shelter, in bad weather, on bad roads. More than four thousand Cherokees died during the march! Few of the seven thousand troops guarding them suffered much. This has been remembered in Native American history as the Trail of Tears. One can only imagine how much crying was heard on this road. It was a death-march. The entire incident is a great shame on America and on

Andrew Jackson. Needless to say, the Cherokees had never previously expressed any particular interest in moving to Oklahoma.

It must be added that there had already been other trails of tears. In 1831 more than three thousand Creeks had died in their forced march westward. This would seem to be a clear warning to government officials that on future marches of this kind, the Native-Americans needed proper provisions and protection. The Choctaws (1830) and the Chickasaws (1830) also suffered forced removal to the west under Jackson. I hate reading about this stuff. Sometimes history is fun. Sometimes it is not.

So in essence, the best behaved tribes were the ones kicked out of their homes. The tribes that had obeyed the laws of the USA, and stayed out of trouble: these were the only Native-Americans that were left to expel. Hang the model prisoners. The Indians of the southeast were up till Tears' time assimilating well, and had been led to believe that they owned some land within the United States.

The only apology worth considering is that all over the world there was a trend towards the expansion of industrialized races, with arrogant Darwinian justification being sufficient. The same thing was happening in Russia where the industrialized Slavs pushed the native Siberians and Uzbeks out of their homelands. The same tragedy of progress was hitting the outback of Australia and the veldt of South Africa. Blame America boldly, but don't blame America first or only. The USA didn't invent greed and invasion.

But ten wrongs elsewhere don't make America right. (Many historians have suggested that Jackson's Indian policy was following the leadership of Thomas Jefferson who had originally promoted the concept of Indian removal to western lands. That's a delicate subject.)

This is from the book, The USA in the Time of Martin Van Buren: 1837-1841

THE GRIMKE SISTERS - SRO TOUR - 1837

In the world of 1837 show business (otherwise known at the time as 'the church') there was a big rock & roll tour by two traveling minstrels: Sarah and Angelina Grimke. They were the daughters of South Carolina slaveholders. The Grimkes had a grim view of slavery. They dared to defy their parents, who loved slavery like I love baseball.

South Carolina cast Sarah and Angelina out of the state for speaking out courageously against slavery. The sisters fled north. The Grimke sisters published influential tracts, and in 1837 went on a sold-out speaking tour of the churches of the North. Scranton had to add a midnight show on Friday. The Grim-girls were truly preaching to the choir. In the South they were persona non grata. If Sarah and Angie had been Sam and Angelo, their lives would have been in danger wherever they roamed, and they never would have gotten out of the South with their original faces.

Old fashioned mores came in handy for many female abolitionists. Women often led the Abolitionists crusader events because the racist men were hamstrung by their own too-conservative value system that forbade violence against women, at least not by a (white) gentleman. How could they solve a problem like Angelina? "Cain't beat her up. Now what we do? Dang!"

On their tour, Sarah and Angelina not only spoke against slavery, they demanded equality for all women, black and white. They were 'two for one' reformers. The Grimkes claimed that the white women in the North had a special bond with black slave females in the South. The Grimkes blended abolitionism and feminism into one batter.

'Grimkeism' caused a rift within the Abolitionist movement. Some Abbies wanted abolition to be the sole goal of the movement. Even those who agreed with tag-along causes, like women's rights, free education, and care for the insane, often felt that the chance for success in any issue would be reduced by an attempt to win several at once.

In 1838, Angelina became the first woman ever to address an elected assembly in the United States. Garrulous Grimke lectured the Massachusetts Legislature on the twin evils of slavery, and the doctrine of male supremacy. Her stories of conditions in the South - conditions that she had witnessed with her own eyes - moved many. The Speaker of the House was crying for half the speech.

Angelina was the first person to speak to these people about slavery from having seen it in person. When she was five years old she saw a slave whipped and went inside crying. By the time she was 13, Angie Grimke was sneaking into the slave huts and teaching them to read and write. She nursed the wounds of the whipped.

Angie Grimke married the famous Abolitionist, Theodore Dwight Weld, on May 14, 1838, in Philadelphia. The ceremony and the service were performed without a minister. Pennsylvania law allowed anyone to perform a legal marriage as long as there were 12 witnesses. Mr. Abolitionist Himself, Mr. William Garrison married the lib lovebirds.

Teddy Weld read a statement into the service about the injustice of too much power being vested in husbands. He condemned the idea that a bride is supposed to "obey." TD Weld declaimed in his prepared statement that a husband has no right over the property or the person of his wife.

"She is not welded to anyone," said Weld.

This is from the book, *The USA in the Month of William H. Harrison: 1841*

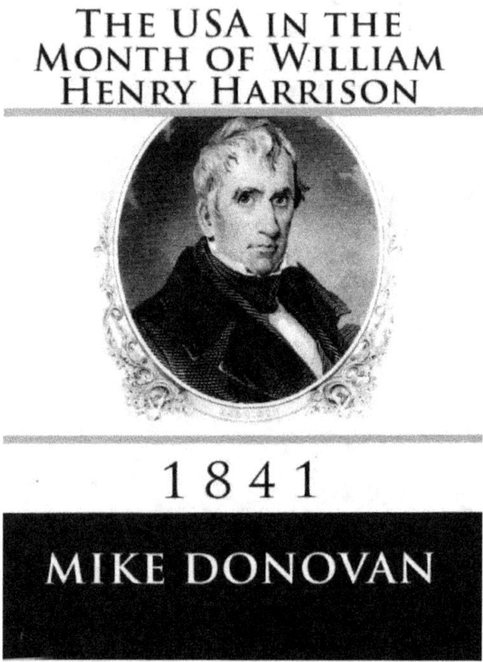

INAUGURATION DOOMSDAY

The Whigs were euphoric between Election Day and Inauguration Day. Who could blame them? They had never been winners before, and now the Democratic Goliath was down and not moving. Little did they know that their choice of a virtual Democrat in the VP slot would come back to haunt them. The death of Harrison, 30 days after taking over, nullified the spectacular victory of 1840. Tyler would be expelled from the Whig party while still President and the Democrats would seem to have won the election of 1840 after all.

Long exposure to a cold rain and wind at the Inaugural may have cost Harrison his life and his presidency. But it is not 100% certain the cold weather killed him. In any case, I like to go with that. The guy should have listened to his mom who surely advised him not to go out without his warm jacket "or you'll catch pneumonia."

Harrison's African-American servant helped him off with his coat as he strode foreword hatless to deliver a two-hour address followed by the swearing in ceremony. Maybe the sly servant whispered in his ear, "Don't worry Mr. William Henry, it's plenty warm out."

Chief Justice (Dred Scott) Taney administered the oath of office.

Harrison had already ridden a horse for two hours through the cold streets before delivering the two-hour speech in the chilly little storm. He gave his talk on the east steps of the Capitol.

Some historians say that Daniel Webster wrote Harrison's Inaugural speech. Others say that Webster edited it. One historian says it was Ted Sorenson. Daniel Webster had tried to edit it down to size but Harrison would not listen. The insufferably pompous historian W. E. Woodward calls the speech "pompous." Webster complained of the excess of Latin quotes that he had to try and cut out. "I just killed 17 Romans," said Dan after one slasher session.

Harrison's two hour talk was a long speech, even by Bill Clinton standards, and was delivered hatless, scarfless, & brainless. William Henry was no spring chicken and his old body couldn't handle it. Harrison developed a severe and ultimately fatal flu as a result, probably pneumonia. (Extremes of heat and cold cost the Whig Party their only two elected Presidents. President Taylor would later succumb to the 92 degree heat of July 4, 1850.)

This is from the book, The USA in the Time of John Tyler: 1841-1845

IS JOHNNY A NEW PRESIDENT?

President Harrison lasted 30 days in office before changing addresses on April 4, 1841, and VP Tyler became the chief.

Many people were angry with Tyler for assuming the title of President. He received many death threats in the mail.

Why were these people so mad at Tyler?

It was understood that upon the death of a president, the vice president would assume the duties of president; but it was not understood that he would take the full title of President. Some felt that a president should be elected, and that the title should thusly be earned. The Constitution, after all, only said that the _duties_ would devolve on the VP. It said nothing about swearing in the VP as the new actual, literal, President.

But John Tyler refused to perform under the title of 'Acting Vice-President.' John demanded that he be sworn in and made the real deal or else he would not so much as sign a single piece of legislature of any kind. The baby got his way. Congress recognized him officially as 'President Tyler.' The system of the Vice President becoming President is based on the Tyler precedent. It could easily have gone the other way.

This is from the book, *The USA in the Time of James Polk*: 1845-1849

ORIGINS OF THE MEXICAN WAR

Mexico won its independence from Spain in 1821. The USA immediately granted Mexico full recognition. The US recognized Mexican independence a lot quicker than the US later recognized Texan, and certainly faster than Mexico recognized Texan independence, since it never did.

What if the US had supported Spain, instead of Mexico, in 1821? Could Mexico have withstood a counter-attack by Spain if Spain had the passive support of the United States? In return for crucial US support in 1821 Mexico took an attitude towards the US in 1845 as if Mexico were a great and formidable nation with a long and glorious military history, and the US had been oppressing Mexico from day one.

In fact, neither nation had done anything special in the military field. The US had won a war of independence by running away from big battles and finding a French ally. Over the long haul, Sam defeated, in scattered warfare, a lot of poorly-armed Indians, and fought the War of 1812 to a draw on its home field thanks largely to British forces being tied down in a total conflagration in Europe. Mexico had thrown off Spanish rule two decades earlier. That was it for their glorious military histories.

Texas initially was a part of the Mexican state of Coahuila y Tejas. Then it sought statehood within Mexico, and this was of course long before it sought independence.

In 1827 Mexico emancipated its slaves. Texas was determined to keep its slaves in chains, and, ergo, the relation between Mexico and the province of Texas was ruined (and that's the first time I ever used the word ergo.) The worst thing that can be said of the USA in the Mexican War is that Texas loved slavery, and that was behind the initial breakup between Texas and Mexico in the first place. One of the reasons that Mexico wanted to reassert its authority over the former province of Texas was to stamp out slavery there.

Texas declared its independence of March 2, 1836, and won it with a military triumph at San Jacinto on April 21 of that same year.

When three US Presidents (Van Buren, Harrison, and Tyler to the near end) rejected the admission of Texas into the USA, the British began making overtures to Sam Houston's gang. Maybe Texas could free its slaves, with compensation from the British. The UK would buy the slaves from Texas if Texas agreed to free them. Britain would move in and become an important trading and political partner with Texas and free the slaves officially.

This so-called Piccadilly Plan scared President Tyler and the Congress into changing its mind about Texas. Tyler and Congress suddenly decided to annex Texas by proclamation in March of 1845, just a few days before Polk took office.

So as both Mexico and Britain were pushing on Texas to give up slavery, Texas fell back into the arms of the only power that seemed willing to let Texas keep it, the United States. Not only that, the

Southern Congressional bloc was going to surely protect slavery in Texas for the indefinite future, and said so.

At the beginning of the 1846 conflict, many international military analysts actually were putting the odds on Mexico to win (Vegas opened with MX at 2-3 - If you bet Mexico you have to put up 300 pesos to win 200.) Mexico had a much larger army, and the USA had dismantled its War of 1812 army long ago. This most recent performance of the American Army had produced a stalemate in Canada and an inability to prevent the British from burning down the White House. Mexico had reasons for its false confidence.

The United States became the big bully only after it won the war. It wasn't seen that way by the world when the game began.

The Mexican conflict had four primary origins but it was even more complex than that. The conflicting interests and the divisions between and within many groups were in play at all times.

The United States was divided internally on many things. It was divided on expansion, divided on slavery, divided on relations with Mexico, divided on relations with Texas, divided by partisan politics between parties, and divided by political factions within political parties, all while being "one nation indivisible."

It was also divided in foreign policy between maintaining friendly relations with European powers, and warning them against interference anywhere in the Western Hemisphere. There were financial reasons to desire good relations with Europe, but there was always fear of entanglements in this age of international power plays. Too much quicksand in European entanglements. It was still the age of conquest. The threat of war with Great Britain, for one, was an item on the table for most of the 19th century. The War of 1812 was not in the distant past.

The official trigger for the War with Mexico was the admission of the Republic of Texas into the United States on July 4, 1845.

Mexico in 1845 had only been independent for a little more than 20 years and was in political chaos. It was a dictatorship maintained by a rubber-stamp Congress to keep up appearances. Santa Anna's Mexico was no friend of Spain, no friend of Texas, no friend of the USA, and no friend of democracy. At least it was against Slavery.

Texas was divided between a desire to enter the USA and a desire to remain independent. Within the group favoring independence there were divisions about which nations to ally Texas with. Britain was in the hunt for Texas.

What Texas was not divided on was slavery. Texas was never half slave half free.

The United States had never been 100% slave. Massachusetts outlawed slavery before Washington was inaugurated. The USA was a house divided, part slave, part free. But Texas was different. The independent nation of Texas had lived its nine years as a slavery republic.

California, which figures prominently in the origins of the Mexican War and the end of it, was in 1846 sparsely populated by various national and racial groups. Any significant demographic fluctuations or sudden deep-probe military exercises had the potential to change Cal's political status overnight. It was weak and beautiful, an obvious prize. The USA, Mexico, Great Britain, and even Russia coveted California. Technically it belonged to Mexico but the hold was weak. There was a potential for Texas-style independence taking Cal-root before one of the big bullies could grab it. The Fremont's 'Bear Flag Revolt' of 1846 almost created a Republic of California (some would say that we have that today).

Here are my top four picks for the causes of the Mexican War:
One: Mexico refused to accept the annexation of Texas by the USA. It adopted a policy of non-recognition, even though it did not have the military force to enforce its view, much like U.S. non-recognition policy towards Red China in 1950, or of Russia in the 1920's. But Mexico went much further. It declared that annexation of Texas by the USA would be *casus beli* (Latin = grounds for war.) In other words, Mexico was declaring a state of war with the United States from the moment if and when Texas joined it. In that sense, Mexico started the war, point blank. Technically, you can argue that Mexico had declared a state of war with Texas, not with the United States, but it certainly was tantamount to a declaration of war against the United States, and Mexico knew that.

History has more cases of Alzheimer's disease than the state of Florida. It has no recollection that Mexico thought it could win a war against the United States. MX did not enter this war thinking it was a hopeless underdog fighting only for Mexican honor. But that's how the story of the Mexican War has evolved in lib history.

Two: Settlement of the exact boundaries of southwest Texas. The US was claiming the Rio Grande as the southern boundary. Mexico claimed the river Nueces. The Rio vs. Nueces argument was to become the visible trigger that started the hostilities of the Mexican War.

The obstacle for a diplomatic settlement in this area was that Mexico did not recognize the recently annexed Texas as American or Texan territory. Therefore Mexico could not with dignity agree to a boundary settlement because the very act of negotiation in itself would constitute *de facto* recognition of the nation/s it did not recognize. Since it could not engage in diplomacy, it could only settle the dispute by war.

Three: Settlement of claims of US citizens against Mexico. Many Americans had lent products on a massive scale to Mexico on a pay later basis and Mexico had failed to pay later. In early 1846, Mexico formally announced that it did not intend to pay at all. (Shades of 1918 and the Allied Intervention when the Bolsheviks tried to get out of all Tsarist debt and the Allies said no way, and tried to help overthrow the Reds.)

Four: A desire on the United States to acquire California and a fear that Great Britain would take it if the USA did not. The British had a great navy and a strong presence in Oregon country. The United Kingdom did not wish to see the United States acquire California. The USA and the UK were like two competing muggers watching a drunk with a fat wallet stagger out of a bar. California was not going to make it all the way home tonight.

This is from the book, *The USA in the Time of Zachary Taylor*: 1849-1850

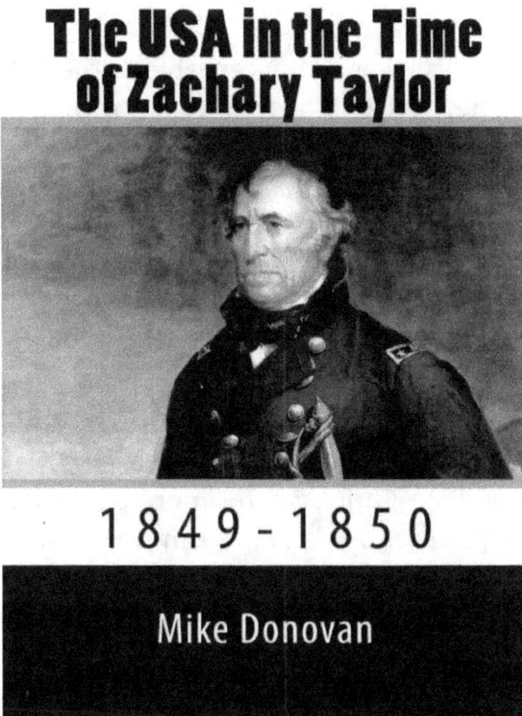

COMPROMISE OF 1850

The Treaty of Guadeloupe Hidalgo in 1848 gave the United States a restart on the slavery controversy just when it seemed to have settled down. Prior to the Mexican War there were 15 slave and 15 Free states. It will be recalled that Massachusetts had let Maine break off and become a new free state in order to maintain the balance in 1820.

The victory over Mexico came with responsibility for administering new territories, setting up governments, and accepting applications for statehood. The slavery issue had to be addressed.

There were three basic alternatives for the USA.

One: Have Congress bar the institution of slavery in the new territory (the Dave Wilmot position), which was of course, unacceptable to the South.

Two: Extend the Missouri Compromise line to the Pacific Ocean. This would allow slavery below the line of 36-30' and ban slavery above it.

But the Mo Compromise was not acceptable to the Southerners for two reasons. For one, it would admit the power of Congress to legislate on slavery. Slaves were property and they were therefore protected by the Constitution. The South sought the right to take slaves into the new territories regardless of Congressional laws on slavery there. As far as the slave-owners were concerned, Congress had no authority on the matter one way or another.

The second reason the South opposed this solution was that the South had little hope of obtaining new slave states below the Missouri Compromise line anyway. The South was not interested in making a concession that would gain them nothing. The South had its eyes on Mexico and the Caribbean for more potential slave states. They weren't looking west to the American desert and beyond for slave gardens.

Not all Southerners shared this opinion. Some felt that some new slave states could be gained to the west. Some Southerners felt that black slaves would be well suited for the mines of the southwest, just as they had so ably worked the cotton fields of the southeast. Some Southerners favored the Missouri Compromise extension even if they could not gain full slavery for California. Having said all that, these Southerners were in the minority. The conventional wisdom was that slavery was not likely to thrive or survive in the new southwest.

The Missouri Compromise extension plan would displease most Northerners who were now feeling that the momentum was turning against slavery in the new age. The free-soil movement was increasing in numbers and what was acceptable in 1820 was not acceptable in 1850. The Northern liberals were now insisting that the

Congress did have the right to legislate on slavery (in the territories) just as surely as the South was insisting that Congress did not.

Some were openly defiant. New York Whig Senator, William Seward dared to say that there was a "higher law than the Constitution." This was a shocker by any standard.

Alternative number 3 was the doctrine of 'popular sovereignty.' This gave each state or territory the right to choose to enslave or not to enslave, by ballot. But the exact mechanisms for this system were always delicate and complex and left as many questions as answers. Did the territories get to vote on slavery as a territory? Could they then seek admission as a free or slave state? Or did a territory have to achieve statehood first and then decide on the slavery issue?

The Democrats deliberately did not answer such questions so that each branch of the party could sell its own interpretation in its respective areas.

Two new complications thickened the plot. The aforementioned gold was discovered in 1848 in California (one week before the signing of the Treaty of Guadeloupe Hidalgo) and soon a mad rush was on. San Francisco went from a tumbleweeds town of a handful of people into the west's new metropolis (and a lawless one at that, one resident said that everyone was generally armed and he personally used a cane with a sword hidden inside it.) California territory would be ready for statehood much sooner than expected, and so a decision had to be made quickly on slavery.

Also the Mormons under Brigham Young had settled in the Utah desert when it was ruled by Spain, and now were Americans. Their well-established and prosperous community called Deseret would also soon apply for statehood. Slavery would have to be decided in Utah Territory too.

It was Henry Clay who first proposed the Compromise of 1850 on January 29th. But Clay tried to do it all at once. He tried to get Congress to pass a so-called Omnibus Bill, which included compromise solutions for several problems.

The Southern radicals, called 'fire-eaters', who were against compromise of any sort, rejected Clay's omnibus bill and called for an ominous anti-omnibus convention of Southern states to meet at Nashville.

Northern rads also rejected the Clay plan because they too were against compromise of any sort on slavery.

Three of the greatest political men of the era would play their last scenes in the great debate that led to the Compromise of 1850: Clay, Calhoun and Daniel Webster.

Calhoun was so old and weak in 1850 that his speeches had to be read by someone else. Calhoun would sit in his wheelchair and listen to his words echoing through the Senate via the voice of a younger man. Calhoun surprisingly demanded that California be admitted as a slave state and even proposed an amendment whereby the United States elected co-presidents, one from the free states and the other from the slave. Yeah, that would have worked real good.

Henry Clay of Kentucky had lost his final bid for the presidency in 1848 and was attempting to continue his notable record of forging compromise in 1849 and 50. Clay would later need compromised versions of his compromise to get his compromise passed. Clay was 73 in 1849.

Daniel Webster supported Clay's compromise. This would cost Webster his place in history as a great moral crusader. The public suddenly saw Daniel as just another effective politician. His star faded faster than the wacky next door neighbor on a cancelled sit-com pilot. 'He's not the liberal we once knew,' went one angry song lyric. Webster felt that avoiding civil war was more important than taking an unequivocal stand against slavery. This choice came at a time when the anti-slavery movement was getting hot and hip. It was the wrong call. Webster's 7th of March speech in support of the compromise of 1850 was considered one of the best of his great career. But the message damaged his reputation forever.

While Webster's Seventh of March speech knocked his star down, the Eleventh of March speech of Senator William Seward of New York sent his rising. His phrase about a "higher law" became an overnight folk legend. In one month, Northern liberal leadership passed from Webster to Seward, where it would remain until Lincoln's Inauguration in 61.

The Compromise of 1850 tried to tackle the following issues:

1)The status of slavery in the newly acquired territories
2) Statehood for California

3) The border dispute between the State of Texas and the territory of New Mexico
4) The Fugitive Slave Law
5) Slave trading on federal property in the District of Columbia (where there were no states-righters to fend off)
6) The general agitation in the South for secession as result of all of these problems.

President Taylor in the meantime was no-nonsense about the Texas-New Mexico dispute. When Texans threatened to occupy the disputed territory and incorporate the land by force in defiance of federal troops, Taylor took a page out of Andrew Jackson's book of 1832. Zachary announced that the US Army would if necessary, march on Texas:

"I will command the army in person and hang any man taken in treason."

Don't mess with Louisiana.
The Clay omnibus bill contained the following solutions.
1: California would apply for immediate statehood as a free state and skip the probationary territorial period. Slavery would be decided in the new territories by popular sovereignty. Utah and New Mexico would be encouraged to prepare for statehood in the short-term future.
2: The Texas-New Mexico dispute would be solved by compromise but with the settlement generally favorable to the aspiring state of New Mexico. The federal government would assume the large state debt of Texas to compensate for its giving in on the New Mexico issue. This was an effective plan because Texas needed the dough. It had lost significant revenue when it became a state because when it was a nation Texas kept its customs revenues. Now it had to hand it over to the feds. Assumption was welcome relief in Texas.
Three: The new and improved Fugitive Slave Law would be strictly enforced. FSL was an incendiary issue. The idea that southern slave-owners could hunt down and arrest runaway slaves in free Northern cities was unacceptable to legions of Yankees. This law would lead to much trouble and would be ferociously resisted. For the South, the

right to do this was important because it upheld its argument that slaves were property and therefore protected by the Constitution. Already there were owners bringing slaves into California. Southerners were insisting that it was their right to do so. (This argument would come to a climax later in the Dred Scott case).

Four: Slave trading would be prohibited in the District of Columbia. Whig Congressman Abe Lincoln had been horrified by the slave auctions going on near his boardinghouse as he walked to work every day at the Capital Building. Slavery itself however would not be prohibited in D.C. You could own and work a slave in D.C., but you had to buy the soul elsewhere.

President Taylor opposed Clay's compromise Omnibus Bill. Taylor's untimely death on July 9 was timely for Clay, Webster, and the entire compromise crowd. New President Fillmore the Fill-in was more amenable to the compromise.

Eventually, with the indispensable help of rising political star Stephen Douglas, the entire Clay omnibus bill was passed, but not in that collective form. Instead its separate parts were proposed, debated, voted on, and passed, one at a time. By itself, as a full package, it would seem too extreme to some. Others who might have an objection to only one part were sure to vote against the entire bill. By breaking it down to smaller parts the plan enabled those who objected to one part to at least be there for yea votes on all the others. So the elements of the Clay omnibus bill were all passed, but without the official participation of Clay, and not in the form of his one super-bill.

It was, in the end, the Clay-Douglas-Fillmore Compromise of 1850 which sort-of belongs more in the next chapter.

It is hard to decipher exactly which elements of the Clay Omnibus Bill that Taylor was so opposed to. It may be that he did not wish to hand the 1852 nomination for President to Henry Clay. A third Clay compromise victory would probably give the aged Clay one more chance in '52.

In the end, Taylor may have been more active in death than in life, as far as his presidency is concerned. The compromise of 1850, intended to settle the simmering secession movement in the South (and I guess it did) might not have made it through Congress under

Zak's watch. Taylor said he would have vetoed it. He even threatened to support a Wilmot position if it came to it. Webster later said flatly that the compromise of 1850 could not have been engineered under Taylor.

News of Taylor's death hit the North hard, and people mourned. In the South there was a chilled equanimity about it. They had been greatly disappointed with their slaveholder ally. Taylor had not exactly come through for the Old South. Maybe it was because he wasn't from the Deep South where cotton was king and slavery queen. Zachary had been born in Virginia and raised in Kentucky. Taylor had northern Southern roots. Perhaps President Taylor even felt guilty about his slave-ownership and tried to lean against the institution as his apology to God. In the end he pleased no political groups. The Cotton Whigs, Conscience Whigs, Democrats, Barnburners, Hunkerers, Locofocos, and the Know-Nothings, all repudiated Zachary Taylor. He died an independent man.

This is from the book, The *USA in the Time of Millard Fillmore*: 1850-1853

SHADRACH MILKINS – FEBRUARY 1851

He was a man of many names. Slaves were flexible when it came to names. Fred Wilkins or Shadrach Milkins, or Minkens: a slave by any other name feels just as persecuted.

Shad was a runaway slave from Virginia who was a waiter in a coffee shop in downtown Boston. On the morning of February 15, 1851, the bounty hunters caught up to him and Boston caught lightning in a bottle.

This was the first time that the Fugitive Slave Law had been enforced in New England. This new federal law, passed in 1850, not only made it legal for slave-owners to hire bounty hunters or employ the U.S. Marshalls free of charge, to catch runaway slaves in the free states; it made It illegal for private citizens not to help them catch them!

The time, effort and money expended to catch a runaway slave in New Hampshire were not cost-effective. No Southern state or individual was really going to make a fortune hunting down isolated runaways. The FSL was about power and its manifestation through a symbolic law.

The entire nation had wondered aloud what it will be like the day a Southern agent arrests a slave in downtown Boston, and it was about to find out.

Milkins had escaped his owner, John De Bere in Norfolk, and was working at Taft's Cornhill Coffeehouse, near the State House. It was just after 9 am when De Bere's agent, John Caphart, sat down for breakfast, His prey asked him how he would like his coffee. "I'll take it black" John said with professional aplomb. A Marshall was fake breakfasting at the other side of the diner. Nine more were outside.

The authorities were well aware of the BVC, the Boston Vigilance Committee: the abolitionist group pledged to prevent the enforcement of the Fugitive Slave Law. They knew they would have to be efficient and quick if they wanted to bring this slave back. It had to be done before the Vigilants could react. (As things turned out, the bad guys did manage to kidnap Freddie before the BVC could react, but they did not count on spontaneous combustion.)

Capart and Deputy Marshall Pat Riley stood in the spot between the kitchen and the seating area. When Shad walked in with that hot muffin they each grabbed an arm and walked him aggressively to the court house two blocks away. It happened pretty fast. By 10:30 am, Shadrach stood helplessly before Magistrate Curtis.

There was a physical as a well as a legal conflict going on. Boston and Massachusetts had passed 'personal liberty laws' which nullified the Fugitive Slave Law, in theory. It was a mini, legal civil war; and Massachusetts was claiming states' rights over intrusive federal laws.

Now the battle began over whose law was law: city, state or fed?

Massachusetts may have been a hotbed of Abolition, but Boston was a hotbed of money. There was a great deal of Beantown moral support for the federal enforcement of the Fugitive Slave Law. Throughout the Shad sage, many local officials knowingly refused to even acknowledge the existence of Personal Liberty Laws. They looked the other way, knowing that they had every right to challenge the feds if they so chose. Justice Lem Shaw refused the pleas of Abolitionist lawyers who demanded the release of Milkins on the basis of local laws that Shaw had sworn-pledged to uphold.

Mayor Bigelow was equivocal. He did not support the Abolitionists but he also would not let Marshall Pat Riley take Shadrach to the Charles St. Jail. Riley then contacted the Charlestown Navy Yard. Since it was federal property, they would take Shadrach at the Navy brig. Nope: just a vague answer from Charlestown (where Senator Foote of Mississippi had bragged that he would personally arrest a runaway slave at the foot of the Bunker Hill Monument.)

Pat Riley improvised. He cleared the courtroom and turned it into a jail until he could get some reinforcements. People started drifting out until there were 15 bad guys, the victim, a priest and one reporter left inside. The reporter was Elizur Wright, ace reporter for the *Commonwealth*. Elizur was acting all innocent observer but he knew that something was going down outside and didn't tip anyone off inside.

At 1 pm the word was on the way to the authorities to bring help, but word had spread much faster in the working class black community of Boston. 150 black men of Boston had gathered outside the building and had done so quietly.

The priest asked to leave. Pat Riley reluctantly cracked the street door just enough to let the priest out, but that was enough. The blacks began to push the door open. Two marshalls pushed back. The reporter Wright grabbed the door, helped push it open and then yelled and waved his arms in a circle yelling "Come in! This way!"

The door broke open and 20 black men rushed in. Riley was crushed behind the door, and seemed happy to hide there. No one resisted the mob that came in and the mob didn't hurt anyone. What they did was pick Shadrach up and hoist him on their shoulders. Then they passed him out to the street. Witnesses said the entire thing took only ten seconds! The speed of this critical action stunned everyone that saw it. It was efficient and violent, and Shadrach, understandably, wasn't sure if they were there to save him or hurt him. Milkens went from the courtroom to the street like a rocket.

Shadrach was weak, and his clothes were torn. He found his feet and marched off towards Cambridge Street with the crowd cheering all about. A carriage waited for him there. The rescue took a minute. Richard Henry Dana, Abbie lawyer, and author of *Two Years Behind the Mast*, witnessed the whole breathtaking thing from his window across the street from the courthouse. Dana joyously described witnessing "a black squall" that passed through Boston. The next day the slave was headed north to Canada on the Undergound Railroad.

It was Boston's Raid at Entebbe.

In the aftermath, several prominent Bostonians, some black, were arrested on various charges, long after the event. The authorities did not forget how they had been defied and they enacted some delayed fuse revenge. Almost all of those accused were acquitted, but the prosecutions did put some healthy fear into Boston's Abolitionists. They knew they were risking much when they stood up for what's right.

One great black man's name has escaped historical credit. This one individual went around the black neighborhoods yelling "The Crackers are coming!" and arousing this mini-revolt in flash time. He was charismatic and he whipped the crown to action with clear, determined leadership. Because he didn't want to get into any trouble, he kept his name out of it, and so did his pals.

Shad Minkins lived a long and free life in Montreal and is buried in the Catholic Mount Royal Cemetery (Mount Royal of course, the name of Montreal in English.)

The South seethed over the Shadrach incident. Even U.S. Secretary of State Daniel Webster was not happy with the behavior of his home state, and said so publicly (check out his charming mug up the back of the book). The Shadrach affair was another factor in the decline and fall of Webster's once holy name. When Webster condemned the actions of his home state in a righteous cause, he took one giant leap towards putting his picture beside the phrase "has-been" in Webster's unabridged.

This is from the book, *The USA in the Time of Franklin Pierce*: 1853-1857

THE KANSAS-NEBRASKA ACT

The Kansas-Nebraska Act legalized slavery north of the Missouri Compromise line all the way to the Pacific Ocean.

The slavery controversy was the dominant issue in the nation from the time Pierce was sworn in until the time he was sworn out. It was ultimate ostrich move for the USA to ignore slavery as an issue in the 1852 election, as it did.

History generally does not think much of Pierce on the slavery issue. Harry Truman, the quasi-historian President, once referred to Pierce in print as a "birdbrain." Like he knew the guy. Well I say Carter was a numbskull; how's that?

Truman was mad at Pierce partly for approving the Kansas-Nebraska Act, which opened up the territories of the entire west and northwest to slavery.

Prior to KN, the Missouri Compromise had been in force, by which no territory could create a slave state above the compromise line. Below that, whip away! But above that line it was a no-go.

Senator Stephen A. Douglas of Illinois, later of the famous Lincoln-Douglas debates in 58, was the primary author of the Kansas-Nebraska act and history has not been kind to him for it. I agree with history.

The Kansas-Nebraska Act was an attempt to influence the location of the long-desired transcontinental railroad. Everyone knew that a great railroad was going to be built sooner or later, one way or another, somewhere. Douglas wanted the eastern terminus to be located at a mid-western city, preferably one in his home state of Illinois. The Senator was hoping to build up the Midwest as the decisive makeweight in the close political balance between North and South. He needed to attract the railroad his way and then use it to build up his Midwest.

Southern Senators for equally selfish reasons wanted the long, long railroad to lay along a southern route with the eastern terminus in New Orleans or Memphis. They wanted Interstate 10.

Stevie D realized that the Southern men in the Senate could easily block his grandiose plans for a Midwestern transcontinental railroad. He had to throw them a bone.

That bone was the *de facto* repeal of the Missouri Compromise of 1820. The MC had had been a great King Solomon's wand cutting a line through the belly of the country, declaring slavery illegal on one side and legal on the other. This Missouri Compromise had been a great victory for the anti-slavery forces even though it was a compromise. True, it had sadly sanctioned slavery in some very large areas, but it had also established the more important principle: that the Congress could legislate on the slavery issue at all. The South was largely against this principle and had swallowed hard to take the Missouri medicine in 1820. Now Douglas was going to give pro-slavery forces back this earlier defeat, and on a platter.

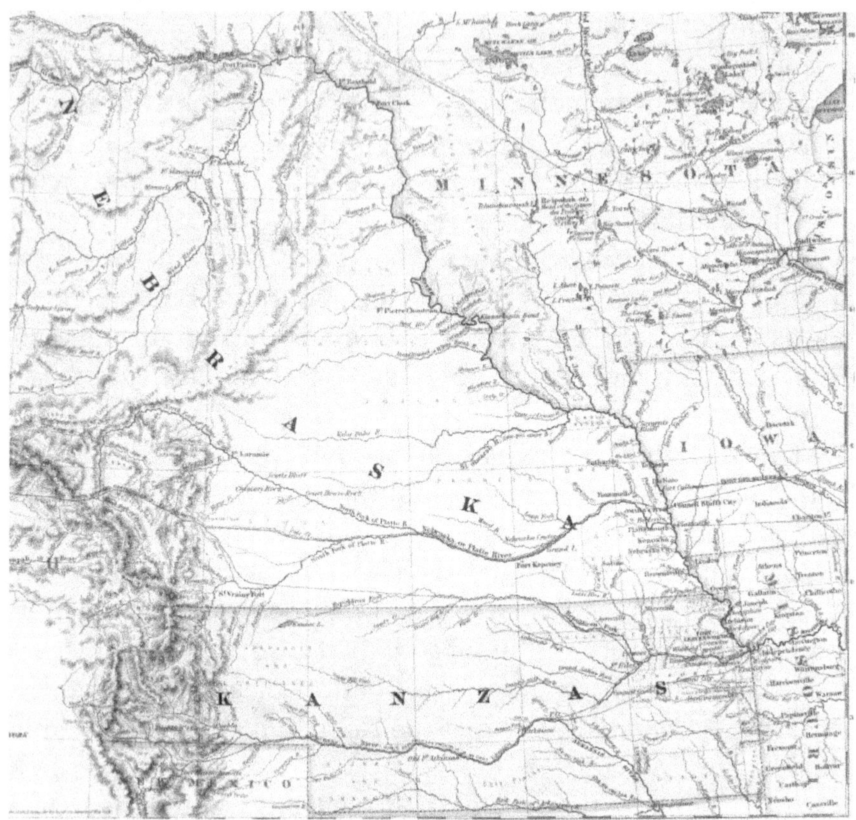

Memorize the names on this easy to read 1855 map

If Congress approved the Kansas-Nebraska Act, it would be overturning its own work. The new law would supersede the old and slavery could now be re-instated in a place (Kansas) where it had once already been effectively banned. Kansas was above the Missouri Compromise line.

What was even more horrific to progressive Northerners, slavery was now legal in the west all the way as far north as the Canadian borderline. Just when the Yankees felt that they were beginning to at least stuff the slavery monster into an isolated Southern box, it snapped out if its cage and spread out over half a continent.

By the terms of the Kansas-Nebraska Act the Nebraska territory would be divided into two separate territories, Kansas and Nebraska. As for slavery, it would be up to the settlers of these territories to decide on slavery. "Popular sovereignty," it was called. Instead of judicial, Congressional or executive decisions on slavery, the local referendum would become the arbiter on this delicate problem in the new territories.

This was in effect an open invitation to make Kansas a slave state, since Missouri, a slave state, was its dominant neighbor. The Douglas referendum system was a drunk fumbling with a cigarette lighter in a fireworks factory. Pro and anti-slavery settlers poured into Kansas for political battle.

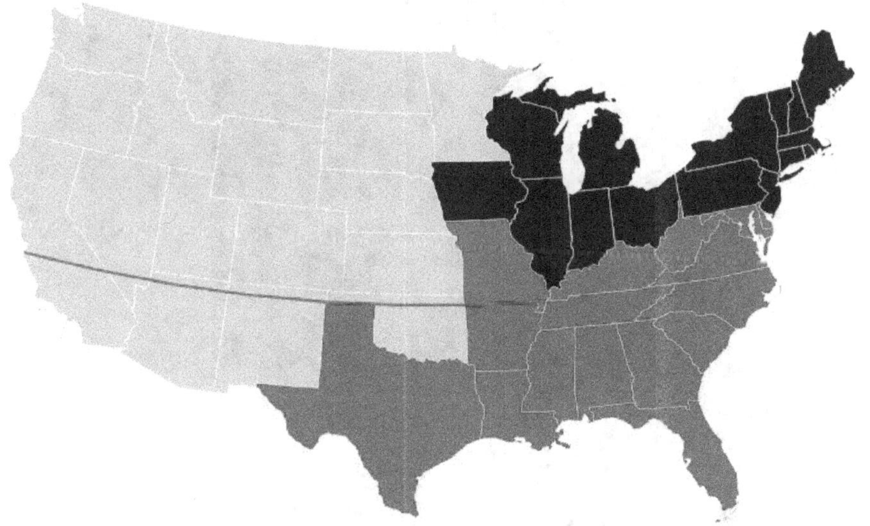

K-N shattered this Missouri Compromise Line of 1820

Senator Douglas misread the American public. He thought that expansion was more important in the public mind than slavery. That might have been true in the early 1840s but this was the do-wop fifties.

The Kansas-Nebraska Act passed the House of Representatives 113-100 and the Senate by 37 to 14.

The Free-soilers, Republicans, and Abbies hit the roof. KN set off a firestorm throughout the North and cost Pierce whatever chance he ever had for a place in history as a good guy. The author of the act, Douglas, took so much flak for the Act that he borrowed an old line from Jackie Jay that he could travel the country at night by the light of burning Steve Douglas effigies.

This is from the book, *The USA in the Time of James Buchanan*: 1857-1861

A DREDFUL INAUGURAL

A hotel messed up the Buchanan Inaugural.

The National Hotel in Washington D.C. hosted the show. The weather in the first week in March was so cold that the pipes froze at the Nat, causing the sewage system to back up. The kitchen help got very ill and began passing dysentery around to the guests. James Buchanan had severe diarrhea for his Inaugural. Thanks, National. James had a doctor close beside him for the entire speech just in case. Many of the dignitaries listening to his speech were just counting the minutes until he wrapped it up and they could get to a restroom.

The slavery question and an impending Supreme Court decision played a major part in Buchanan's Inaugural speech.

The hot controversial question was: Does Congress have the right to legislate on slavery in the territories? All agreed that Congress did not have the right to decide on slavery in the states; but what about the territories? (And by the way, read that carefully. All agreed that Congress did not have the right to legislate on slavery in the states - so much for the Southern excuse on secession that the North was trampling on states-rights over slavery. What the South really seceded over were territorial-rights; the rights of slavery in the federal lands.)

If Congress had no right to legislate on slavery in the territories, then the Missouri Compromise would logically have to be declared invalid. That 1820 ruling had divided the territories into north and south with slavery allowed to the south and prohibited to the north of a line of death. But many Southern Democrats were prodding the Supreme Court to declare the Missouri Compromise unconstitutional. There was a case pending before the Court involving Dred Scott, a slave who had lived in free territory briefly, and was now back in slave-country. This man wanted to go Scott free and he was taking his case to court.

The Democrats were confident that the Southern-dominated Supreme Court of 1856 would rule against Scott in this specific case. What they weren't sure of was whether they could nudge the judge into holding a grudge on African slavery, while they were on the subject. The Dems wanted the Court to void the Missouri Compromise.

Buchanan was hoping that the Court would judge Dred before the Inauguration so he could avoid the issue by declaring it settled.

Fate intervened a little bit to delay the Court proceedings, and deny Buchanan his wish.

Justice P.V. Daniels of Virginia was going to a boring formal ball with Mrs. Daniels. She wanted to look pretty for the occasion and it was getting a little late. P. V. called upstairs, "Are you ready?" Then he heard the worst sound in the world. The sound of his wife screaming in terror. Her grand gown had caught fire. The wife of Supreme Court Justice Daniels died in the flames. The Court recessed for several days to honor her memory and his loss. This delay pushed back the Dred Scott decision until after the Buchanan Inaugural.

Buchanan had written to Justice Catron asking anxiously when Dred Scott was going to be settled. He wanted to know which way to write his Inaugural speech, and that depended on the Court. Buchanan prodded Justice Catron to try and make sure that the court ruled on, not only the Missouri Compromise, but on the larger issue of whether Congress had the right to legislate on slavery in the Territories. The justices would almost certainly rule in the South's favor if they ruled at all, so Buchanan was trying to get himself off the hook and get Southern support from his very first day in office. He wanted the North to know he had nothing to do with it. He wanted the Court to do it.

But two Northern Justices argued on the side of decency, and the Court had to spend many days deliberating before setting down an official decision. More delays.

Buchanan was, by now, however, beginning to realize that he had nothing to worry about. The court was going to rule in his, and the South's, favor. No one actually tipped him off, as has been written, but he was influential enough that he knew that his correspondence with Catron was creating a self-fulfilled prediction. The Court could rule on larger slavery issues because the President-elect was privately prodding it to do so.

Just minutes before the Inaugural address, Chief Justice Taney went over to Buchanan and whispered in his ear. Some history books say that Taney was tipping him off that Dred Scott was in the bag; but Taney was merely instructing Buchanan on some procedural matters during the ceremonies. People at the time thought that Buchanan was making a corrupt deal. The erroneous historians got their cue from them.

If Buchanan was going to make a shady deal with Taney, he certainly would not transact it in front of three thousand people. Buchanan was guilty of collusion, but his deal with the Court was understated.

In his Inaugural Address, Buchanan said of slavery that he would "cheerfully submit" to the decision of the Supreme Court.

This is from the book, *The USA in the Time of the Great Civil War*: 1861-1865

MEXICO

North and South sent a diplomatic representative to Mexico, seeking diplomatic recognition. The North had the advantage, since Mexico already had diplomatic relations with the United States. The U.S. envoy in Mexico City was Thomas Corwin. The North was just looking to maintain what it already had, and the South was asking for ... the South was asking for a lot.

The South had a long hill to climb to get Mexican recognition. Not only was it a daring and risky step for Mexico, there was also the slavery issue. Mexico had abolished slavery in 1829 and did not look too favorably on the CSA.

Certain historians can say that the Confederacy was not about slavery - but the Rebel envoy to Mexico, Anthony Pickett, had a tougher time with that claim. Pickett had to deal with the reality of the time, which was that his Confederacy was an over-the-top slavery empire. Pickett had to somehow convince Mexico that this was not true. Mexico treated him with studied discourtesy.

The Mexican government agreed to see Tony Pickett, informally, only once or twice, and it made it clear to him that he was whistling Dixie in Mexico City. Mr. Pickett continued to plead and cajole the Mexicans into recognizing the Confederacy. They weren't very nice to him, but he had to turn the other gray cheek because he had a job to do. Pickett couldn't just tell them all off and go home. This Kentucky Southerner (a relative of the man who became famous in the 1863 'Pickett's' Charge at Gettysburg) was basically on a mission to convince the Mexican government that the sky was not blue, and that the Pacific Ocean was 11 miles wide.

In the meantime, Mexico treated USA Ambassador Tom Corwin well. Mexico didn't exactly love the Northern Union. After all, it was the USA, not the CSA that had waged the war of 1845-6 against Mexico. But compared to the pro-slavery Confederacy, the Union was superb, and it was easy for the Mexican foreign office to reject Pickett's side. Mexican support for the USA didn't mean overt help for the Union, but it certainly meant non-recognition of the Confederacy.

There was something else that made things much worse for Pickett in his quest for recognition. The dim-wit was sending vicious letters back to Jefferson Davis ripping the Mexicans to shreds. Pickett's pen was calling the Mexicans every name in the book, and in every sentence. The Mexicans were intercepting and reading these letters, and then not even passing them on to Davis. Pickett was poison-penning himself into a corner, killing what little chance he ever had for success by calling the Mexicans a whole slew of racist names.

Pickett's purloined pouches proved that his diplomatic mission was malevolent and dishonest, and that Southerners were apparently only slightly less racist towards Mexicans than towards blacks.

Lincoln's choice of 'TC' Corwin to head the Mexican diplomatic mission was a shrewd and excellent one. Corwin was already a legendary hero in Mexico for his famous left-wing comments during the War of 1845. Corwin was in the U.S. Senate at that time, and was so ardently against the Mexican War that he said that if he were a Mexican he would be only too eager to "provide a hospitable graveyard for the invaders." The comment became famous, and hurt Corwin's chances at higher ambition; but he also became a hero of the left. Horace Greeley thought that Corwin was an excellent choice for the White House. Greeley once officially nominated Corwin for President, but nothing came of it.

All of this made Tommy in 1861 the ideal Ambassador to Mexico during the Civil War. The Mexicans loved Corwin, seeing him as the only important American who really had stood up for them during the clash with the USA. Mexico treated Tommy like royalty from the time he arrived in Vera Cruz. In Mexico City he was practically a visiting crown prince. Tom Corwin had a lifetime pass to all the bullfights.

In the middle of all this, Mexico defaulted on its foreign loans, creating an international crisis. The Mexican government didn't have a peso to its name and the bill was due on some hefty foreign loans to France, Spain, and England, among others.

There was a standard procedure for these situations in these times. The creditor nations would gather up a punitive expedition to take over the biggest port city of the defaulting nation and take the owed money from customs revenue. The United States did this, well into the 20th century, in the Caribbean. It was no shock to the United States, the Confederacy, or Mexico that in 1861, France and Britain prepared to sail to Vera Cruz and collect their vig by force. And it was only the vig that was due. The Mexicans were obviously not able to pay the principle on their foreign loans. What the Europeans were demanding was the payment of 3% interest that was now due on these loans. Mexico couldn't pay for a tab at Applebee's.

The last thing Seward and Lincoln wanted right now was a European military presence on the North American continent during the Civil War.

Seward and Corwin came up with a good idea. They presented it to Lincoln, who approved. What if the United States loaned Mexico the money to pay the interest on its foreign debt to Europe? Then the French and British could stay on the other side of the ocean, and Mexico would be free to treat with the United States on various maters without this European 'dunning expedition' mixing up the batter.

Mexico really appreciated the gesture and became that much friendlier to Union Corwin. The USA did ask for collateral however. Mexico would have to put up four of its northernmost states to guarantee the US loan. If Mexico defaulted after six years it would have to turn over Sinaloa, Chihuahua, Sonora, and Baja to the Yankees. Mexico did not act offended by the terms.

In taking hostage collateral lands, the USA seems just as avaricious as the CSA, but there were differences. The South had been preaching about expansion to the south of the South for decades, and the North had not. The South was openly and avowedly going to expand to the Latin-American south: an empire of slavery. The North was offering a loan to save Mexico for now. The CSA was offering nothing but conquest, while feigning friendship, and fooling no one. The North was by far the lesser of two vultures. Besides, the impending possible turnover of Sinaloa to the USA meant that the South couldn't intrude there with impunity. Mexico might accept the fallback position of throwing one province under the bus to save the country from the Montgomery slave machine. I'll sacrifice Sinaloa to block.

The loan however, still had to be approved by the United States Senate. The Hills Brothers debated it at length. Many months went by and finally the Washington Senators rejected the loan. But the loan was a success story because the United States collected Mexican good will while it was being debated. By the time the loan was voted down in the U.S. Capitol, a new president was in power in Mexico, the North had won a couple of battles, and the Confederate Ambassador was in a Mexican jail.

France and Britain meanwhile had decided that even if the United States paid for the interest due, Mexico was still in default on the principal, so they would still send the dunning flotilla to Vera Cruz, and they did.

In the middle of all this comes a grand, but too real to be called grandiose, scheme by the French to take over Mexico.

Napoleon III and his gold-digger girl-friend were going to take advantage of the temporary weakness of the United States. They would defy the Monroe Doctrine and re-establish French colonial power on the American continent. Nap's woman was always on him about restoring French greatness in America. She convinced him to take over in Mexico and to set up a puppet French emperor on the throne of a French-Mexican kingdom.

The bill-collectors expedition went down, providing the opportunity for Nap 3 to make a quick strike. GB went back to GB after collecting some gold and property in Vera Cruz, but France stayed on and marched to Mexico City like Winfield Scott in 1847. France eventually set up a colonial government and became the ruling power of Mexico.

The Confederate Ambassador, John T. Pickett, was not thrown into a Mexican jail for spying, and his arrest was not a political reprisal against the pro-slavery regime he represented. Pickett was jailed because of a personal brawl with a Northern big-mouth who was in Mexico City on business at the time. Pickett did 30 days in the Mexico City drunk tank because of a fistfight he started by giving a critic the standard Southern slap across the face. This wasn't the place to do stuff like that. This wasn't Milledgeville, you idiot.

Pickett got slap happy because the other guy had been drinking in bars in Mexico City saying loudly that the Confederates were "traitors." That was his crime. Pickett found out where the guy lived, knocked on his door and when the man opened his door Pickett stepped forward, called him a "Yankee Scum," and slapped him hard. Pickett at this point presumed that the guy would now do the proper thing and accept this as a challenge to a duel. The two of them would meet the next morning with their seconds. But the other guy was from Utica and didn't get it. He instead grabbed a fire iron and tried to crash Pickett's skull with it. Pickett rushed forward into the guy and the two of them went into a knock-down drag-out movie-fight in the guy's front yard that lasted until the Mexican police arrived.

Pickett honorably admitted that he had thrown the first slap. The Mexicans released the Utican and told Pickett that he had to apologize and pay a fine. JT refused to apologize to "that ignorant Yankee salamander," so Pickett did 30 days and only got out when he bought his way out with a sum that was larger than the original fine he had refused to pay.

As soon as he got out, JT went home to his wife, dog and picket fence. He recognized that the Southern quest for recognition was, like all TV commercials, a complete waste of time. The Mexican government was clearly against the Confederacy and in favor of the USA.

Hooray for the Mexico!

This is from the book, *The USA in the Time of Andrew Johnson*: 1865-1869

MEMPHIS & NEW ORLEANS - APRIL 30 AND JULY 30, 1866

The problem of racial violence began quickly in the Johnson era. On April 30, 1866, a 3-day race riot erupted in Memphis. It would be more accurate to call it a race massacre. It started with some scuffling between black US Army troops and local white police. White mobs joined the police. They initiated an indiscriminate attack on every black person they could find. Forty-six black people died, some of them women and children. Eighty were seriously injured. On the other side, one white person was injured. The cops and robbers burned 4 black churches and 12 black schools to the ground.

Then on July 30, 1866, another massacre: this time in New Orleans. A state convention had been called for a special session to vote on a volatile plan to give the franchise to blacks and take it away from ex-Confederate leaders. A crowd of blacks cheered for the new legislature as it entered to do its work. This crowd was attacked by a bigger mob of enraged whites. 34 black people died along with four liberal whites.

These riots are not famous in American History but probably should be. They were famous at the time and the entire North was aroused. The Radicals cited these riots as proof that the South was simply never going to behave as if it had lost the war unless it was forced to.

This is from the book, *The USA in the Time of Ulysses S. Grant*: 1869-1877

COLFAX MASSACRE IN LOUISIANA - APRIL 13, 1873

1873 and 1874, the state of Louisiana was in a virtual state of civil war. The following two stories showcase the awful problem of Reconstruction.

One Louisiana carpetbagger governor switched and went over to the (racist) conservatives. For this he was impeached by the group supporting the Radicals. It was on their platform that he had won.

The conservatives formed an alternate, rebellious legislature, declaring the Radical one illegal. The state of Louisiana now had two legislatures, one conservative and one Radical.

US Army troops went in to support the Radical side. This led to much violence, as you might have guessed.

Colfax is a little town, far from the big cities of Louisiana. I go there for the annual Pecan Festival. (It's one of the best, not quite as good as the one in Anderson, SC.) Colfax was named for the sitting Vice President, Mr. Shuyler Colfax. And Colfax was the county seat for Grant Parish, named after Ulysses. The white Redeemers didn't like these new names and decided to take a stand at Colfax.

The election of a local sheriff started a race war. All over the state there were dual election returns, by Republican and Democrat counting boards. In Grant Parish, a man named Christopher Columbus Nash felt that he had been robbed of his win by corrupt counting methods. He organized the angry white dudes in three counties and made himself a little army.

A lot of blacks heard that the whites were planning on seizing the county courthouse at Colfax to install Nash, and every other Democratic candidate who had lost. So about 100 black men surrounded the courthouse and began digging trenches. These black volunteers, many of them local officials, were going to militarily defend the standing legitimate Republican-backed government of Colfax, Louisiana.

For several days the blacks dug in, with numbers growing. Nash knew he had to strike before their defenses became too strong.

At exactly high noon on Easter Sunday, 1873, more than 400 heavily armed whites, half on horseback, attacked 150 blacks trying to defend Colfax Court House. After an initial charge, the whites took a siege position and started firing. For about an hour it was a shootout with only a few casualties on either side. But the whites had one piece of heavy artillery, and when they got it in position, the playing board changed. Two shots blew holes through the black defense and killed several. There was panic in the ranks. The Colfax defenders lost all discipline. Most of them fled the courthouse, while others tried to find some corner to hide in.

The whites chased down the fleeing black men and murdered them in various ways and places. Their bodies floated down the Red River and flattened a spot of crops. Most of those inside the courthouse were killed. Near sundown, 50 black men were rounded up, set aside and allowed to live. Near midnight Satan got back to work. The 50 black prisoners were all executed in cold blood.

This was the worst atrocity in the history of the Reconstruction. Altogether, more than 120 black men were killed. Two whites died in the Battle of Colfax Court House. They really could just add this to the list of the Battles of the American Civil War.

Two of the white men who killed black people on Easter Sunday were tried before the United States Supreme Court and acquitted. The Redeemer hero was a man named Cruishank. That decision was rendered in 1876. More on that later.

The Colfax Massacre is certainly one of the under-publicized episodes of American History. Most people who like to read history don't know about it. In the last few years two new books about it have been published, giving it more ink than it's had in some time.

The movie *The Great Escape* makes much of how the Germans executed 50 American PW's. That was In a declared war, and the escapes were draining German resources in the hunt to catch them, thus inflicting German casualties indirectly. What happened at Colfax was much worse. The blacks were only defending a public building from armed aggression, they were completely just, and it was American against American; and everyone who inflicted this murderous injustice got away with it.

The Great Escape says at the end, "This Film is Dedicated to The Fifty."

This little book is dedicated to The Fifty.

This is from the book, *The USA in the Time of Rutherford B. Hayes*: 1877-1881

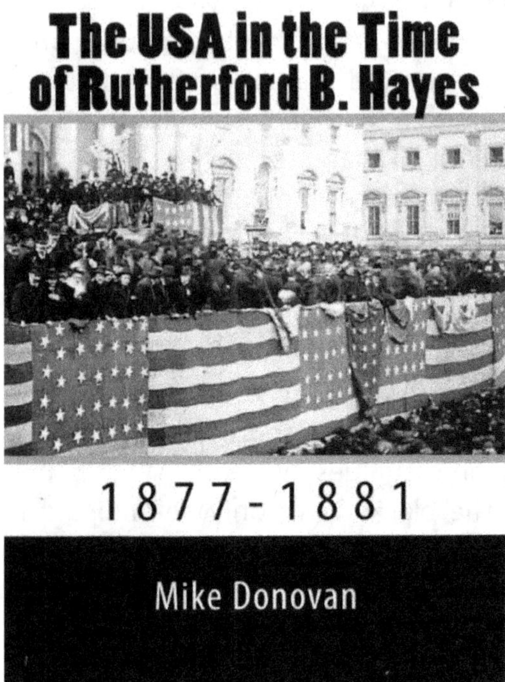

ELECTION OF 1876

It was a good year for Cin city. In 1876, Cincinnati hosted the Republican Convention; its favorite son, Hayes became the nominee; and the Cincinnati Reds baseball team began their first season as a member of the brand new National League.

The Democrats, at their convention, nominated Samuel Tilden, of New Lebanon, New York. New Lebanon is about a mile from the Massachusetts border. 'Tildo' started in politics as a young man by campaigning in 1840 for the unpopular President, Martin Van Buren. Hayes might have had some geographical prejudice, as Van Buren was from two towns away.

Sam Tilden dropped out of Yale, yet made himself a multi-millionaire as a corporate lawyer. Tilden was the only bachelor among the all the losing nominees for president in US history. This was not because Sammy T. liked to play the field. He simply never seemed interested in the ladies at any point in his life. This is not the kind of person I could ever have voted for.

Sammy T made his name in politics largely by standing up to the corrupt NYC boss, Thurlow Tweed, of Tammany Hall. 'Boss Tweed' would end up in jail during a later presidential administration.

Tilden's biggest problem - besides being a member of the racist Democratic Party - was his personality. Tilden was colder than a Point Barrow March midnight, and no one denied it, not even Tilden.

On Election Day night, Tilden the Democrat initially seemed the clear winner in both the electoral and popular votes. But the Republicans challenged the results in three states: Florida, South Carolina, and Louisiana. The Republicans also disputed one electoral-vote from Oregon.

The Republicans used fast math to decide which controversial state returns to contest the most vigorously. The party used power and influence to control the decisions of these 3 state elections' boards, and the boards suddenly decided that Republican Hayes had won.

The country was stuck in a great controversy. The Democrats were enraged. They threatened: "Tilden or War."

It was finally agreed that an 'Electoral Commission' would settle the issue. It would be composed of: 5 men from the US Senate, 5 from the House, and 5 from the Supreme Court.

The ten Congressmen evened out at five Republicans and five Democrats; so it was up to the Supreme Court Five, fortunately, an odd number: Someone was going to win. Two of the justices were Democrat and two were Republican. Justice David Davis was an 'Independent Republican' and his judgment would be more or less the deciding vote. Both sides trusted Davey Davis to remain neutral in conscience.

But then the Democratic Illinois Legislature got too clever for its own good. It voted Davis to the United States Senate. The Illinois Dems thought that this would force Davis to side with the Democrats when deciding the election controversy. But instead, Davis showed the independence he was already known for. He took the Senate seat but resigned from the Electoral Commission! The Democrats had shot themselves in the foot. Dave's Supreme Court replacement on the commission was a Republican sympathizer named Joseph Bradley. From then on, the vote on everything went 8-7, Hayes over Tilden. All the disputed state electoral votes went to the Republicans.

The Democrats were still capable of continuing the quarrel but the two Parties made a behind the scenes deal at the Wormley Hotel.

The Democrats did not accept the Hayes presidency in return for the removal of federal troops from the South. That is commonly believed, even by many historians.

Hayes had made it known several times during the campaign that this removal would be his plan if elected.

In the deal that was agreed upon, the removal of federal troops was the least important concession from the Republicans. Both sides knew that was a given. The Democrats accepted Hayes for four bigger favors than that.

One: Federal funding for the Texas & Pacific Railroad, with large land grants in the South.

Two: Southern local control on federal job handouts.

Three: A Southerner or two in the Hayes cabinet.

Four: Major federal money and aid for internal improvements in the South, especially roads, bridges, and harbors.

The South basically wanted economic integration with the North and federal money for business growth. The Wormley deal on the removal of troops was a smokescreen to sell the larger deal, which was the new co-operation with Washington towards the Southern economy. The troops were leaving anyway, but it was easier to sell the public a supposed corrupt bargain for the removal of federal troops, than it was to admit the true corrupt bargain of railroads, land, cabinet posts, and federal spoils in local areas. The 'bloody shirt' angle was a matador distracting the bull, while the big money deals went down.

The election of 1876 was not settled officially until March 3, 1877, only two days before the Inauguration!

Hayes made one gesture of conciliation with respect to the disputed results of '76: He pledged to serve only one term. In 1880 he kept his promise. His hat was not in the ring.

This is from the book, *The USA in the Time of James Garfield*: 1881

SHOOTING OF GARFIELD - SUCCESSION CRISIS

Garfield was shot on July 2, 1881, after only four months in office.

For 79 days, Garfield lingered on in frail condition. This opened up an important controversy about the line of succession in the White House.

The country held out hope, but the victim knew better. On the day he was shot he told his doctors, "I am a dead man." Between July 22 and September 19 Garfield performed a singular act of Presidential duty. He signed one extradition paper. Then he collapsed from the effort of that one signature. It wasn't looking good.

The question now arose as to whether or not Vice-President Arthur should assume the duties of president, without in fact becoming President. Should he be given the oath of office, thus supplanting the president? Another question had to be addressed. If Arthur were sworn in, would Garfield then be allowed to return to office if he recovered; and if so by what legal written authority? The matter came to a formal discussion at a cabinet meeting on Sept 2, 1881, and the honchos came to this conclusion. For now, Garfield would continue as president and they would consult with Garfield before making any important decisions ('squeeze my hand if we should attack, squeeze it twice if we should try diplomacy first.')

Fortunately, there were no crucial decisions on war and peace in the late summer of 1881. Lord knows how a real national emergency would have gone down. The succession issue was still unresolved when Garfield solved it by dying at his home in Elberon, New Jersey, on September 19th.

This is from the book, The *USA in the Time of Chester A. Arthur*: 1881-1885

GERONIMO'S WAR

The leader of the Apache's finally gave up in December of 1886. Geronimo had gone off the reservation several times. This time, he and his small band of brave troublemakers decided to fight no more.

The Apache Wars had been going on for more than 20 years. They had gone through many phases, but the white invaders kept growing stronger and the Apache's weaker. Confined to the Fort Apache Reservation, all they could do now is 'go off the reservation' and rebel that way. They could no longer sustain a real war against the whites.

Native-Americans who left the reservation, lost all legal status. They were not recognized as United States citizens and thus could be apprehended by anyone claiming legal authority. A mall security guard could arrest an Indian or shoot him in the back while he ran away and then claim self defense ("the Indian was going to get a gun.")

By the time of Arthur, the few Indian War stories left to tell are sad beyond words. The situation for Geronimo was typical. He is going to war against 10,000 white soldiers by hiding in the hills with 25 warriors and 120 women and children. Once in a while, his 25 does a hit and run on a couple of white settlers and the alarm goes out across the countryside to stop this menace. But it is essentially a pathetic scene. It's hard for me to root against the Indians in these times, even when I read about them going berserk on innocent settlers. Their situation is just too sad. An entire race, barely enough to fill up a jazz club, shivering in the snowy hills, exchanging long-distance rifle fire with Caucasians and actually wondering if the race will still exist one month from now: this was the state of the last decade of the "Indian Wars." Reading about the Apache Wars and their ilk makes me pine for the good ol' days when the American Indian had a fighting chance under Little Turtle or Powhatan. These final-frontier years were just a humiliation; and the native culture still carries the scars of resentment. Try telling these people to "go back where you came from!"

This is from the book, *The USA in the Time of Grover Cleveland*: His First Administration 1885-1889

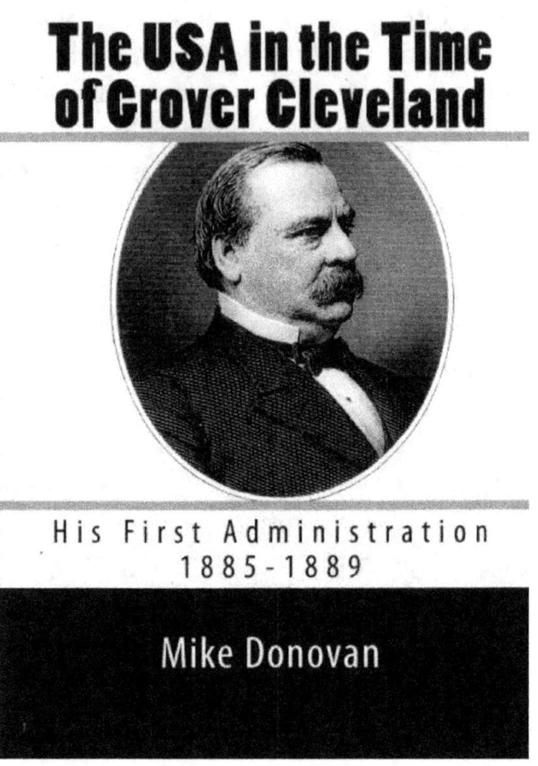

BACKWARD BELLAMY - 1888

His name was Ed Bellamy. His book *Looking Backward,* was a smash best seller in 1888. Edzo was a native of Chicopee, Mass.

The book was the fictional reminiscences of a Bostonian in the year 2000. In Bellamy's Boston of 2000 there was no longer any poverty, and the rich had to share their wealth. Everything was put to good use, and there was no industrial waste. I lived in Boston in 2,000 and I could tell you that his dream was just that, a dream. While he was at it Bellamy might as well have added that there was no traffic congestion or noise pollution, that everyone was always cheerful no matter how much snow fell, parking was free and easy, and everyone enunciated their words correctly.

Bellamy referred to his visionary system as 'Nationalism,' but many of his contemporaries considered Bellamy a socialist. Edward knew that he was a little bit socialist, but disavowed the organized Socialist movement with vehemence. He wrote to a friend that:

"I may seem to out-socialize the socialists, yet the word socialist is one I could never well stomach. In the first place it is a foreign word itself and equally foreign in all its suggestions. It suggests the red flag with all manner of sexual novelties, and an abusive tone towards God and religion."

This is from the book, *The United States in the Time of Benjamin Harrison*: 1889-1993

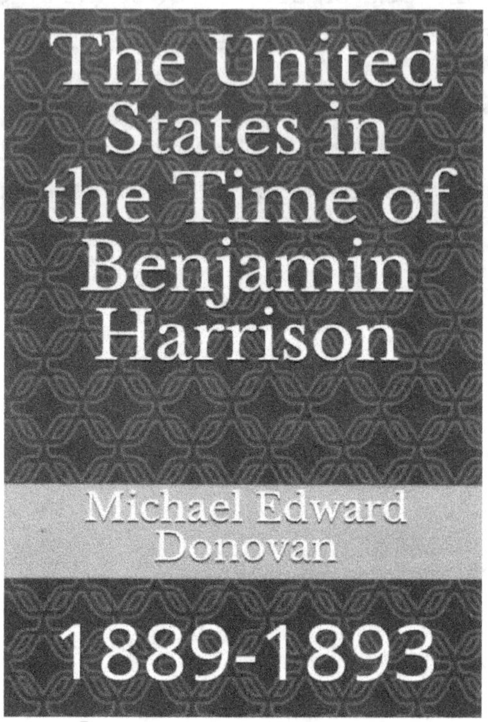

THE SOONER THE BETTER - 89

The Oklahoma Indians had, by and large, supported the Southern Confederacy during the Civil War, and for this they had to be punished. Other Indians tribes were therefore forcibly settled on Oklahoma Indian lands. The arid Oklahoma area was useless for agriculture anyway, so no one was worried about it, at least no white one. The western OK panhandle was so useless that even the Indians had never settled there.

In time, however the value of the central Oklahoma lands was revised upward, and so it was time to resume the punishment. The government suddenly designated two million additional acres in the center of the state for white settlement.

The eager pioneers lined up on the Oklahoma border on April 23, 1889. It was like the beginning of the Boston Marathon. On foot, or by horse and wagon, everyone was set to go. A train was loaded and ready to rumble, hundreds of people holding places on the roofs of the RR cars.

A starter's gun fired at noon. Thousands of horses and wagons went racing westward across Oklahoma territory, while yelling dumb stuff. No less than 50,000 crazed crackers stampeded over the Indian lands on the first day alone. Soon instant Oklahoma cities, made of tents, sprang up. They had names like Guthrie, Norman, Lashua, and Kingfisher. Many would grow into permanent cities that are still bustling today.

There was, however, one downer surprise waiting for the new stampeders. Thousands of white settlers had cheated, beating the rush by sneaking out ahead of schedule, and staking out their claims illegally. They were already squatting on much of the best land available. These white sleaze-bags had arrived 'sooner' than the legal start of April 23, 1889. From this is derived the nickname the Oklahoma 'Sooner.' Every time an Oklahoma football defensive lineman is called for an off-sides penalty he is living up to his team nickname.

4.23.89 marked a key milestone in the relentless slap-around of the American Indian.

This is from the book, *The USA in the Time of Grover Cleveland II*: His Second Administration 1893-1897

GOLD DIGGER PIERPONT MORGAN - 1895

It was an accepted formula that the USA needed at least 100 million dollars in solid gold to operate. When the gold supply dipped below that figure, and continued to plummet, President Cleveland had a little private panic of his own. By the beginning of 1895 the gold supply had dropped to 42 million dollars.

On February 7, 1895, the President and a few close advisors met with millionaire banker J. Pierpont Morgan to discuss plans to stop the bleeding. JP suggested that the government buy a hundred million dollars worth of gold with bonds, under the legal umbrella of a law passed way back in 1862. Sure, that law was passed under the emergency of war, but this crisis was legitimate too. So why not? Cleveland and his advisors approved the plan. The millionaire banker JPM began buying all the gold he could, all over the world, and then loaned the gold to the United States government in exchange for US bonds, redeemable at about 4%.

The scheme worked. The one-way-street flow of gold out of the country stopped at long last. The gold standard was saved and retained. The nation began to show signs of rising from the depths of the depression of the 1890's. J.P. Morgan is a great hero! Okay, not exactly, but some credit is due, sure.

Morgan made seven million in profit from loaning the gold to the United States, and for this, all the modern historians put him in a sleeper hold. Liberal history respects J.P. Morgan about as much as a gas station owner charging 700% for fuel during a hurricane.

Morgan's percentage was not exorbitant by any banking standards, then or now, and he had no selfish need to make the investment.

The neo-left pundits, none of whom had to live through the Panic and Depression of the 1890's still consider this incident one of the blackest stains on the history of the planet. J.P. Morgan's name is now synonymous with greed, so there is little chance his golden deed will ever get any credit for saving the US economy when it was possibly the only thing that could have.

Morgan later recalled the White House meeting with Cleveland (and Onley) on February 7. He said Cleveland was upset that the banker had him over a barrel. The robust President paced about the room complaining that Morgan was forcing him to do what he did not want to do. Cleveland knew the kind of criticism he would get from the left, although he probably did not imagine that it would get worse with the passage of a hundred years.

Interestingly, Cleveland's account of the meeting is kinder to Morgan than Morgan's own account. Writing in 1907, Cleveland was hardly seething with resentment towards the vilified baron of big business:

"I found that I was in negotiation with a man of large business comprehension and of remarkable knowledge and prescience. In an hour or two of the preliminary discussion I saw he had a clear comprehension of what I wanted and what was needed, and that,

with lightning rapidity, he had reached a conclusion as to the best way to meet the situation. I saw too, that with him, it was not merely a matter of business but of clear-sighted, far seeing patriotism. He was not looking for a personal bargain, but sat there, a great patriotic banker, concerting with me and my advisors measures to avert peril, determined to do his best in a severe and trying crisis."

This is from the book, The *USA in the Time of William McKinley*: 1897-1901

EVANGELINA COSIO CISNERNOS - 10.7.1897

A marker on the road to the Spanish American War was the dramatic rescue from a Cuban jail of an 18 year old woman named Evangelina Cisneros.

Evangelina was very attractive, and she supported the Cuban rebels. She also had a few American friends who knew William Randolph Hearst.

Evangelina was arrested while conducting agitation for Cuban freedom on the Isle of Pine Combs. While Miss Cisneros was a prisoner, a Spanish Colonel Jose Ferrero made sexual advances towards her to a degree that would make Billy Bush shudder. Eve screamed in panic. Five Insurrectos heard what was going on from the outside and broke into the jail. They tied up Colonel Ferrero.

Within the hour the Spanish made a counter-rescue of the Colonel, and made Evangelina Henrietta Cisneros a prisoner again. This time they took her to a notorious and more secure prison, one reserved usually for lunatics and undesirables.

US newspaper magnate William Randolph Hearst got wind of this and sent down a team of reporters with instructions to rescue the young lady. Go make a spectacular story and report it at the same time! The lead reporter, Karl Decker, and his team of five men had plenty of guns. They did it. They went in, and busted lady Cisneros out of jail on October 7, 1897. Two days later she slipped off the island in disguise on the steamship *Seneca* (she was disguised as an ugly old woman.)

Evangelina Cisneros

When Evangelina reached New York she became an American heroine. EHS published a book that sold 200,000 copies called *No, Way, Jose!* Hearst made sure that Cisneros got all the royalties.

Some historians say that the whole thing was probably an elaborate hoax, a big fat publicity stunt. But recent scholarship by a professor from American University concludes the story to be true. If so, it's time for someone to write the movie script.

Evangelina Cisneros married one of her rescuers six months later. Would she do that if it was all a fake?

This is from the book, *The USA in the Time of Theodore Roosevelt*: 1901-1909

COAL STRIKE OF 1902

A common expression going around in TR's time was 'Roosevelt's luck.' Any person could use it to describe positive turns of fortune. TR had lucked out into the Presidency, survived San Juan Hill, survived the trolley crash in Pittsfield, and had been born rich and lucky to begin with.

Roosevelt's luck would hold out once more during the national anguish that was the coal miners' strike of 1902. It was a close call, and it could have hurt him, but in the end, Roosevelt emerged more popular than before.

The miners of Pennsylvania hadn't had a raise since 10,000 B.C. Working conditions were dangerous and cruel. Employees had to buy at the company store because they were paid in company scrip rather than US cash. The company store didn't give its employees a discount. They charged them more than they would have to pay at a public store. The operators gave the miners the shaft.

The workers were paid by the tonnage they produced. So the owners decided that a miners ton was 2,500 pounds, not 2,000 as is taught in the schoolbooks. The average miner made $501 a year in 1901. The job was deadly dangerous. About 600 miners died a year in accidents, not to mention the long term damage to their lungs. Miners who wanted to sue would lose all their gains to lawyers' fees, so there was no point in trying.

In this corner, weighing 200 million tons of coal and millions of bucks was George F. Baer, head of the Philadelphia and Reading Coal Co. Baer had a heart of coal. Any miner who even complained was declared a socialist agitator and fired without a hearing. Miners who even talked about joining a union had better sleep with one eye open.

In this corner, weighing millions of American miners was John Mitchell, the head of the largely unrecognized UMW, the United Mineworkers Union.

The owners and the workers had slugged it out during a short strike in 1900. The government played mediator, and the compromise settlement left both sides miserable. The laborers felt they had been shortchanged by light concessions, while the owners were chewing nails over the fact that they had allowed government arbitration of any kind. They had sacrificed the sacred principle of lassaiz faire in order to keep their books in the black, and some had second thoughts about it when it was too late.

It was the Republican Party bosses that had pressured the coal barons to back down and make concessions in 1900. The R leaders pleaded that it was an Election year and the reaction could do all conservatives more harm than it was worth. 'You guys don't want Bryan in there, believe me!'

Next time, they privately grumbled, they would eat their losses if that's what it took to show those no-good dirty workers. They got their chance to in 1902. 1902 was not an Election year.

On March 18, 1902, the coal miners called for a strike. They appealed to the owners to make some concessions and avoid this, but Max Baer said "bring it on." The strike began in earnest on May 12. 150,000 men and women walked off the job. Strike headquarters was Hazelton PA, but soon the whole state, and beyond, was a non-coaling region.

The strike made the nation very unhappy. The USA could survive for the summer, but what was going to happen if the thing lingered on, and the cold weather came on? People could freeze to death and schools could close.

The national sentiment was generally, but not yet overwhelmingly, on the side of the miners. Religious leaders wrote to Baer asking him to see this thing through, reasonably. Max, will you please compromise?

Baer wrote one of them back a heartfelt letter in which he made his philosophy quite plain. That letter turned out to be a big mistake. The Baer letter was arrogant and over the top in its disdain for the working man. Baer's pen was so insensitive that when it was first printed, many questioned its authenticity. The man who received the letter had to have it photocopied and reproduced in its original form. When the Baer letter was proven true, and pasted on page two of a hundred major newspapers, the nation came down firmly against the coal barons, although this is not say that it ended the trouble.

Here is what Baer, the owner of Reading Coal had to say to a religious leader; the words that got him in trouble:

"I see that you are a religious man. But you are evidently biased in favor of the right of the working man to control a business in which he has no other interest than to secure fair wages for the work he does.

I beg of you not to be discouraged. The rights and interests of the laboring man will be protected and cared for – not by labor agitators, but by the Christian men to whom God in his infinite wisdom has given control of the property interests of this country."

The country reacted badly against that letter.

In June, TR asked Secretary Knox if the United States could sue the coal interests for restraint of trade under the Sherman Anti-trust Act.

In the meantime the coal owners were asking if they could prosecute the labor leaders under the terms of the Sherman Anti-trust Act. All of which proved that the Sherman Anti-trust Act was weak. It would be many more years before the Act would straighten out its act, and find direction and authority.

President Roosevelt had to get this coal thing settled before the fall elections and the winter cold. He wanted to enlist the support of other sectors of big business. If other rich greedy businessmen could convince the coal bosses that what was bad for the American economy was bad for all big business, maybe the logjam could break. Certainly the coal strike, if it went on long enough, would set off a negative chain reaction that would hurt all big businessmen in the pocketbook. The rising price of gasoline today often drives up the price of food and other important commodities and is has ripple effect on the entire economy. It was a similar situation in 1902 when coal, not oil, drove the railroad trains and heated the buildings. Coal was the life blood of the American economic machine.

TR was saddled by his famous reputation as a trust-buster. How could he ask big business to assist him now when he had been doing them harm for a year and half? They didn't owe him a nickel. His only hope was that through personal intervention he could appeal to their patriotism (lots o' luck) and their selfishness (now you're talkin').

The first to cross the big businessmen picket line was J.P. Morgan. This millionaire was willing to treat with Teddy the trust-buster because JP knew that his own fortune would suffer if the coal-pigs refused to compromise. Mark Hannah, the powerful Republican leader, and a potential candidate for President in 1904, told TR the good news that Morgan was willing pitch in to work for a compromise settlement. The bad news: to everyone's surprise, Max Baer gave the thumbs down. Coal was against compromise per se. The coal-pigs (Emma Goldman called them that) were still mad that they had even accepted compromise in 1900 and now actually wanted to get back their losses. They were way past merely not being willing to compromise. It was Max Baer vs. Teddy Bear.

TR knew that he had no legal authority to force a compromise. It was a free country. This wasn't Nicky's Russia. This was the USA with its three famous national colors of green, gold, and silver. But there was nothing to prevent TR from trying to work for a settlement in his capacity as a private citizen who just happened to be the President.

Roosevelt managed to arrange a meeting at Lafayette Place (the White House was closed for renovations) for October 3, 1902, between the angry parties. The meeting was a matter of high publicity, with throngs of reporters watching the celebrities pulling up to the temporary White House like movie stars. It was Coal Strike Oscars night.

The meeting lasted all day. The reporters, and the public mob with them, had only one moment of excitement when a man in a wheelchair (TR was still injured from the Pittsfield trolley crash) went whizzing by a window showing spectacles and a lot of teeth. Everyone cheered. It was the one and only in the flesh!

They might not have cheered so loudly if they knew how badly the big meeting was going.

There are no official records of the meeting, but two things are clear: John Mitchell of the UMW behaved like a perfect gentleman for the entire meeting. Max Baer did not.

The UMW was more than ready and willing to compromise. Baer was not only unwilling to compromise in the tiniest bit, he also behaved like a perfect boor the entire time towards everyone. Baer repeatedly accused the UMW of revolutionary socialist violence that had never happened anywhere. The Coal King repeatedly insulted John Mitchell in a needlessly personal manner. Baer said, for example, that he resented being called to Washington to meet with a criminal, no matter how important the person who wrote the invitation. Baer not only didn't show any deference to the President, he insulted Roosevelt in a personal manner more than once. Big mistake.

Teddy was not a man that took to insults well. By once account (I'm not joking) the President picked up a chair and hurled it at Baer! Not close enough to hit him but enough to create a hush in the room as the chair rocked and rolled to a rest. Baer didn't flinch and sat there with his arms folded in defiance.

TR later wrote that he wished he wasn't in a wheelchair at the time because he "might have picked Baer up by the scruff of the neck and hurled him through the window to the street below." Note the word "through" as opposed to "out." I would have paid good money to see that. Teddy also told a reporter that, "Only one of the three principals at the meeting behaved like a gentleman and it was not I."

TR later insisted that he "didn't mind so much that Baer in at least two cases assumed a manner towards me which was once of insolence. This was not important," he lied, "but it was important that they should absolutely decline to consider matters from the standpoint of the public in any way."

Here he spoke the truth. By the time of this meeting, several schools in New York City had already closed for lack of heating coal.

When this meeting became national news the public and the politicians turned against Baer and his rich friends.

Senator Lodge of Massachusetts, normally a friend of big business, said that if he met a coal baron in public he would walk away without speaking to him.

The strike dragged on.

The President proposed another idea to Mitchell. If John Mitchell would get the men to go back to work, TR would then appoint a commission to work out a compromise settlement once the coal began to flow. Mitchell had to say no. The UMW leader said that if the settlement favored the owners, then Baer would agree to it, but if the settlement favored the workers, Baer would simply not honor it. Mitchell had a point.

The government intervened in small increments. By now there were 10,000 militiamen in the coalfields of Pennsylvania. Maybe they will soon work the mines. But could TR ask them to actually start digging for coal, or were they limited, legally, to protecting the sites from violence? The strike lasted through the summer and well into the fall. The price of coal jumped from 5 to 30 dollars a ton.

Elihu Root said that TR could invoke the old common law that if you're freezing to death, it was legal to cut wood from your neighbor's forest. It bothered neither man that no such common law ever existed in the US or in old England. TR jumped at the idea anyway. The President informed Baer that the US government would soon take over the mines; and would produce the coal that the nation needed. He told Baer about the old common law about the neighbor's wood. President Roosevelt believed that he *was* the law in an emergency.

Baer now began to listen more when TR proposed arbitration. Baer however, demanded that he, not the President (and certainly not the miners) would determine the make-up of the arbitration panel. It would have to be a five-man panel consisting of:

1 - An Army engineer
2 - A mining engineer
3 - A Federal Judge from Pennsylvania
4 - A Coal mining businessman
5 - "An eminent sociologist."

Baer wanted a loaded panel in the favor of the owners. Ted said no can do and the Coal Crisis of 1902 was stuck in the mud all over again. TR made a counterproposal. He would make it a seven man panel. Baer could name the first four. The fifth would be former president Grover Cleveland, and he, Roosevelt, would pick the last two.

"No!"

Then TR had a brainstorm. He calculated that it was really all about Baer's pride. The President would name the persons he wanted, but under Baer-pleasing titles that they really weren't entitled to. TR would get the panel he wanted, and Baer would look as if he had made TR do his bidding.

A priest; and a leader of the conductor's union were named to the panel under false titles. Another labor leader was named as the "eminent sociologist."

To almost everyone's surprise, Baer agreed to this panel of arbitration. TR was the only one not shocked. It took one to know one. A big ego knew how to manipulate another one.

The arbitration panel did its work over the next four months and made its official finding on March 22, 1903. The miners would get a 10% raise and some other concessions on work conditions, especially on safety issues. But the United Mine Workers union would not get recognition. It was a three-year deal.

The settlement came just in time and the ongoing effort helped the Republicans immensely in the Congressional elections of 1902. The coal settlement fueled TR's chances for 1904. Now, Teddy was not only a trust-buster, he was a friend of labor as well.

This is from the book, *The USA in the Time of William H. Taft*: 1909-1913

A TARIFFIC START - PAYNE-ALDRICH 1909

Now for that ever-exciting subject: the tariff. Please try and control your emotions.

Taft had promised a revision of the tariff if elected, and everyone knew that 'revision' meant reduction. Many Americans blamed the high cost of living on the high tariffs, which hadn't changed substantially since sky-hi Dingley in 1897. It was common thinking in 1908 that the high tariff led directly to more monopoly in business; and since everyone was against monopoly except Rockefeller and Morgan, it was safe to pledge tariff reductions in any campaign.

In practice, tariff reduction had to pass the Congress. Big business had its hands deep into the pockets of many members, so it was always hard to get real tariff reductions, even if the public supported them.

The House passed a bill for serious tariff reduction on March 15, 1909. Then it went to the Senate, where Nelson Aldrich of Rhode Island led the obstructionists. Hundreds of amendments were attached to the bill, which reduced the practical effect of the original to nothing. Most amendments were for increases in tariffs on exceptional items. It added up to no gain for the low tariff movement even though Congress was about to pass a bill that ostensibly lowered it.

This is from the book, *The United States in the Time of Woodrow Wilson*: 1913-1921

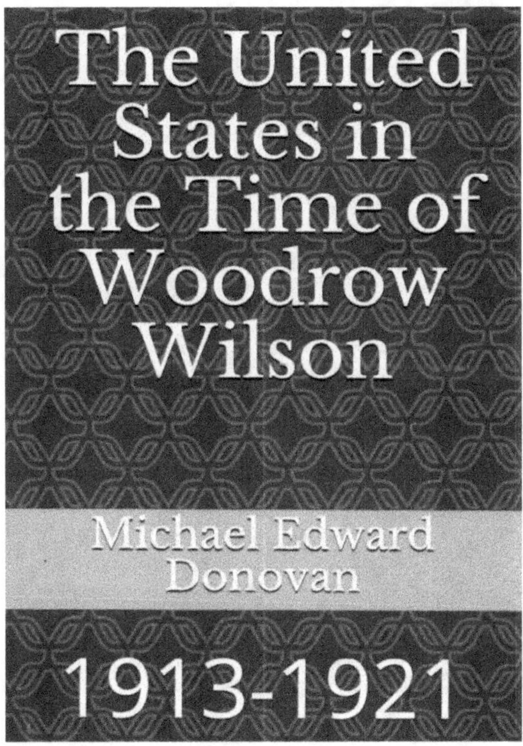

WHIPPING UP SUPPORT FOR THE WAR - 11.7.17

Well, at least they didn't kill them.

A story now about war bonds, a story in the spirit of 76. Bonds paid for more than half the war. It was every American's patriotic duty to own at least one bond.

Judge Thomas Evans in Tulsa Oklahoma declared it a town law that everyone had to buy one. "War bond or bail bond, you're choice," he told citizens. 12 men from the IWW refused to buy a bond and Evans had them all arrested. While awaiting trial, a mob of Patriots broke into the jail and brought the Wobblies out to the woods. They tied the dirty dozen to a tree, one at a time, and whipped them with a cat-o-nine-tails; and then gave them the ol' 1773 tar and feather treatment.

Disgusting, especially considering the weak reasons America got into this war in the first place.

These regulators hated anyone who didn't stand up for war. All had to buy bonds and support the war, in the name of America's freedom.

This is from the book, *World War One in 1914*: Clash of Empires

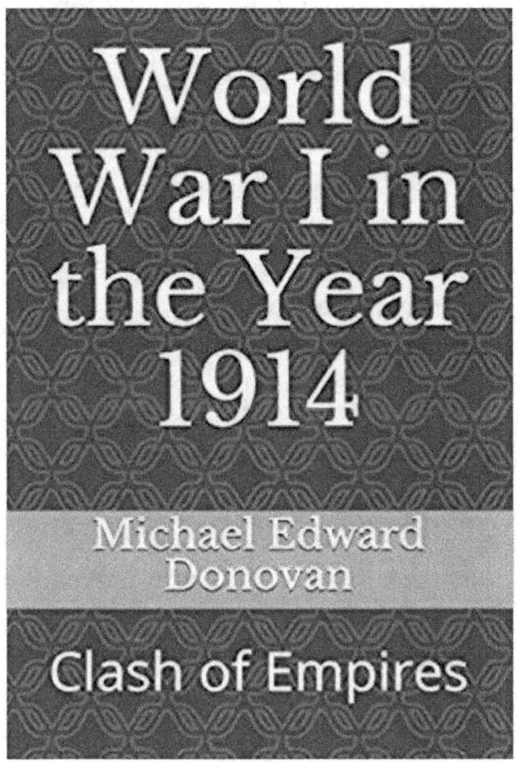

18 REASONS (PG. 18) WHY GERMANY BLUNDERED INTO WAR
 Wilson had his 14 Points. Bush 1 had his thousand points of light. Here's my 18 points of darkness, 18 reasons why Germany stumbled into a disastrous war.
 Austria and Russia mobilized first, but everything revolved around Germany. All the great powers were terrified of Germany mobilizing and moving before there was time to react. In that sense, all the mobilization that led to German mobilization was still, at the core, a matter of Germany.
 At face value Germany (25 almost autonomous states comprising the German Empire, and not really a nation called 'Germany') was

insane to help start a war cheerfully, a war that would waste 2 million Teutonic lives. If it knew what it was getting itself into, the German wolf would have stayed in its lair and put a stop payment on the blank check it gave Austria in July of 1914.

A combination of the following 18 miscalculations added up to a smart nation doing something very stupid. 12 of them are based on the opinions of US Ambassador to Berlin 1913-1917, James Gerard. I added six more.

I list them in approximate reverse order of importance. You will see that the last two seem to contradict each other; but these polar opposite forces worked in tandem to bring on the catastrophe:

18. The Kaiser's dream of Germanic-Islamic Empire

The Kaiser surprised everyone, especially Russia, by declaring in 1913 that he was now the protector and defender of Muslims all over the world. This was a direct threat to Russia, where many Moslems (old spelling) lived under the Tsarist rule.

The Kaiser ruined his hope for an alliance with Russia with this gesture. Wilhelm more or less chose Otto over Nicky. Wilhelm had become quite taken with the idea of a strong permanent alliance with the Ottomans. A Germano-Islamic condo could stretch from Belgium to Persia and back to Morocco.

The Baghdad Railway would turn the dream to reality. Germany sought a railroad from Berlin to Baghdad which would anchor an Empire. When Turkey lost the Balkan War, it messed things up. Serbia, Montenegro, Bulgaria, Greece, and Romania were now blocking the tracks. If Germany and Austria-Hungary made a war, won it, and made all southeast Europe German-Turko condo-ruled, the Berlin to Baghdad Express would be 'Eastdown and Bound, loaded up and truckin'. The greedy desire for this imperialist goal was a danger to peace.

17. The Kaiser's Big Mouth

The Kaiser, from 1896 to 1913, had the bad habit of talking too much and expressing his ambitions too openly. The announcement that he was going to be the godfather of oppressed Muslims is a prime example. The other powers took his big talk more seriously than he did, and were counter-arming for war in response. The

Kaiser was a publicity hound, and his need for constant publicity helped stir up the pot for war. Basil Liddel Hart stresses this point in his book, *The Real War*. The Kaiser was pulling the walls down in on Europe with his endless headline-seeking threats. He didn't actually want a war, but he wanted to enjoy threatening everyone by telling everyone that he wasn't afraid of one. The rest of Europe took that to mean that he wanted one and prepared for war in response.

16. Italy - The Germans were counting on Italian intervention, or at least support. The Axis of World War One on opening day (8.1.14) was the trio of Germany, Austro-Hungary, and Italy.

When the Italians did not come in on the side of Germany, and remained neutral, it was a strategic disappointment to the Kaiser. When Italy joined the Entente in 1915, it was a lot more than a disappointment. Italy tied down half the Austro-Hungarian Army for three years and even forced the Germans to send divisions to help there. The Germans would/could have had these 30 or 40 Austrian divisions helping out on the western front.

The presumption that Italy would remain in the 'Triple Alliance' was a tall German blunder. The help of Italy had figured in Germany's calculations for war.

15. The Arms of Krupp - In the case of Germany, the charge that munitions manufacturers more or less actually wanted the war is true. William Manchester wrote a book about it. Like US Steel, what was good for Krupp was good for Germany. I do not, however, agree with those who say that American and British munitions makers wanted to start a war for the sake of profits.

The Krupp's armaments industry influenced German military and political leaders. They thought they would make millions on a war and instead they lost it all. The Kruppsters did not expect a four year stalemate and a defeat to wrap it up.

14. Ireland - The German Ambassador in London reported to Berlin in early 1914 that a serious rebellion was about to break out in Ireland. Not only that, but if Britain dared to go to war to protect its continental allies, Ireland would take that opportunity to rebel. England was going have its hands full soon without joining a war; to

join one would be that much more out of the question. Germany counted on a green deterrent that didn't exist.

Ireland did not erupt in rebellion until the spring of 1916. The Easter Rebellion was contained with only incidental damage to the war effort.

13. British neutrality a given - The German Ambassador to London assured Berlin that even without an Irish rebellion, London would simply stay neutral, period, in a continental war.

Wrong: Britain had a long standing policy that no continental power must ever be allowed to dominate the continent. So in fact, Britain had no choice but to get involved. Hitler made the same blunder when he invaded Poland in 1939. Ribbentrop, the arrogant Nazi Foreign Minister, had guaranteed Hitler that England would not intervene, and it did, and for the same reason.

12. Taking French pessimism at face value - Many politicians in France were lamenting how woefully unprepared France was for any sudden war. Germans in the peanut gallery were taking notes and taking all this 'woe is us' talk too seriously. They reported back what they wanted to believe and what their bosses wanted to hear.

France was far stronger than its worst pessimists said it was. (Same with the USA: the defense sky has been falling here since I was old enough to read the papers. Even at the height of the Ronald Reagan military build-up, books were published declaring and proving that Russia could beat NATO in a war and it was time to panic.)

11 - Belgian conscription - The German war-plan was to get behind Paris by way of Belgium, but Belgium was in the beginning phase of instituting conscription, the draft. If Germany waited too long, Belgium might be too strong. The 'Schleiffen Plan' might not work if Belgium doubles the size of its army. Better a war sooner than later for this reason.

10 - The Russian Railroads - France had loaned Russia a ton of money to build a railroad that ran right up to the border with the German Empire. That railroad was under construction at the end of 1913 and Germany, which already had a completed railroad system that went

right up to the border with Russia, felt it needed to attack Russia now, before that Russian railroad was completed. The military balance was all about railroads and this one was a key system in the east. We'd best use ours, before they get a chance to use theirs.

It wasn't just the Russian railways; it was the rising economic power of Russia. The Kaiser was quite plain in his conversations in the pre-war years about the need for a war with Russia before Russia becomes too strong. Many German leaders agreed. These crazed Heinie hawks spoke of the need to attack Russia *before Russia attacks Germany*. The former thought-pattern allows for peace through strength; but the second does not. The second almost requires a pre-emptive attack on Russia.

The bimbos in Berlin projected their own aggressive intent on the enemy. Russia had no intention of attacking Germany. Russia *could risk* war with Germany if Russia moved on Constantinople, but Russia never presumed there was some big showdown inevitably coming with Germany, and Germany felt that way in reverse. Germany was probably blundering in thinking there had to be this great showdown between Slav and Teuton: but it was definitely blundering in thinking the Russians saw things the same way.

Besides, you have Poles to block. Here we have some key linkage between the Kaiser and Fuhrer. Both were convinced that in the final analysis, everything, including the rotation of the earth, revolved around the great mass military showdown between Teuton and Slav. The need for this showdown, which Russia did not exactly share, inspired two world wars.

Maybe there was some subconscious rationalizing, and the Great German General Staff had just convinced itself that Russia was planning to conquer Germany because the Staff boys had toys and wanted to use them. They wanted any reason to put the world's best war-machine into action, so they exaggerated a vague threat into a do or die showdown that had to happen.

The new Russian railroads were defensive and good for the economy. They were the only indication of Russia supposedly preparing for the big attack on Germany.

The Kaiser and the generals also thought that the time to attack was now, not tomorrow, because today, Austria-Hungary was a strong ally. What if we don't have A-H with us later on and the showdown with Russia comes and we are alone?

Russia was the 'Great Satan' to Germany, not France. France was the hated Lesser Satan. Alsace-Lorraine was bitter, and a cause for the war, but not as serious as the German perception that the Russians were planning on wiping the German race, state, and culture off the face of the earth. The Germans planned a war in the West to plan the realization of its dreams in the East. France was supposed to bend its will to Germany but not become Germany. White Russia and the Ukraine were a different story.

I'll throw in here the general point about 'war by timetable.' All nations, including Germany, were in the 'war by timetable' trap. The states of the continent were all afraid that if they hesitated so much as a day when someone else was mobilizing, it could mean a sudden defeat for the home team. So the armies and the railroad systems were all timed to go into overdrive the moment war was declared, and start rushing 100,000 troops here and there as rapidly as possible, lest the other side get the drop like the Rebs did at the first Bull Run. This led to the political leaders losing control of events about three hours after war was declared. Whatever chance there was to pull back was lost one it got in the hands of the army and their requisitioned railroads. I'd make this a separate point, but about six countries were guilty of war by timetable, so I won't tack it on to a Germany list. I believe the phrase 'war by timetable' comes from A.J.P. Taylor.

9.   The Russian Revolution - The German Ambassador to Russia convinced Chancellor Bethman-Hollweg and the Kaiser that Russia was so close to imploding, that the start of a serious war would set it off. All Germany had therefore to do was attack Russia and within a month there would no organized Russian state to oppose it.

Wrong, you dip. The start of the war made the Tsar's hold on power stronger, not weaker. Russia held strong for 3 years and when it finally overthrew the Tsar in the spring of 1917, the new government continued on with the war against Germany. By the time of the Russian implosion, Germany was already losing the food war, and America was taking its shirt off for the fight. The second

Russian Revolution in November 1917 almost pulled the Kaiser's chestnuts out of the fire, but almost don't count. So there was some logic to point 9, but eons too much time passed before it materialized. The miscalculation was that Russia was tottering on Revolution at the end of 1913.

The Germans forgot about 'wag the reindeer.' A war is as likely to solidify a shaky government as topple it over. The Germans thought a war would topple the Romanovs.

8 - German overestimation of the strategic power of its three new super-weapons: poison gas, Zeppelins, and flamethrowers.

   None of the three proved capable of winning a campaign. The flame-thrower and poison gas were of some initial value at the local level (tactical value), but the British and French made their own version as copy-cat killers, and the trick plays were all non-decisive. They only added to the great stalemate. The Zeppelins were supposed to destroy British cities and bring the London government to the negotiating table with trembling hands. The Zeppelin bombers proved to be a highly overestimated weapon whose only value was terrorizing and then angering the British people. The only thing they accomplished was forcing the British to bring some fighter planes back from the continent to play home defense.

   Germany was ahead of Britain in machine gun technology, but not enough to think it had a super-weapon advantage there.

7 - The Leipzig Monument - 1913 was the 100 year anniversary of the great Battle of Leipzig in the Napoleonic wars. The Leipzig Monument was dedicated in late 1913 and stirred much of the population to new heights of martial pride. The LM contributed to the bizarre scene in August 1914 of thousands of doomed civilians cheering the news of war at last.

6 - The false belief that history repeats itself

   No one could truly foresee the horrific stalemate that defied sanity and decency from 1914 to 1918. Wars were always clearly won or lost at some point, and soon enough. The other nations that went to war in 1914 shared this Kaiser miscalculation, or else none of them would have cheered in the streets about the declaration of war.

Military analysts had seen a glimpse of stalemate in the American Civil War, but the Siege of Petersburg broke and the Union won, and they concluded that the permanent stalemate was a non-starter. If any of the nations that went to war in 1914 could have pictured Verdun and the Somme, there wouldn't have been a First World War.

The corollary to the blunder is the economic price of stalemate. All the Great Powers could have told you ahead of time that their nation could barely sustain the costs of a five month war. The thought of a war lasting more than four years was unthinkable financially as well as militarily and morally.

As it turned out, everyone ran out of both money and credit by the spring of 1917 and American intervention saved the Entente by making it solvent at the very hour it was about to bust. The Central Powers didn't have an Uncle Shylock to bail them out.

5 - The sitting ovation - The Reichstag insulted the Emperor in December 1913 by refusing to rise as one when he left after giving a speech. This had never happened before and it indicated that the Kaiser (same person) was not as popular as he thought he was. Wilhelm was livid. He was now extra-anxious to start a war to put these liberals in their place. A war would see to that, and it did. All internal opposition to the Crown ceased in August, 1914. The capital-S Socialists didn't start any more trouble until 1919.

4 - Incident at Zabern, Lorraine, or how an insult started World War One - When Germany won the Franco-Prussian war in 1871 it grabbed the departments of Alsace-Lorraine and made them German provinces. France planned the next war with getting them back as priority one.

Since all 25 German states were almost independent, the two new provinces could not be given to any one state without the objections of others. So Alsace Lorraine became autonomous regions not affiliated with any state, and not states themselves, A-L didn't become the 26th state.

There was a mix of Germans and French, and plenty of mixed blood, in Alsace-Lorraine. Alsatians were proud of their race.

Like the n-word in America, there was a volatile "w-word" in Alsace Lorraine which was okay for the natives to use on each other; but outsiders would risk needing a new nose if they used it. The term was *"wacke"* and it meant "square-head." Alsatians could call each other wackes, but if an outsider did it, they might get whacked.

The German administrator of Alsace Lorraine was a 20 year-old Lieutenant Forster, who looked about 16, and the locals teased him about it. Forster was young and foolish and he tossed the w-word around while training some local troops. When the word got out about the w-word, there was quite the to-do about it.

A local Zabern yokel, an older man, confronted Forster on the street about his big mouth. Forster drew his sword and cut the old codger down, causing a severe injury but not killing him.

Within two hours, 2,000 Alsatians and Lorrainians gathered near Forster's headquarters, chanting evil things. The whole thing came to a showdown, and Forster ordered the angry mob dispersed. The Prussian guards made their presence known and charged into the miscreants. No one was seriously hurt, but a lot of people got pushed around a bit and a few skulls grew lumps. The German troops never actually opened fire.

Word of the riot over a rank-out spread all over France and Germany. This led to a Reichstag proposal to censure the crown! Unprecedented! The Kaiser had a few things to say about this threat by the paper tiger Reichstag. He dared them.

They would and they did (the incident at Zabern was what the Kaiser was speaking about when the Reichstag refused to stand when he left. He was defending the action of the troops at Zabern while they yawned and he boiled.)

The day after the Kaiser got the silent ovation, the Reichstag stunned him, and the nation, by voting to censure the crown. The vote was a Kaiser-kicking 293-54.

This added more fuel to the fire for war. The Kaiser was now more eager than ever to wag the dog, start a war and put the socialists in a box.

Socialists led the censure but were not alone.

3 - Happy memories of recent wars - The last time Germany had gone to war, it had beaten France in less than two months. That was

in 1870. Before that, Germany had battled Austria, Saxony, Bavaria and others in 1866 and beat them all, adding Nassau, Frankfurt, and Hesse-Cassel to the Empire. Before that, in 1864, Germany had fought a war with Denmark. Take a guess who won that one. It was over in three days.

So the German people, from peasant to admiral, had really good vibes about going to war, based on past experience. That's a definite factor in the German blunder of thinking it could/would win a great war in 1914.

2 - Lust for war - Let's face it, the German Empire had a love of war and all things military that was second to none. Children from the age of four were trained to obey and respect the military. A noble woman would marry a second lieutenant quicker than an industrialist with money. A second lieutenant might rise to real power some days, but a businessman will always be just a businessman. Anyone in military uniform could cut to the front of any line in a German city and be as thuggish as they want, if that was their bent. All citizens backed off when a military man walked down the street.

Crown Prince William told a close friend of the American Ambassador that, "if we don't have a war in my father's lifetime, we will certainly have one if I ever become the Kaiser." - The woman asked him. "Why do you say that?" - To which he replied, "Because it is my duty and besides, it would be fun."

1 - Fear of socialist rebellion from below. - The Kaiser and friends heard the progressive footsteps threatening their power long before the wacky incident at Zabern. When the Reichstag disrespected him on purpose it sealed his mind up in a place it was heading to anyway. The rising demand for popular voting rights threatened him.

The newspapers of Germany were infested with people saying it was time to end Prussian militarism. It was time to overthrow it. That movement was growing stronger by the month.

Points 2 & 1 might seem to contradict, but just like in any other era, the lefties and the righties unpeacefully co-exist. Germany was not all macho-man. It was on a balance beam for its future, and war determined which side it was going to come down on. Point 2 is fairly well known, but this last point is unfairly forgotten. A movement was growing to challenge the way the military ran the government. The Kaiser was happy in the summer of 14 to join in the new war because it was a chance to crush his internal as well as his external enemies. It worked for the duration of the war but when the war was lost, the crown went down.

This is from the book, *World War I in 1915*: Stalemate

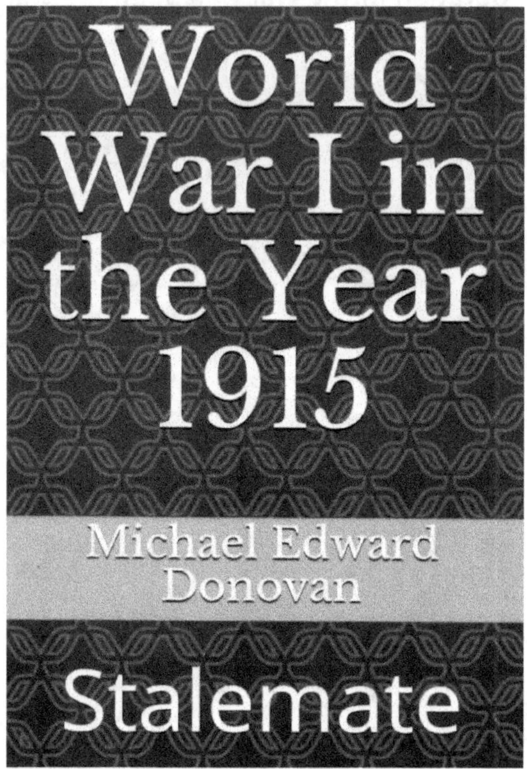

RUSSIA MISSED THE BOAT AT THE BLACK SEA

An astonishing fact of the entire failed Gallipoli campaign was Russia's refusal to help. Russia had fought a war with France and England over Constantinople and the Dardanelles, and did not want to see them victorious there now, even though they were allies! Russia could have attacked Constantinople at the same time the West was attacking Gallipoli; and the idea was, of course, proposed.

Tsar Nicholas was the loser. The Tsar's very survival depended on Britain and France breaking through the Dardanelles to the Black Sea, yet Russia would not help save its own skin. It was all the more bizarre because the initial impetus for the Gallipoli campaign was a January Nick request for help, as he was under military pressure in the Caucasus. By the time the Gallipoli campaign was in its opening round, the Tsar had already informed Britain and France that this help was no longer needed in the Caucasus. But wheels had been set in motion; and threatened Russian dreams of taking Constantinople.

The real threat, that Nicky didn't get, was the boiling Red revolution. The failure of Gallipoli meant starvation and lack of ammo for Russia, and those two led to revolution and military defeat (and it's hard to say which came first.)

This is from the book, *World War I in 1916*: The Sausage Machine

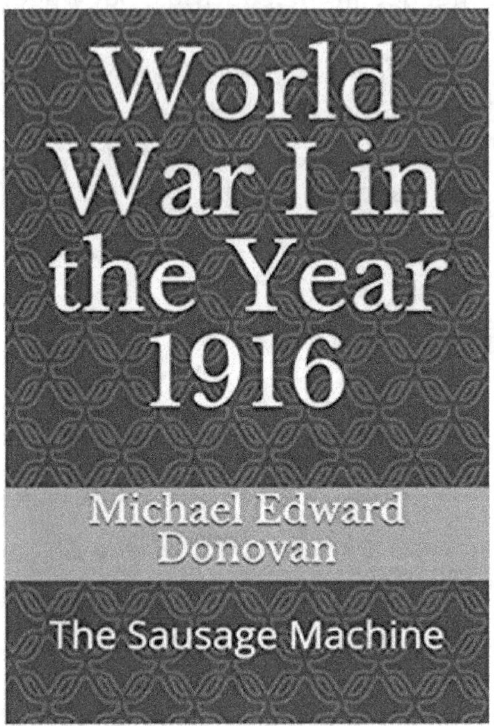

THE HELL OF VERDUN - FEBRUARY TO DECEMBER 1916

The Entente and the Central Powers planned great offensives in 1916. Each knew that this new one would win the war. Each was going to attack the other at around the same time, and neither knew of the other's plan. The Allies messed up by delaying their offensive on the Somme. Instead of attacking in late February, the Somme was postponed for a few weeks. Then the Germans attacked at Verdun and the Somme was postponed for a few months. But initially the plans were coincidentally timed, so that The Germans were going to attack at Verdun around the same time the Entente was going to attack on the Somme.

The Germans planned a full-scale assault on the fortress town of Verdun. 'Big V' was on a salient into the German lines, so the Huns felt that they could attack it on three sides, giving the offense an advantage it did not find elsewhere.

Verdun had more symbolic importance than strategic. Sure, it was at a railroad crossroads, but the Germans had cut off most of those lines that went north and south from Verdun. Two thirds of the French garrison had long been evacuated.

The Germans did a remarkable job in massing an historic amount of artillery opposite Verdun without being detected. Two French officers pleaded for days with their higher ups that a big attack was coming at Verdun, but they were ridiculed as "Ver-Dunces."

General Falkenhayn commanded the dark forces of evil. The opening German artillery attack set a new world's record. 85 trillion shells were launched, or something close to that number.

The attack had some initial success, but the front was too narrow to exploit at anything more than a divisional level. Falkenhayn could not force a corps through a bottleneck even if that bottleneck was secured.

So the Battle of Verdun went on for months as one German regiment after another hurled itself through a narrow front against an old, useless fortress that was a salient into the German lines. That salient made little difference either way, and surely Falkenhayn knew that. Both sides did. It was just a mass slaughter because it was campaign season and we all might as well give it a shot. Verdun was as good a place as any. Some French generals had actually discussed withdrawing from the Verdun salient voluntarily, long before the German attack.

The Germans never reached Verdun. Outer French forts fell. Some fought and fell, and one fort just fell when the 23 man garrison was caught sleeping.

There was some initial success for Germany, but then the defense solidified and the lines held. It was a battle that lasted almost a year.

Verdun had about 300,000 killed on each side. That's an entire corps of corpses. It was becoming painfully clear that infantry on the attack was no match for nests of machine guns in a series of trenches behind barbed wire, with artillery to the rear of that. The defense was just way too ahead of the offense. The tank had not been deployed in combat yet it would re-invent the battlefield when finally deployed on some scale in late 1917 at Cambrai - but for now nothing could break the enemy lines. Both sides were in a tankless position.

The segment title comes from what people called it for years after the war: The Hell of Verdun.

The one thing that saved Verdun was the Somme. Erich Falkenhayn's mince-meat strategy might have worked at Verdun if not for the Somme. The Allies didn't plan the Somme in order to save a desperate crisis 100 miles to the north, but it worked out that way. It was somme solution. When the Allies attacked along the Somme, on July 1, 1916, the Germans immediately began to switch Verdun divisions south to meet the crisis. Germany would not send any more troops to the Verdun sector for the rest of the war, although fighting continued until December. The Somme was hardly a success, but at least it saved *Le Grande Vee*.

The French counter-attacked in the fall of 1916, taking back more than half the lost ground by mid-December.

The arrival of generals Petain, Nivelle, and Mangin saved Verdun and made all three men famous. They all became the heroes of Verdun, and two of the three went to their graves as heroes forever. One died a snake. Guess which one?

This is from the book, *World War One in 1917*: Revolution and Intervention

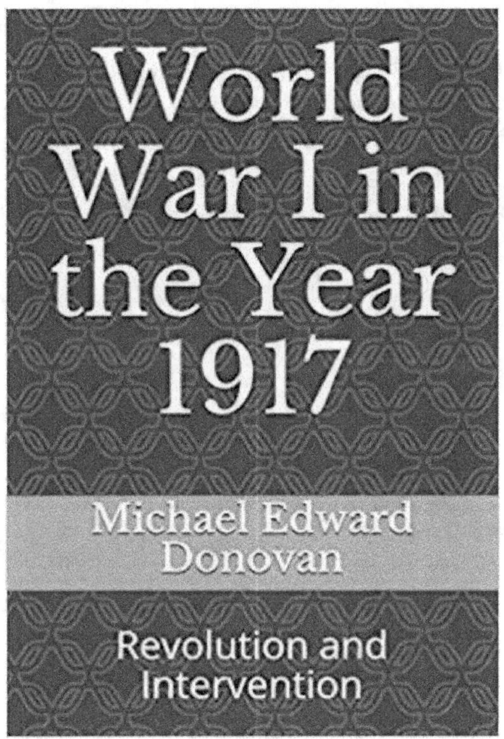

THE BLOKE OF THE BROKE - APRIL 21

The German Navy raided the Dover coast three times in the spring of 1917. The big German ships were afraid to come out and play but the smaller ships were not. A raiding force of a dozen destroyers and torpedo boats harassed shipping and shelled towns on the Dover coast on February 25 and March 17. Then they beat it. The RN intercepted the third German attempt to raid the Island.

Commander Edward Evans, the captain of the British destroyer *HMS Broke*, won the Victoria Cross for his actions that April 21. The Broke went straight into the German raider-line, sinking one destroyer with gunfire and then ramming another one in a near suicidal assault. The German flotilla scattered in fear of this one DD wrecking ball, and the villagers on the coast slept peacefully.

For the rest of his life, the hero of the day was known famously as "Evans of the Broke." The poor fellow tried to get people to stop calling him that, but there was no stopping the thing. Everywhere he went it was, "Hey! There he is! Evans of the Broke!" - He got sick of it. "I've done a lot more than that! Stop calling me that!"

I don't blame him for being annoyed. E.W. Evans was a world-famous Arctic explorer before the war, but now this one courageous act in combat buried his fame for what he really wanted to be remembered for. Pop culture got the best of the poor bloke of the Broke.

This is from the book, World War I in 1918: The Defeat of the Central Powers

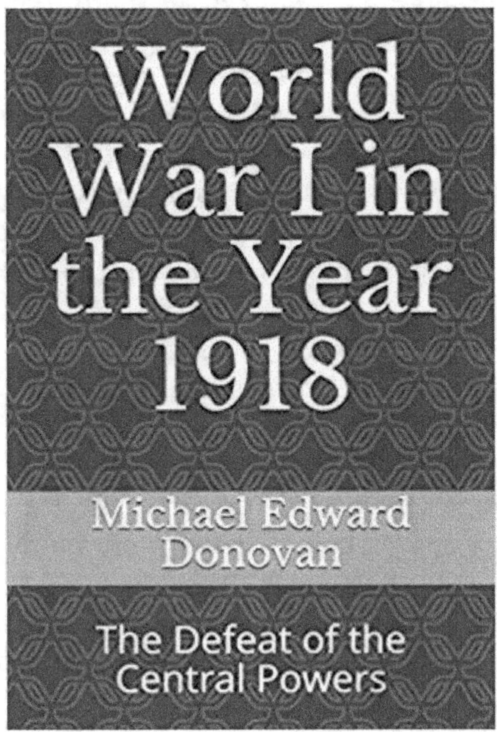

OIL AND BAKU

The Germans bragged about their superiority in coal and steel, but they forgot to fill up the oil tank before starting on a four year war.

There was no oil energy crisis for either side in the first two years of the war, but by the middle of 1916, the world had turned sharply towards oil. Suddenly both sides had to fight for an energy weapon they had never fully appreciated before, as a war component.

Britain had a severe oil shortage by the beginning of 1917, but at least it had the USA, which produced 62% of the oil in the entire world in 1914 and 67% in 1918.

The Central Powers, meanwhile, had an oil crisis, not a mere shortage. Oil hurt the already hurting German effort at crunch time in World War I, and would do the same in World War II.

Romania did Germany a favor by joining the war in late 1917 and getting beaten down. Germany took over a heapin' helping of Romanian oil, some first-rate sabotage by the retreating Romanian army notwithstanding. By the summer of 1918, everyone was on the lookout for oil, wherever they could find it, and Britain was suddenly a little happier that it had forces in Mesopotamia, even though some military men said it was a waste of troop strength.

The grand prize in the east was Russia's Baku oil-fields, on the Caspian Sea. They are still one of the grand prizes of the earth. The Bolsheviks controlled them in early 1918, but the Turkish army was closing in.

In March, 1918, the Germans inserted a Baku clause in the surrender terms for the Bolsheviks at Brest-Litovsk. The Krauts requested permission to march on Baku. The Bolsheviks were so afraid that the Turks would destroy the wells, and massacre 5,000 people, that they agreed under duress, that yes, we would like it if you would just take our oil. In exchange for our permission, will you now please restrain your Turk allies? We'd like to have the oil-fields standing in Baku when the war is over, and maybe a few people too.

The Turkish army ignored German diplomatic notes and just continued to march on Baku, competing with their own German allies to get there first. The Turks reached the outskirts of Baku in early August 1918, and captured some of the peripheral oil-wells. Baku held and then went under. The Bolsheviks reached out to the capitalist enemy, Britain, for help. The old alliance revived itself for expedience, and Britain said, yes, you stabbed us in the back and left the alliance and now you want our help to save you, and we will, but only because we must deny this oil to the Germans.

A British military force marched up through Persia to the Caspian, clashed with Turkish troops, and secured Baku for another five weeks before the Turks broke through and forced the Brits back to Persia. The Turks came in and massacred 2,000 Armenians who worked in the Baku Oil-fields. The Germans at least convinced them not to destroy the place.

The British intervention in Baku was one of the most decisive events in the course of the war. The one month shut-off of an oil supply that Germany was counting on in August made a difference. On August 10, the Kaiser and his H-L dual military-monarchy got the bad word that the German Navy could hang on for a short while on coal, but German air power would disappear totally from the sky by November for a lack of oil. All German mechanized transport would stop. Railroads and battleships could function, but no planes, tanks, or trucks. All of yesterday's dynamics were still up and running, but today's energy needs could not be met. In the middle of this comes the word from Baku that the oil deliveries expected from there by the beginning of September, would not be arriving, if at all, until mid-October. This put a downer on the whole situation.

The Baku setback at crunch time influenced the ultimate decision in Berlin to end the war in early November. Ludendorff says so in his memoirs.

A final oil-sticky-note about BP, British Petroleum: In 1913 BP was a German company, owned by Anglo-Persian in London. When the war broke out, the British expropriated BP and made it genuinely British. There was no compensation for the German owners, whose country was dropping Zeppelin bombs near the Westminster offices where the appropriate decision to expropriate was made.

This is from the book, World War I: The Medal of Honor: The Recipients of the CMOH: 1917-1918

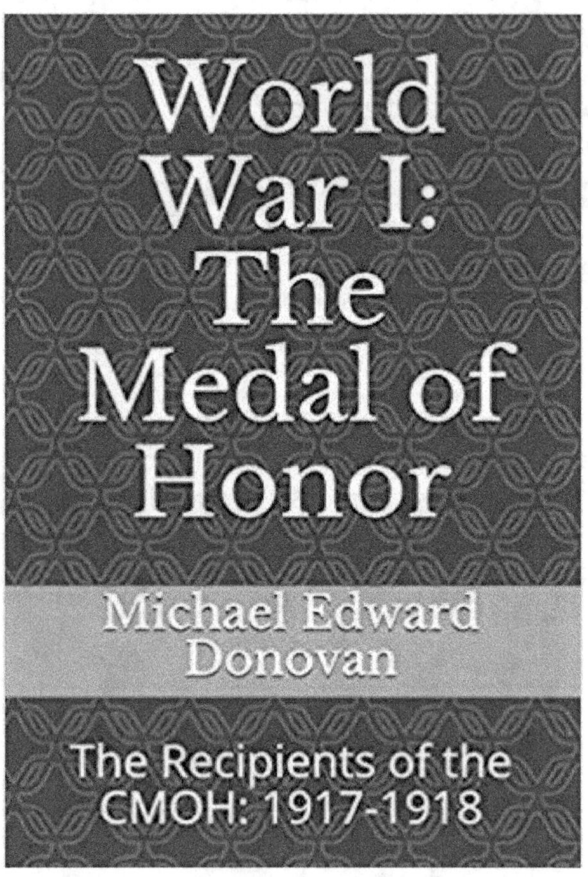

Mike Perkins

October 27, 1918: Private Michael J. Perkins of the 26th Divisions was a one-man army on 10.17, at Beilieu Bois. His platoon was pinned down by a nest of five German machine guns, plus a pillbox, which kept opening the steel door so two Germans could throw hand grenades, and then shut it.

Private Perkins, on his own initiative, and all alone, managed to quietly get on the roof of the pillbox. The next time the door opened to throw out hand grenades, the looming hand of Perkins threw one in. After the explosion, Private Perkins went inside with a knife and inflicted several casualties. Mike took some PW's, and then he attacked some nearby machine guns and took three, taking still more prisoners. The wounded Perkins was killed by an artillery shell the day after his courage already had earned him the greatest medal.

Mike Perkins was nuts. Of course was. He was from South Boston, my home town. MP was from 247 E-Street, to be exact.

This is from the book, *The USA in the Time of Warren G. Harding*: 1921-1923

VERSAILLES TREATY REJECTED

The United States shocked the world when it rejected the Versailles Treaty and the League of Nations. The United States after all, had been the one nation that had introduced high and mighty morality into the First World War, and now it was the first to abandon the idea of collective enforcement of it.

Prior to World War One, no nation in Europe really fancied themselves morally superior to the other states. Power was its own reward, and there was no need to justify it with moral pronouncements (mission statements.) Only the United States was spewing that nonsense from across the ocean and no one outside the United States took it very seriously, even though Sam did.

The whole game in Europe was 'balance of power' - everyone understood balance of power politics and accepted it as a fact of life. Many had tried to control Europe by empire. When 'peace through empire' was finally recognized by all as a failure, as an unattainable goal, the next step was the balance of power system of alliances.

If a number of relatively equal selfish greedy states were left to their own devices, surely war would break out regularly between them. The only way to prevent war was to have each of these states join one of two greater alliances. These two alliances would each be strong enough to deter any states in the other alliance from starting serious trouble. If you mess with any state, you will have to deal with all its big brothers.

Two giant groups thus emerged from all the states of Europe, and for a while this worked well enough. But no one in either alliance fancied themselves to be in that alliance for idealistic missionary reasons. It was just national survival. Power without dogma.

The system worked because every time a crisis arose, one of the quarreling states would back down under the threats of the other guy's big brothers.

But in the summer of 1914, a crisis arose in which a number of states decided this time they were all not going to back down. So now, instead of preventing the larger war, the system of grand alliances created the largest war ever. Talk about a dismal failure. Balance of power politics put 20 million people into an early grave and left 30 million destitute in the aftermath. Nice goin' balance of power.

So now enters the United States, which had never believed in balance of power politics, had never participated in it, and worse, had an uppity attitude because it thought it stood for higher principles than anyone else on the globe.

Of course, the only reason the United States had never participated in balance of power politics, and could dish out preachy rhetoric, was that it was safe and unthreatened in its hemisphere, surrounded by weak nations and two moats of thousands of miles each. If the same US leaders had found themselves located in the middle of Europe, they would have dropped the high and mighty rhetoric and joined one of the two systems of alliances in a heartbeat.

The Europeans thought Wilson and the Americans naïve about the difference between rhetoric and reality, and they never took the moralist pronouncements of Wilson too seriously. But the Limeys and Frogs needed Yank help to win the war so they paid lip service to Wilson's words in order to get their hands on his weapons, and one of the great ironies of the war is that the Entente wanted American weapons more than American troops, but it was American troops that prove decisive, while American weapons failed to get there in time. The Americans flew French and British planes and French 75mm artillery. 50,000 Doughboys died in combat.

When the Entente won the war, the Euros were faced with a new dilemma. They never had any intention of really establishing a new moral world order. That was to help get Wilson and the American knee deep into it. They really just wanted to defeat the Triple Alliance. But how could they do this and still maintain the veneer of moralists adhering to Wilson's vision? They had to make it look good. They needed to drag the United States into their balance of power world, but needed to pretend they were dragging the US into an idealist crusade for a new world of peace. If they made it look like what it really was, a restoration of the same 'might makes right' power game, the United States would surely back out of it.

The Versailles Treaty and the League of Nations preached forgiveness and progressivism but practiced the opposite. The terms given to the defeated powers were no less punitive than those of any other war since the time of Rurik. If the European victors had demonstrated by their deeds, that Wilsonian ideals were being respected and applied, then the Election of 1920 might have gone to the Democrats. And if the Republicans had won in 1920, and thought the Europeans were behaving, they would have got on board with the League and the V Treaty.

But the Republicans of 1921 didn't like the picture and made the call.

The obvious historical view is that the United States failed the cause of humanity when it failed to join the League for the simple reason that if the USA had joined, there never would have been a World War II.

But what was the United States being asked to join in 1921? Was it a cause of greater justice than the world had ever known? If so, the USA should have joined.

But what were the signals coming out of Paris?

The Arab states had been promised independence during the war. They got instead a "mandate," a system of administration from outside and above. In other words, France and England had completely reneged on the promise. They set up puppet states and asked the people there to try and imagine they were independent. The western powers could now own these places, yet ask the locals to do the work of running the place in the name of their "independence." The mandated states would have been better off as colonial property. At least the ruling states would be responsible for picking up the garbage on Mondays.

In Africa, the French and British conquered German colonies and kept them for themselves: new overlords for old.

What kind of new Wilsonian order was being implemented in Germany? The victors were seizing German territory, industry, money, and populations as if Wilson and his words had never existed. Who wants to join this phony League?

What about Turkey? Western power was taking everything from the Ottoman Empire but the kitchen sink of Anatolia. If this was 'peace without victors,' then Don Knotts played fullback for Princeton, and so did I.

This pattern of the vicious victors made Wilson's 14 points seem like a practical joke being put over on the world to amuse diplomats in Paris and London. Yet history has condemned the decision of the United States to reject the League. The judgment is based solely on the 25 years of events down the road, while ignoring completely the perspective of those making decisions in Washington in 1921.

This is from the book, *The USA in the Time of Calvin Coolidge*: 1923-1929

THE INHERITED TERM - 1923-1925

Calvin Coolidge was at the old homestead at Plymouth, Vermont, on the night of August 2, 1923. He was in the upstairs bedroom with Gracie when they were woken up by the sound of his father calling his name.

"Calvin, wake up son! Wake up! This is urgent!"

"It had darned well better be," grumbled the VP as he put on his night-robe and lit a candle.

The old man's voice was trembling as he came up the stairs and announced, "Harding is dead, son." Then he entered the room and said with deliberate drama, "Or should I say, Harding is dead ... Mr. President."

Calvin returned his father's stern stare and said "Don't worry Dad. I think I can swing it."

The two political men dug up a Bible, and a copy of the Constitution. They read the document closely to make sure there was no legal reason why the father, a legal magistrate, could not administer the oath.

Just then, an emissary from Washington arrived and asked Coolidge to come to DC to take the oath, but father and son declined. They both agreed that it would not be wise or proper to go to Washington and take the oath of office there. The country would be two days without a President, and there was no reason that should be.

An hour later a little group of witnesses gathered at the Coolidge household, including Senator Dale who happened to have been visiting.

And so, by gaslight, in his father's living room at 2:27 a.m. on August 3, 1923, Coolidge became the only President sworn into office by a family member, and the only president who took the oath in New England. There is an accurate drawing of the event, but no photos. After the 'so help me God' he turned to his wife Gracie and hugged her. She had been shedding quiet tears through the ceremony. There were eight witnesses including one member of the US Congress, James Thatch Hutt. (Calvin only mentions Senator Dale in his memoirs, but another account says that Hutt was there too.)

Coolidge served without a Vice-President for the remaining 20 months of the Harding term.

The USA was somewhat lucky that every time the nation has ruled without a Vice-President, the new sitting Prez remained alive. Tyler, Johnson, Arthur, Teddy Roosevelt, and now Coolidge were collectively veepless for all or a part of 22 years (1841-45, 1865-69, 1881-1885, and 1901-1905, 1923-1925.) There was absolutely nothing in the Constitution about what to do if a VP succeeds a dead President and then dies too! We will never know how the USA would have solved that one. There was no further succession to the

Presidency past VP by law until 1947, and no provision to appoint a new VP until 1967 with the 25th Amendment.

This is from the book, *The USA in the Time of Herbert Hoover*: 1929-1933

AMERICAN COMMUNIST PARTY

When it comes to Communism, American history today is all about the Red Scare or McCarthyism. The thing that these two overreacted to barely gets a mention.

There were plenty of Communist activities in the USA, long before Joe McCarthy. The Communists tried their best to overthrow the United States government and the capitalist system through revolutionary agitation.

In 1929, the Communist Party of the USA was alive and well and living in all 48 states. It called for the overthrow of the Hoover government in Washington and the installment of the Communist "worker's dictatorship." Doyeee.

The American Communist Party worshipped the USSR. American Communists were the Kremlin's pet dogs.

But they had a problem: When the Kremlin became divided on the issues, what were the American Communists to do? Answer: They had their own USA Communist schisms, in lackey mirror reflection of the Kremlin schisms.

Nick Bukharin was a Russian Politburo leader who wasn't getting along great with Stalin (if you can believe that.) Bukharin broke with Stalin in Russia. Now the American Communists sort of had to pick a team, (and this style split had already happened in the American Communist Party earlier, when Stalin split with Trotsky.)

So part of the American Communist Party sided with Bukharin. For this they were expelled. They then had to form their own party. They made signs and logos which read:

"American Communist Party (Opposition.)"

The leader of this pro-Bukharin ACP faction was Jay Lovestone. His followers were called Lovestoneites.

The Lovestoneites made an impact, at least within the left. The Lovestonites were in the middle of hundreds of political fights and labor strikes, well into the 1930's.

Any political history of the era has their name coming up all the time. "We were battling the Chicago cops and the Lovestoneites showed up to help." or "Later we battled the Lovestoneites" The Lovestoneites were the rightist opposition and the Trotskyites were the leftist opposition.

American Communists were facing long odds if they were striving for a united party. Dividing itself up three ways over Stalin's murderous cat-fights in Moscow was not a productive move.

History has forgotten how serious and massive the Communist revolutionary movement once was in the United States. Just because it died down during and after WWII to the point where it is today a miniscule army with an office in both Greenwich Village and Harvard Square, doesn't mean it wasn't a serious force in Herbert Hoover and FDR's time. The political reaction to the Great Depression was manifest in the rise of the Communist Parties in the United States. When the war, and the post-war boom, saved the national economy, it ended the threat that "The Commies are coming." It's easy to mock it and laugh at it now, but it was real enough to anyone living in Hooverville.

This is from the book, *FDR and the Great Depression*: 1933-1939

THE BRAINS TRUST

The group of advisers around Roosevelt was nicknamed 'The Brains Trust.' It's usually called 'The Brain Trust,' but Rexford Tugwell, who was one of them, insists in his book that the proper term was actually 'The Brains Trust,' so that's the one I'm going with. Rex wrote a book in 1933 about the Brains Trust. Its title? *The Brains Trust*.

Technically, the Brains Trustees were the men hired to win the campaign for the presidency in 1932. A few key members left shortly thereafter. Historically, the term has come to mean all the genius advisers to FDR through the 1930's, and the term applies a bit less in the war years, but it still hung around. The careers of the Brains Trust before, during, and after their service under Roosevelt, spread a wide path through much of American history. Some had served earlier under Woodrow Wilson, and some would serve later under Lyndon Johnson.

The concept of the Brains Trust was politically unorthodox. Past presidents had always chosen their advisers from the ranks of experienced politicians, or from close friends in the business world.

Speechwriter Sam Rosemann suggested to Roosevelt that the great minds of America's universities were an untapped resource. The FDR team should interview candidates from cool schools who might be interested in joining the President's team. What professor would not be dazzled at the idea of even an interview for such a job? FDR loved Sammy's idea, and soon a bunch of eggheads invaded the White House and Roosevelt was, figuratively speaking, back at Harvard with his own private faculty. The BT met and worked on problems, and proposed new ideas around the clock, then presented them to Roosevelt for rejection, acceptance, or revision.

The three top Brains Trusters were Rex Tugwell, Ray Moley, and Adolph Berle.

Moley would later break with Roosevelt, join the Republicans, and write a book criticizing FDR severely. It was called *After Seven Years* and was published in 1939. After seven years looking for it in the used bookstores, I gave up. But the internet gave me the whole thing for free. A-7 is an amazing book and Raymond scoffs at the story that I just told you that the Brains Trust was Rosenman's idea. Moley's attitude is that if Rosenman wants to spin that story and if people want to write history that way, whatever. But he laughs it off. Moley claims that this Brains Trust idea was in the works long before Rosenman supposedly suggested it to Roosevelt.

Rexford Tugwell was a brilliant economics professor. Rex eventually broke with Roosevelt too, but not severely, not the way Ray Moley did.

This is from the book, *Origins of World War II*

KELLOGG-BRIAND - THE PACT THAT MADE WAR ILLEGAL

In 1928 the leaders of several nations signed a pact amid great ceremony; a treaty that made war illegal.

It was called the Kellogg-Briand Pact, and is the funniest thing that ever happened on this planet.

Yeah, that'll work.

When Japan, Germany, and Italy began to take other people's territory, they were often reminded that they had violated the Kellogg-Briand Pact.

Von Papen said after the war, that the only time he had ever seen Ribbentropp really laugh was when someone reminded him that he must not violate the Kellogg-Briand Pact.

KB was a joke because the decent nations could not enforce it, but it became a serious prosecutorial weapon after the war. When the Nuremburg and Tokyo Tribunals convened, the prosecution charged the Axis trio with waging illegal war. Defense scoffed "As if war was ever illegal." The prosecution was then able to cite the Kellogg Briand Pact of 1928, and squash that defense angle. Indeed it was primarily for conspiracy to wage illegal war that the Nuremburg and Tokyo criminals were punished, and not for specific war crimes once it started.

Frank Kellogg of the USA and Aistide Briand of France are the full namesakes at the top of the pact.

This is from the book, *Who's Who in World War II*: The Americans; The British; The Chinese; The French; the Germans; The Japanese; The Russians; And the Rest

KALTENBRUNER (1903-1946)

Ernst Kaltenbrunner replaced Heydrich in 1943 as head of the RSHA: The SS police.

He was born in northwest Austria. The town of Reid im Innkreis is only 40 miles west of the town of Linz, where Hitler was so poorly raised.

The famous Nazis like Hitler, Hess, and Goebbels were mostly from southern Germany and northwest Austria, the Bavarian cream of the crop.

This also goes to the heart of why the old-school Wehrmacht generals and admirals disliked and disrespected the Nazi leaders and mocked them among themselves when SS people weren't around. Prussian militarism may have been largely responsible for the Franco-Prussian War and WWI, but Bavarian reactionary 'wild in the streets' style militarism caused WWII. The civilians dragged the Prussians into it this time around, a stark reversal of the classic pattern. Men outside of the army started World War II in Germany, which surely shocked the dead bones of the founding members of the Great German General Staff, and the fact that "great" is in the title should tell you how much they figured they control things.

Ernie Kaltenbrunner was the 'Scarface' of the Nazi Party. He claimed his scars were caused by constant dueling as a young man, but it might have been from a drunken-driver car crash, with Ernie as the designated drunk driver. He was six feet seven inches tall and 220 pounds.

When the Allies assassinated Heydrich in Czechoslovakia, Kaltenbrunner took his place. He replaced Heydrich and Himmler was afraid of him. That about sums up Kaltenbrunner.

Near the end of the war, Hitler bumped many of his police leaders up to military generals. Kaltenbrunner became a full General of the Waffen SS, perhaps to protect him and his officers from criminal prosecution after the war. Kaltenbrunner was once in charge of a plan to assassinate FDR, Stalin, and Churchill at the Teheran Conference in 1943.

The Allies hanged the hangman at Nuremberg on October 16, 1946. His last words were, "Bow to your master before you hang him!" One of the guards said something back that is unprintable and then said, "and furthermore! ..." Then he pulled the trap door. In 2002 someone found Kaltenbruner's personalized medal of the SS. EK had thrown it into Lake Zurich at the end of the war hoping to escape justice.

This is from the book, The History of WWII, 1939: From Poland to Finland

ROYAL OAK - SEPTEMBER 14

There aren't many famous trees in history but the Royal Oak was one. The RO was the tree where King Charles II climbed and hid to avoid the Roundheads who were out to capture and behead him in 1688. Two Roundhead chumps stood below the tree looking for him, and then walked off.

The Royal Navy named a battleship the *HMS Royal Oak*. The BB fought well in World War One. In 1939 the *RO* was still in service, but relegated, because of its age, to rear-guard duties.

In October the *Oak* sat quietly in the bay at Scapa Flow on the northern tip of Scotland. More than 100 very young men manned the ship along with 1,200 men. The Royal Oak doubled as a training ship.

Scapa Flow was an important naval base for Britain. A small island protected the harbor and made the entrance very thin. The Royal Navy also sank a couple of old ships side by side to make the entrance virtually submarine-proof ... or so it thought.

On October 14, Captain Gundy Preen, in a daring feat of skill, slipped his *U-47* into Scapa Flow. Once inside he looked around for the fattest target and spotted the *Royal Oak*. A battleship would do just fine. His periscope was so close to the land that he saw a guy on a bicycle ride by on land flip a finished cigarette aside as he pedaled.

Preen fired four forward bow torpedoes at the *Royal Oak*. Only one hit and it did so little damage that the crew didn't realize they were in mortal danger, and no general quarters sounded. *U-47* did a U-turn and fired four more torpedoes, one at a time, all of them missing. Still undetected was Preen. He U-turned again, took his time re-loading the forward tubes and fired four more. This time he was closer. He confidently looked away from his periscope and at his officers. He displayed one finger at a time with a smile as the explosions timed to matched his fingers. "One (blam!) - Two (kaboom!) - Three (va-room!) - Four (nothing)"

"Three out of four will do, men. Now lets get the hell out of here!"

U-47 dodged past the sunken ships at the entrance in a repeat performance of navigational skill. The *Royal Oak* capsized and sank with 883 KIA's including 100 16-year-old boys. Less than 300 crewmen survived.

Captain Preen won the Iron Cross for creating the iron coffin. *The Royal Oak* still sits capsized in 98 feet of water as an official war grave. The hull is only 15 feet below the water line. Divers are not allowed to go near it.

The news from the Flow lifted German spirits and depressed British. Coming on the heels of the *Courageous*, this was very bad indeed. Was the German submarine fleet going to pick off all the capital ships of the Royal Navy one at a time all over the globe?

In reality, the *Royal Oak* was an old wagon, and its loss didn't change the balance of naval power by one half of one percent. But the press on both sides ran with it as though it was big stuff.

Many British general histories of the war fail to mention that the *Royal Oak* was an obsolete BB on the edge of mothballs. They love to exaggerate how bad things were in the early days and describing the loss of a first-rate battleship makes for better reading than that of a leaky old rust-bucket being used for training teenagers. It's similar to Pearl Harbor where most American historians include the loss of the battleship *Utah*, deliberately failing to mention that it was a *target ship,* and that the Japanese attacks on that unmanned ship were a net gain for America that day, a waste of bombs that could have been dropped on oil tanks or submarine pens.

This is from the book, *The History World War II: 1940*, Axis Ascendant

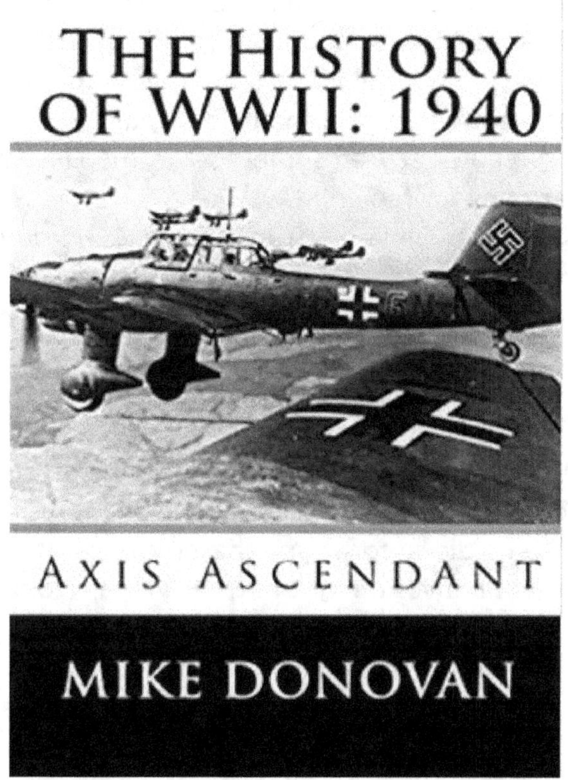

GERMAN NAVAL LOSSES IN NORWAY CAMPAIGN

Germany did not want the Norway campaign. It did not want to get involved there, it just wanted supplies and a secure flank. Britian threatened on both counts and the Nazis reacted with invasion.

Norway was a victory, but it tied down troops and airpower needed to administer another country. The Germans lost too much of their compact navy in the Norway campaign, and this had a direct influence on world history. Hitler's admirals might have went along with Operation Sea Lion, the invasion of England, if not for the losses in Norway. They told the Fuhrer that they couldn't protect a German invasion force crossing the Channel, thanks to Norway.

Scattered small engagements added up to half a Jutland loss for Germany.

First, the Norwegian shore batteries sank the *Blucher*.

Then a destroyer, the *Glowworm*, did a kamikaze on the *Hipper*. Two big Germans were chasing this one litte British destroyer. *Glowworm* hid in a fog, then appeared at ramming speed. It smashed a hole in the *Hipper*, then pulled back and blew up. There were 38 survivors. *Hipper* went back to Germany for repairs.

The RN cruiser *Renown* scored some hits on the *Gneisenau*, which went back to Germany for repairs.

Three Fairy Swordfish biplanes from the *HMS Furious* sank the *Konigsburg*.

The submarine *Truant* eliminated the *Karlsruhe* near Christaiansand.

And the sub *Spearfish* scored a torpedo hit on the *Lutzow* which limped back to Germany for repairs.

All in all, with such a small navy, the collective losses here were a dealbreaker in considering the invasion of England four months later. That was your do or die escort right there, lost in Norway. Raeder wanted a wide front invasion of South England, from Ramsey to Folkstone, but didn't have the capital to insure it.

This is from the book, World War II in 1941, From the Desert War to Pearl Harbor

BATTLE OF CAPE MATAPAN SQUARE - MARCH 29

The Italian Navy decided in the spring of 1941 that it had to make a showing in the Mare Nostrum.

Hitler was already employing Rommel to rescue beaten Italian forces in North Africa. Italy was glad that Germany came to the rescue, but being rescued was also humiliating. Italy needed a victory of its own, to show Hitler that it was a strong little brother, not a weak one.

This was the essence of the Italian naval plan to steam to the area around Crete in force, engage the best the Royal Navy had to offer and win a big one. The Italian Naval HQ in Rome, the 'Supermarina' heard false reports that the three British battleships in the eastern Mediterranean had been badly damaged by Luftwaffe attacks. This disinformation baited the trap that in the end took the Italian Navy off the board for the rest of the war in this one disastrous naval battle, the worst defeat in the history of the Italian Navy.

Before all the smoke had cleared on March 29, 1941, three Italian cruisers, the *Pola*, *Fiume*, and *Zarex*, plus two destroyers went down to Mario Lanza's locker. 2,878 Italian sailors and officers were dead. After Matapan, the Italian Navy never came out in force again (unless you count the day in 1943 they steamed out in full dress to surrender and were attacked by the Luftwaffe!)

This is from the (oversized 16-font) book, *Mike Donovan's History of World War II: 1942*, From Bataan to Stalingrad

JAPAN ATTACKS INDIA - APRIL 1942

Churchill had predicted, early in 1942, that Japan was going to launch a major offensive against India, and felt that all military force in South Asia should therefore be placed under British command for this impending war. He cabled FDR to this effect. FDR cabled MacArthur for a response to this, as if MacArthur was going to say, 'Yes, please take my authority away from me here and give it to a British General.'

The Mac-Ego was a factor, but MacArthur was also right when he asserted that Japan did not have the resources to stage a genuine invasion of India. The whole idea was absurd. He said that Japanese might invade India at some later date but only after having achieved complete victory in the South Pacific, and then only after consolidating its gains. Japan was not capable of it in the spring of 1942, period.

What Japan was capable of, was raiding India with a carrier task force.

The six heavy carriers that attacked Pearl Harbor were on a roll. Since the *Zuikaku, Shikoku, Hiryu, Soryu, Kaga,* and *Akagi* left Japan on November 26, 1941, they had ripped up Pearl Harbor, and covered the invasion of the Bismarcks with impunity. Now they were going to continue on into the Indian Ocean and try to clear the British Navy out of there while attacking two important bases on Ceylon. They would make the Indian Ocean a Japanese Sea and turn a few British warships into fish-bars. That was some tall order. And they did it.

The carriers were needed elsewhere, but the raid into the Indian Ocean was nevertheless a smashing success.

There is a joker in the deck. The Maldives are far to the southwest of the Indian Peninsula. The British had a base in the Addu Atoll in the Maldives. The British thought that the Japanese knew of that base, but they were wrong; Japan did not learn of its existence until after the war.

This affected the upcoming naval campaign in two ways. First, Admiral Somerville guessed/gambled that Ozawa's carriers were headed for an attack on this Addu Atoll, so he ended up in the wrong place at the wrong time during the first J-raid on the west coast of Ceylon. Then he headed to Addu for gas on the false presumption that raid was over, so his force was not in a position to help when the Japanese launched a later raid on Ceylon's east coast.

So the Addu factor helps explain why a formidable British force led by an indomitable commander such as Somerville did not rise to meet the enemy. The six Jap carriers hit and ran like total pros and came back without a scratch. But if Somerville's forces had been in the right place twice at the right time, the IJN might have lost the *Hiryu* and *Soryu* three months before the Yanks dunked them at Midway.

Somerville's Royal Navy Indian Ocean Force included battleship *Warspite*, the heavy cruisers *Dorshetshire* and *Cornwall*, the light carrier *Hermes*, and the heavy carriers *Indomitable* and *Formidable*.

That's a lot of punch. But the problem here was that the British carriers carried antiquated planes that the Wright Brothers had helped to design. Even with perfect carrier tactics, the Misubishi Zeroes would have torn those poor blokes to bits in huge dogfights. Somerville needed the courage to be afraid. He wanted to wait until British and American factories delivered his great ships some competitive combat aircraft before he took on 120 Zeroes in the Indian Ocean. Somerville didn't rule out an attack on Japanese carriers, but he basically didn't want a showdown right now. The raid in the Indian Ocean was the high point of Japan's greatness.

The first carrier raid on Ceylon was against the west coast port of Colombo. The Japanese were hoping to catch the British Indian war fleet in harbor. It was supposed to be another Port Arthur/Pearl Harbor surprise party.

It was almost a replica of Pearl. 340 planes from the same six carriers struck without warning at 8:00 am on Easter Sunday, April 4. They dropped all their Easter eggs on one Colombo basket.

The raid was only a partial success because it was not a surprise. The war was well under way and so were the British cruisers and carriers. Somerville had taken the fleet out for a southerly stroll. If attacked, they would fight, but they were basically trying to sail away from getting sunk.

Japanese planes sank a few small harbor vessels, and went after the oil storage tanks on shore. They were not going to repeat the mistake at Pearl Harbor when the second wave attacked heavily defended USN ships while huge oil storage tanks sat untouched all about the Honolulu area. Scouring the Ceylon waters, the Japanese sank a miscellaneous 90,000 tons of enemy shipping.

The Brits had handled the raid well, but now they blundered. They presumed that the raid was over. The two huge British carriers headed southwest out of the combat zone to get gas, and the other task force that had left Colombo to dodge, turned around and headed back to Colombo. It might be a little beat up, but good ol' Colombo was still home. Somehow the British didn't figure that the Japanese would simply return to the carriers, re-load, and head out for another go. They just thought the Japanese were trying to hit and run, and would fear the British carriers enough to do nothing more than that. The Japanese airfleet came back to Colombo and found a grand prize of several British warships.

Nagumo's bombers and torpedo planes sank two cruisers, the *Cornwall* and the *Dorsetshire.* The next day his birds found the aircraft carrier *Hermes* and sent it to the ocean floor. *Hermes* was old, weighed only 10,000 tons, and had obsolete bi-planes on its wooden decks. But a carrier was a carrier and *Hermes* was a nice big stuffed animal for Kate to take home from the fair.

HMS Hermes sinking in the Indian Ocean

The Japanese six-pack of carriers had battleship and cruiser bodyguards; and they now had the east Indian Ocean entirely to themselves. They had destroyed the British force that had sallied out for fresh air to dodge the raid, and the main British naval force was headed in the wrong direction for gas and because it thought the Japanese wanted to take the Addu Atoll.

The Japanese had the run of the house. They steamed around to the eastern side of Ceylon and attacked the naval base at Trincomalee. A big air raid did the damage.

Then the big gun-ships took a cruise up the east coast of the Indian mainland and bombarded two cities and several installations. Indians went into a panic thinking the worst. Everyone knew what had happened at Nanking and Singapore when the Japanese took over. The people in those two Indian cities had no idea this was just a bombardment of opportunity.

The April 1942 strike into the Indian Ocean made it a <u>World</u> War for sure. The earth trembled. If the Japanese could bomb India, the next logical step was linkage between the Nazi and Japanese empires. Some Rommel guy was threatening the Suez Canal. People in a hundred lands heard about the Japanese attacks in India and freaked out. It was totally conceivable that totalitarianism might conquer the world. Churchill milked this Nazi-Tojo hook-up in India fear for a couple of years. He used it to justify sending more British cruisers to Madagascar and making the United States replace those ships in the Atlantic (when Nimitz was pleading that they were needed in the Pacific - indeed the several British ships sunk by the Invincible Six were preparing at Tricomalee for an invasion of Madagascar.)

But the threat that Japan was going to put India in the Co-Prosperity Sphere was a bit much. Yamashita and Rommel weren't going to dine joyously together in Kuwait. The fear itself was real, but it was based on the reality of one carrier raid and a cocky guy in goggles thinking he can beat 30-1 odds at the gates of Egypt.

On the way back to Truk the sailors of the Pearl Harbor Six were feeling pretty good about themselves when startling news reached them. The men stopped singing their triumphant war songs and stared at each other. American planes had bombed Tokyo.

This is from the book, *The History of World War II: 1943*, From Casablanca to Tehran

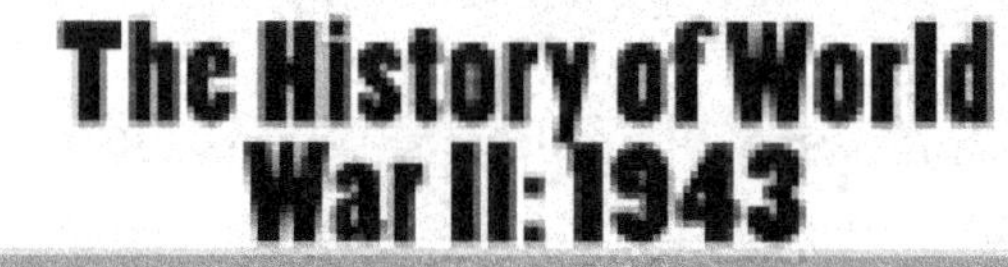

POP THE CORKSCREW - PANTELLARIA IS FREE - 6.11

Before they could safely attack Italy, the Allies needed to seize the small, strategically located, Axis-controlled island of Pantellaria. Even if the armed forces of the Axis were not a threat from there, the ability of Pantellaria to deliver intelligence about Allied invasion fleet movements made the little island a big thorn. Pantellaria airbase provided superb recce (slang for reconnaissance) for the Axis. The conquest of Pantellaria would not be easy because there were no beaches to land on, only cliffs.

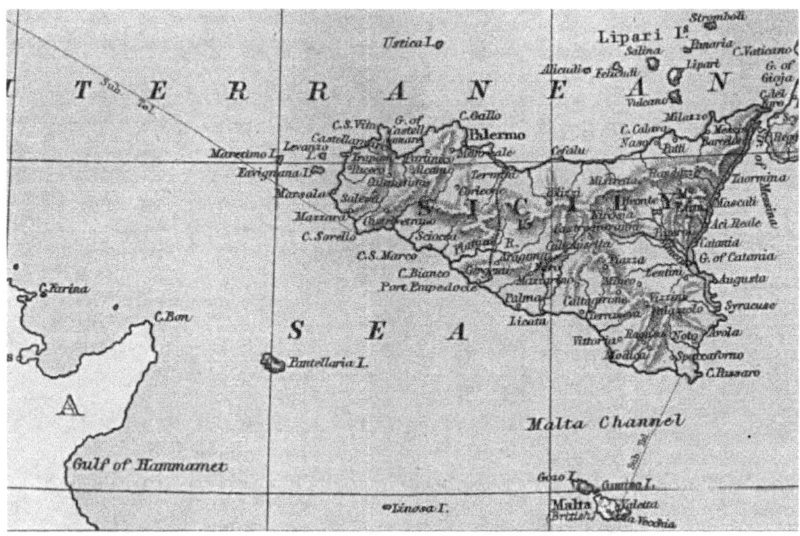

Sicily, Malta, Cape Bon, and Pantellaria

In late May and early June Allied bombers hit Pantellaria hard. They pounded the 21 batteries and the 12,000 Italian troops there for more than ten days. The air power boys bragged that they could force Pantelleria to surrender without any necessity for the planned amphibious assault slated for June 11.

Negotiations for surrender fell short. Soon a hundred British landing craft puttered towards Pantellaria. They were going to storm the cliffs. This was going to be Bunker Hill in the Mediterranean. Then, just in time, a white flag came up from the highest mountain on the island. The Italians had surrendered Pantellaria. There would be no casualties incurred, unless you count the one British soldier who was bit by a donkey. True detail. It was obviously some pro-Mussolini jack-ass.

In Italy there was panic over the loss of Pantellaria in spite of its small size. Although the new Italian Empire had been under counterattack for two years, this was the first time in all the fighting that the Allies conquered Italian soil. Pantellaria was not close to home, it *was* home. The Germans, on the other hand, were furious over the way their ally had surrendered this tough Island fortress position without firing a defensive shot.

CORKSCREW was the code-word for the operation to take Pantellaria.

This is from the book, The History of World War II: 1944. From the Marshalls to the Bulge

LAFAYETTE! WE ARE JUST PASSING THROUGH!

Paris was liberated on August 25. Soon thousands of American soldiers were marching down the Champs Elysees while joyous Parisians smiled and cheered. You've probably seen these famous photos.

But the grunts in the photos are not smiling. It's not that they weren't happy to liberate Paris. They were simply tired and sad from the hard fighting, and knew that they still had, almost immediately, much more work to do which might kill them.

In fact there is more to these pictures than a thousand words. De Gaulle had asked Ike for two US divisions to maintain order in Paris. Ike said no, but he had an idea that might be of assistance to the proud General. There were American divisions just west of Paris that were headed east to resume the fighting. Ike could have them march in parade down the main avenue with Bradley and De Gaulle at the reviewing stand. They would not lose a step in their movements towards the battle while at the same time lending authority to the tall French patriot. This is what happened. It may have been the only instance in the history of combat that full divisions marched in a ceremonious victory parade while on their way to a hot war zone. The Americans who marched past De Gaulle that afternoon were literally in the midst of a full scale battle later that same day! They were marching past the reviewing stand, not parading past it. The parade was part of a live action local theatre.

This is from the book, *The History of World War II: 1945*, From the Bulge to the Missouri

PRIVATE WATERS - HAMMELBURG - MARCH 26-29

The U.S. Army had liberated Cabanatuan PW camp in the Philippines in a spectacular raid; so in March of 1945, General Patton decided he was not going to be outdone. He planned a daring raid, 55 miles deep inside German lines to liberate the Allied troops of OFLAF 13, the German PW camp at Hammelburg.

The Hammelburg raid was a complete disaster, and Patton claimed later that it was his only major mistake of the entire conflict. Patton said that if he had only been assigned more forces for the raiding party, it would have succeeded. Yeah, of course. And if Washington had 3,000 more troops at Brandywine, he would have won there too.

Patton assigned 300 men and 57 fighting vehicles to 'Task Force Baum'. All they had to do was fight their way 55 miles to the town of Hammelburg, and then turn south to attack the combination training camp/prisoner of war camp the Nazis were running just south of the town. The armed column would then smash in the gates of the camp and free the jubilant prisoners. With the entire region now alerted and closing in on the intruders, Patton's raiders, with liberated men clinging to the sides of the vehicles, would fight their way back to American lines another 59 miles. Sounds like a plan. It has similarities to the failed mission of Jimmy Carter in the Iranian desert in 1979: In a best case scenario it was going to be a brutal firefight in, and an even rougher one coming back out.

Colonel Abraham Baum was given the task of forcing his way to Hammelburg. Baum he wondered why he had to go do this when no other prisoner of war camps had to be liberated in advance. Why this one? Weren't these PW's close to liberation anyway?

It turns out that the only reason for the mission to Hammelburg was that Patton's son-in-law, Jack Waters, was one of the prisoners. Patton took care of his family. His daughter would see her beau soon, and people will die for the favor.

The column battled its way to Hammelburg and took some losses on the way. Tanks crashed through the gates of the camp and there was a battle all around. Prisoners came out in jubilation.

The column had now been through two phases of fighting, and was shrinking. The third phase was the road back. The Germans were swarming all over the column now.

It was a total whipping. Not one vehicle made it back to the American lines. 32 Americans were killed. 35 Americans made it back to the American lines and only six of these were liberated PW's.

Some revisionist historians now claim that Patton didn't even know that his son-in-law was at Hammelburg, and that the story was contrived by "Patton-haters." So why is there a group of "Patton-haters" in the first place? There certainly isn't a flock of "Bradley-haters."

A couple of Hammelburg sideshows, now: Guess who was the first prisoner that greeted the tanks at the gates of OFLAG-13: it was none other than the man they were all there to save, John K. Waters. It was pure coincidence. Jackie W. got wounded while trying to get back and was taken prisoner again. He survived the war.

Sideshow 2: At one point in the chaos, an American PW priest held Mass. He held it at the barracks while the two sides were in the middle of a terrifying tank and infantry fight. An atheist soldier tells this story: he looked up from the ground during the explosions and saw the priest reciting the Latin Mass while bullets and bombs flew all about. The shattered windows and the mix of shadow and sunlight gave the Father the look of a mystical icon as he prayed while bullets whizzed by his head. The soldier didn't say if this scene converted him to believing in God, but the priest did survive the Mass.

The mission created more new American prisoners than it rescued!

Life magazine has an amazing photo of a jubilant line of men emerging from Hammelburg at the very moment of the rescue. Few of them could have realized that this was the beginning of a very bad turn of events. Many who would have been liberated in a month were killed in the running battles. They were like the jailbird who makes his break with two months left on a 20 year stretch. Bad timing, bad decision.

Virtually every commander involved in the fighting resented Patton for sending them on a near suicidal mission so that he could save his in-law.

Patton even sent one of his top aides into the danger zone because he was the only man who would recognize Private Johnny Waters by face.

One of the tank commanders who led this foolish mission was Lt. Col. Creighton Abrams. He was such an intrepid leader and fighter that the current Abrams Tank in the Army is named after him; but Colonel Abrams was disgusted with the nature of the mission and the incredible selfishness of Patton in ordering it.

And Patton openly talked about his competition for glory with MacArthur. "I'm going to make Cabanatuan look like boy scout hike," he boasted before the mission began. Mac had saved 500 Americans in the Philippines, and Patton needed to be number one in that competition, just like when Patton based his actions in Sicily, not on military wisdom or studied patriotism or dedication to the Grand

Alliance, but simply to show the world that he was at least as good as MacArthur.

This is from the book, the USA in the Time of Harry Truman: 1945-1953.

RIOT AT KOJE DO - MAY 7, 1952

The biggest issue in the second half of the Korean War was PW's. The military front was frozen, and reduced to mutual harassment operations. Casualties during this stalemate were heavy at times, but little actually changed, strategically.

There were three fronts now: The skirmishes along the battle lines, the negotiating tables, and the PW camps.

Korean Communist prisoners were well organized and very unruly.

The USA had stuffed a large off-shore Korean island with C-PW's. The Koje-Do Prisoner of War Camp held 150,000 unhappy Communists.

On May 7, 1952, the prisoners rioted and took the American commandant hostage. General Richard Dodd became a prisoner in his own PW camp. For 72 hours the North Korean prisoners held an Army general hostage. They had many demands, ranging from food, freedom, American admission of war crimes against Korea, and a bottle of champagne for each prisoner.

General Colson arrived to negotiate for Dodd's release. The rebels especially insisted on apologies for war crimes. Colson issued an American apology, and the prisoner of the prisoners were released. Dodd was unharmed. Colson then released a statement that the apology was made under duress to obtain the release of an American general, and should be disregarded.

The new Commander in Korea was Mark Clark, replacing Ridgeway who had replaced MacArthur. Mark Clark arrived in the middle of the Koje-Do Crisis. Clark was furious that General Dodd had allowed himself to be taken captive. Upon reviewing the whole USPW system, Clark concluded that everything was a mess and it was time to overhaul it from top to bottom.

During the months leading up to the Koje-Do riot of May 1952, there was a civil war within the ranks of the enemy prisoners. Many North Koreans had been forcibly conscripted and wanted to stay in South Korea or, better yet, go to America. They did not want to go back to North Korea.

Then there were the true communist soldier-believers.

These two groups of PW's slugged it out at a dozen camps all over South Korea, and hundreds died in the fighting. I did say hundreds. There was no law behind closed prison barracks doors.

The prisoners defied their jailors. North Korean prisoners used to hang insulting, profane banners denouncing America, capitalism, and Truman's sister; and Dodd didn't do a thing about it.

The prisoners created military units, complete with platoons and companies, and they had an arsenal of weapons that defied all norms of PW control. The US guard squad was already intimidated, and back on its heels. It wasn't going to enforce discipline within the ranks of the violent Korean PW's.

Dodd came close to getting off the hook for Koje Do. He was the victim here, right? But Clark was out to get both Dodd for getting captured, and Colson for daring to dishonor the word of the United States … and both for letting it all happen in the first place. Mark wanted to make sure no one dared run a sloppy, timid, overcrowded PW camp ever again.

General Clark ordered several smaller PW camps built, and made sure that new prisoners, especially, went to the new camps. That's because one of the reasons for the Koje-Do uprising (and a few smaller ones like it elsewhere) was the use of PW-plants. The People's Republic of Korea controlled the rebellions of UNPW camps by planting communist fighting commissars near the front lines who got captured on purpose! It hadn't dawned on Dodd to do something to defuse this danger. The public felt bad for Dodd. Clark made sure he got demoted to Colonel Dodd.

For what it's worth, the weapon of choice in Koje-Do was the tent-pole fashioned into a cross between a large knife and a small spear.

This is from the book, *The USA in the Time of Dwight Eisenhower: 1953-1961* (Note: The tanks on the cover are from the 1956 Hungarian Rebellion)

THE U-2 INCIDENT - MAY 1, 1960

The U-2 overflight program was authorized when the plane was merely a dream; in 1954. A Harvard and an MIT professor told the President that the improvements in photography and airplane design made high-altitude spy planes feasible. Defense Secretary Wilson and J.F. Dulles were there to back up the eggheads. Ike slept on it and then said "we go."

The U-2 was up and flying by June of 1956. Lockheed took less than two full years from concept to deployment, a fantastic achievement, especially for such an advanced plane, and one that would last.

The program belonged to the CIA, and the USAF didn't like that. The Air Force tried to take over the U-2 spy overflight program, but Ike supported the spyboys. The CIA could have its own private air force, based around one great new spy plane, the U-2. It flew at 70,000 feet, and had the best zoom lens in the Solar System.

Eisenhower studied the flight plan for each mission. The first space spy flight over Russia took place in June of 1956. Ike and the CIA were thrilled when they pulled it off, but they presumed, wrongly, that the Russians wouldn't even know they had been spied on. The USSR sent a diplomatic note to Washington about the violation of Soviet air space. American radar had not been able to track the American U-2 but Soviet radar was apparently better. Ike authorized very few flights over the USSR, but he didn't let Soviet protests stop him from doing one once in a while if he felt it was in the best interests of American national security. He used a U-2 flight to make sure that the Russians weren't landing the Red Air Force on Syrian airfields during the Suez Canal Crisis. If they had been, the entire world would have been on the brink of war. Eisenhower authorized another U-2 overflight during the 1956 Hungarian rebellion.

U-2 in Action

The Soviets did not want to protest openly because that would advertise to the world the helplessness of their position. The U-2 could fly to where the air was thin and the sky dark at noon. The US claimed, in justifying the over-flights, that in the outer atmosphere there was no national airspace. The legal difference between light and darkness was a gray area.

Russia quietly threatened to shoot the U-2 down, the first chance they got. Military analysts did not think that Soviet anti-aircraft missiles could ever reach the mighty U-2. Eventually, a Soviet SAM did catch up to a U-2, and it was a sensation.

It happened on Mayday, May 1, 1960, over the Ural Mountains, near Sverdlovsk. A U-2 plane, piloted by a private citizen employed by the CIA took a SAM to the fuselage, and the black bird came crashing down.

The Washington brains trust heard that the pilot had not returned, and presumed him shot down and dead.

Moscow held its tongue. The CIA told the press a silly lie about a missing weather reconnaissance plane that had obviously strayed off course.

A few days later Krushchev stood before the Russian Supreme Soviet and proclaimed that they had the plane and the pilot. Worst of all, the pilot was talking. His name was Francis Gary Powers.

The feeling in America was that he should have committed suicide. But that was not part of his instructions.

Powers eventually stood trial. The world followed the legal drama like OJ. The Soviet court convicted Powers of espionage. Powers 'admitted' he was sorry in the Soviet courtroom. The Russians sentenced him to ten years. If he hadn't said he was sorry, he would have faced a longer sentence.

Powers went to Lubyanka. America was angry with him, not angry on his behalf. He was a traitor and a coward for not killing himself. Then he did his Wally Cox impression before a Soviet Court. Powers later defended his actions by saying that he had given the Russians much false and misleading information during his numerous interrogations.

In 1962, the USA swapped a captive Russian spy, Rudolph Abel, for Gary Powers. The U-2 man became a traffic copter pilot for a Los Angeles TV station.

Overall I side with the people against Powers. The charge that he should have killed himself is completely unfair, but the charge that he stood less than tall in court is, to some extent, fair.

The 1976 made-for-TV movie about this affair, *Frances Gary Powers*, starring Lee Majors, is excellent (Whit Bissell is convincing as Bissell, but Mr. T is a bit miscast as Khrushchev.)

This is from the book, *The USA in the Time of JFK*, 1961-1963

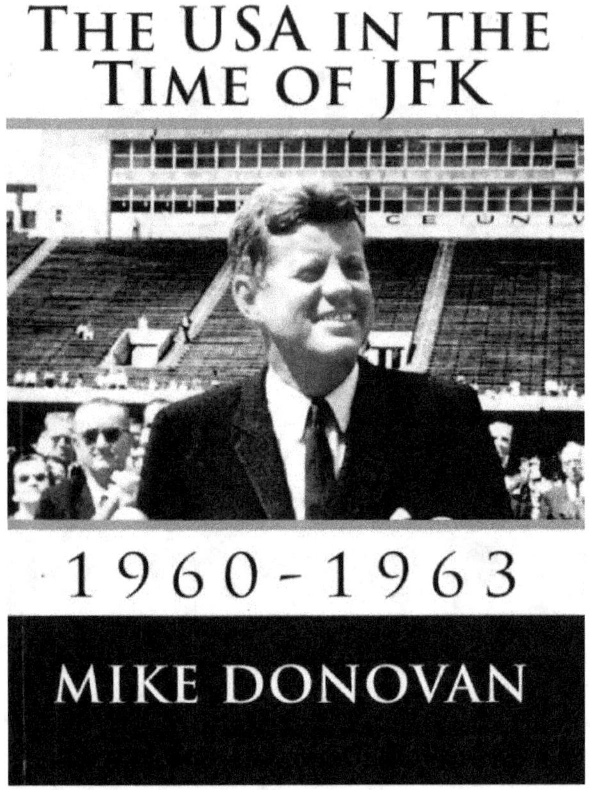

JUPITER

The wild card in the Cuban Missile Crisis of 1962 was the Jupiter missile. In 1959 Eisenhower put 15 medium range jumpin' Jupiters on the ground in Turkey, a NATO ally. That was a direct threat to the Soviet Union. These shorter range nukes were as threatening to Russia as much larger and more expensive ICMBs in the Dakotas. Krushchev spoke often of these missiles as a NATO provocation. The Jupiter missiles would factor into the final settlement of Cuban Missile Crisis.

The Jupiters were considered obsolete. I read that often. That's easy for pen-pushers to type up. But the Russians feared them; and the Turks obviously did not think of them as laughable. Turkey liked having them for defense, and America liked having them in Turkey for offense.

Kennedy had recently discussed unilaterally removing the J's in the interests of better relations with the USSR, but he did not let the Russians know this. If he did remove the Jupiters, he wanted to get something in return. Since he knew he wanted to remove them anyway, he preferred to hold that card as a bargaining chip. The Jupiter missile was an inaccurate first-generation nuke missile. If you set one up in New Haven and aimed it at Yankee Stadium, you'd be just as likely to hit the Vince Lombardi rest stop on the Jersey Turnpike as the Stadium. The Jupiters were highly vulnerable. Small arms fire could detonate them before they got off the ground. A punk with a 22 could blow up a Jupiter.

The Turks and the Russians took the Jupiters far more seriously than the Americans. The Turks considered them status symbols of the highest order. They had just come on-line in Turkey and the Turkish leaders were pretty excited about them.

Krushchev hated the Jupiters with a passion. When Robert Frost was a guest at the dacha in the Crimea, Krushchev handed him binoculars and told him to look out at the Black Sea.

"What do you see?"

"Well, Mr. Krushchev, my eyes aren't so good, but I only see the peaceful shining glittering sea, coated by a refreshing natural sweep of winds, their soft touches poignantly reminding man of his immortality and the calming presence of ..."

"Yes, I get it. Well put." interrupted Krushchev, "Now let me have a look."

Krushchev took the binoculars and stared out to sea.

"That's not what I see, Mr. Frost. I see American Jupiter missiles pointed right at my dacha!"

It turns out that this was a standard act-out Nikita did with all his guests. Krushchev was permanently steamed about the Jupiters.

During the Cuban Missile Crisis, UN Ambassador Stevenson, and a couple of reporters made Kennedy angry by suggesting that the US offer to remove the Jupiters from Turkey if, in exchange, the Cubans agreed to remove their rockets from Cuba.

You might think this would please Kennedy, since this was his actual plan, but it required skill to make it happen, not liberal blurt-outs. Kennedy wanted to use Jupiter removal as a bargaining chip, to be played at as late a moment as possible, or not at all ... or in secret. He was having trouble controlling Stevenson's liberal instincts. In the interest of international progressive good-will, the mature egghead was going to prematurely give away all of Kennedy's leverage with the Jupiters.

This is from the book, *The USA in the Time of LBJ*: 1963-1969

MAYBE IT WASN'T ALL IN VAIN

As a boy in the Johnson Vietnam years, I thought America was winning. I was rooting for the good guys on TV, in the paper, and while I was reading World War II books. Every week there was a graph bar showing something like 924 Viet Cong killed and a little graph bar at the bottom showing something like 24 GI's killed. I can still see Cronkite 200 times telling me how much we were winning. I don't recall any sense of media negativity towards the war, at least not until 68. They reported the protests, but I never sensed that the media was rooting for the hippies.

Although Vietnam involved several Presidents, it is generally considered to be Lyndon's war, or sometimes 'McNamara's War.' That is totally fair and called-for. When LBJ took office there were 16,000 USA troops in Vietnam. When he left office there were almost 600,000.

Coincidentally when he entered office the approximate size of a big campus protest against War, and 'the bomb' was 16,000. By the time he left office a good demonstration tallied about 600,000 people.

There are more than 3,500 books about the Vietnam War. So if anyone boasts "I read all the books about the Vietnam War" you should walk away from that person. The arguments about Vietnam are endless and hopeless.

There are two historian camps, both absolutely sure of themselves.

The majority of about 95% 'know' that the war was wrong, that the protesters were right, and the USA was the bad guy in Vietnam, even if it was with good intentions. They don't think it, they know it. There's nothing to discuss. Only a pathetic ignoramus could look back on the Vietnam War and come to any other conclusion.

The minority camp of 5% is miffed because the war was not conducted with victory in mind. They feel that Johnson conducted the war with a mixed message of powerful yet limited military force, combined with diplomatic and political weakness. This group feels that America fought the war "with one hand tied behind its back." They are astonished that Johnson never thought to occupy enemy territory. They felt that this would have been a sound military and political strategy, and are amazed that the USA was just there to take hits, not give them back. 'We were not allowed to cross the 50-yard line.' That is tough on the morale of soldiers. This 5% believes that the stop and start quality of the bombing campaign was a blunder. The 5% believe that American soldiers behaved, on average, far better than the enemy, just as surely as did American GI's in WWII compared to the Japanese and the Germans.

In his first weeks in office, President Johnson gave much consideration to withdrawing from Vietnam, but, like Kennedy, he didn't want to jeopardize the 1964 Presidential election by 'losing' Southeast Asia. Withdrawal or escalation could hurt his chances in

1964. It is no coincidence that Johnson escalated American involvement in 1965, not 1964. His fears for 1964 were confirmed in 1968 when his escalations in Nam cost the Dems the White House.

The successor to the assassinated South Vietnam President Diem (11.2.63) was a man named Huong who didn't last four months. There were ten regime changes in the two years after the coup that downed Diem. Killing Diem created a leadership hole in South Vietnam that the United States had little choice but to fill. To stand back and do nothing would be to invite disintegration and defeat for South Vietnam, and a few billion bucks down the Mekong drain.

The North Vietnamese Communist cause was set back by the assassination of Diem in an ironic way. Indigent local rage at the Diem regime came to a screeching halt and suddenly a lot of peasants who had been sympathetic to the Viet Minh wanted nothing more than to get back to rice farming. The entire C-revolution in the South suddenly stalled. The North Vietnamese, as a result, decided to send in regular army troops to the South to destabilize the improving situation and give chaos a chance.

The introduction of regular NVA troops into South Vietnam changed the entire dynamic of the war for Johnson, Rusk, McNamara, Bundy and the rest of the Blood Hound Gang. Without Diem's strong hand, the South Vietnamese army and police were now less effective. With this weakness combining with NVA infiltration, the situation was becoming precarious. As Washington perceived it, the war might be flat out lost if the USA did not intervene in force.

Johnson was in the same bind as John Kennedy. Lyndon was trying to be an oxymoron; a liberal hawk. Complete liberal withdrawal might have been a productive solution in the long run. Aggressive military intervention might have been a productive solution in the long run. The worst choice, the one he made, was a middle ground of limited military intervention. This pleased no one on the left or right, and set up a war without end in Indochina, an "escalating stalemate."

Johnson should have listened to Ike, who abhorred the concept of limited warfare. While LBJ played it half way, Ike asked him, "When are you going to go after the head of the snake, instead of the tail?" Johnson went after the tail for six years in Vietnam.

Historian Michael Lind disputes this analysis of the war, which is my own view generally. I respect the orthodox view, only a fool would dismiss the consensus as totally wrong, but I'm with the 5%.

Lind has a radical view: He happens to think that the middle ground was actually the only choice available to Johnson, and that LBJ made essentially the right call. What is even more annoying is that he argues his case well. After all, it is a pleasure to look down on the Vietnam performances of Kennedy, Johnson, and Nixon; especially Johnson. Don't be a spoil sport, Lindy.

Lind's logic is that a withdrawal would showcase a democratic and American global retreat both politically and militarily. On the other hand trying to win the war would have been a burden not worth the cost. The aftermath of administrating conquered communist southeast Asia would have been a nightmare. Johnson according to Lind, had only one option and he took it. It is a radical, yet simple argument.

Maybe it's true. Did the USA take the equivocal middle course and actually do the right thing in dragging out this war until January 1973? The argument goes: The US could not win the war, but it could not afford to lose it. If the United States had withdrawn its support for South Vietnam, the Communists would have won in short order. Thailand, Laos, Malaysia, and Indonesia might have then fallen to Communism. World-wide China-Sov sponsored communists insurgencies would have sprung up all over the world, inspired by the Communist victories in Asia. Latin America might have produced several Communist trouble spots which would never have arisen without the morale boost of an exciting Communist win in Vietnam. Communist Parties in Europe would have grown in numbers and power, and threatened the stability of the NATO alliance.

By marking time and holding the line, the USA got the message across to the world that Communism was not the wave of the future.

So the stalemate in Vietnam was something of a victory because it prevented the contagious wave of other newly inspired C-wins. Everyone likes a winner, especially unhappy big populations of poor people in third world countries who observe closely who is winning. By the time the Communists crashed through the gates of Saigon Palace, in May of 1975, too much time had passed without any Communist victories elsewhere. The Communist Super Bowl celebration party in 1975 was limited to Vietnam, when the goal had once been world revolution. Vietnam was small, remote, had a poor economy, and was not that great of a prize to show off to the rest of the Communist world. Yes, the bad guys won, but they took a beating doing it, it took forever, and along the way, the governments of Malasia, Thailand and Indonesia successfully suppressed their Communist rebellions. Could these countries have won if the USA had withdrawn from Vietnam in 1964 as everyone now in hindsight thinks it should have?

The nuclear arms race in the meantime became so serious that by the time the mid-70's came around, the USSR was more concerned with preventing the total destruction of the human race than it was in fostering revolutions. This opened up the door for new realistic political cooperation between the USA and the USSR and between the USA and China. Between 1964 and 1974 the power and accuracy of nuke missiles more than doubled, plus their numbers increased. This was a wake-up call to the superpowers to stop wishing for hot spots to erupt in revolutionary warfare. By the time the US left Vietnam in 73 there was an entirely new dynamic in super-power relationships.

If the USSR and China had a clear winner in Nam in 1965 because Sam left and let the Communists win, both these Communist giants might have seen the world through a different set of glasses and might not have reached out to the US at all, as they both did in the mid 1970's.

Lind is essentially saying that the 58,000 Americans who died in Vietnam did not die in vain; that they served the cause of freedom and helped hold off the Communist avalanche that was threatening to snowball into something truly horrible for humanity. I hope he is right. He might be!

I still feel that the United States should have occupied Haiphong and crossed the DMZ at the same time. Perhaps in 1965 this would have been a bit drastic, but by the time Johnson had 595,000 soldiers in South Vietnam, it seems militarily illogical to ask them to sit still, penned in, while the enemy dances all around the edges in perfect freedom. At that point you have to let them bust out and do something. Give them a chance to be soldiers instead of constables on jungle patrol with an M-16. Let the United States Army cross the DMZ like an army! Maybe the same number of men would have died, but at least the enemy would have clearly understood which side was on the offense, and that would have altered the course of military and political events.

This is from the book, The *United States in the Time of Richard Nixon*: 1968-1974

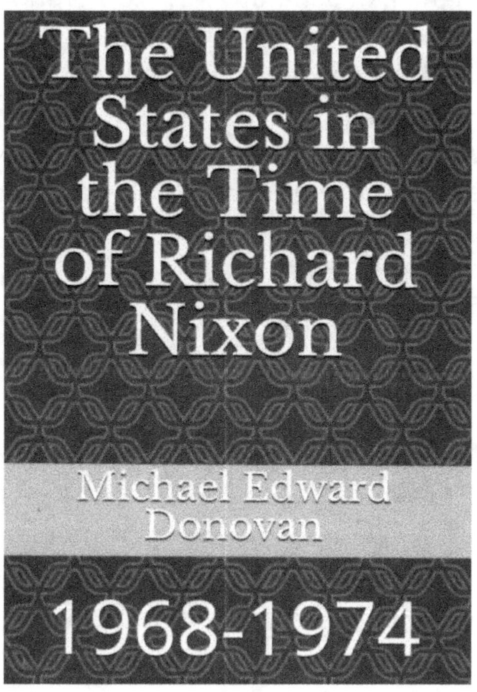

THE TEUTONIC TRIO

For the Establishment, the three most powerful players in Washington, besides Nixon, were all of German blood, so they acquired the less than adoring nickname: 'The Teutonic Trio.'

They were Henry Kissinger, John Erlichman and H.L. Haldeman. Kissinger had the most power, as you might guess. He was Special Advisor to the President, and was the real Secretary of State. William Rogers was just a figurehead Secretary of State and eventually resigned over this. Haldeman and Erlichman were not household names, and they liked it that way. They each wielded almost as much back-door power as Harry Hopkins under FDR, but *Time* and *Newsweek* were not itching to put them on the cover every other week, and they liked it that way.

Nixon was not only advancing the power of the Executive over the Congressional, he was also increasing the size and scope of Executive crony power, and the power alarmed some liberal observers. And Harry Hopkins had never been very secretive. Haldeman and Erlichman were. They both eventually went down with the Watergate ship, resigning in separate new conferences on the same day.

Haldeman and Erlichman decided who the President would see and not see. These twin guardians of Nixon's sacred time schedule were called 'The Berlin Wall.' And any plan to get past them and to Nixon directly was referred to as attempting to 'pole-vault the Berlin Wall.'

This is from the book, *The USA in the Time of Gerald Ford*: 1974-1976

PATTY HEARST - 1974-76

The unluckiest chump in the Ford years was Stephen Weed. One day Weed is young, happy, and engaged to a pretty young heiress. Then, armed men break into his house, beat him up, and kidnap his fiancée. The bride to be then joins up with the kidnappers, robs banks for them, and has sex with them, and never so much as kisses Stephen again. That's some serious bad luck. Even a bad week at the craps table in Atlantic City can't compete with that!

Her name was Patty Hearst. She was 20 years old, rich, slim, and single. Her grandfather was one of the richest and most famous men on earth, the newspaper magnate William Randolph Hearst (Citizen Kane.)

When Patty Hearst was kidnapped it was headline news all over the country. Where was she? The poor young woman! Poor Stephen Weed. For days the search for the missing Hearst was on. The nation feared for her life and worried for Weed.

Then, all of a sudden, on February 4, 1974, a gang of armed robbers sticks up a California bank with machine guns. Guess who's holding one of the tommy-guns. Who's that in the bank camera picture? Is it...? Can it be...?

Good Lord, Patty Hearst is holding bank employees at bay with a machine gun just two weeks after being kidnapped. Then the police get a mailed recording of Patty Hearst saying she was now a happy member of the SLA, the Symbionese Liberation Army.

Patricia Hearst became the personification of "Stockholm Syndrome" where the victims of kidnappers develop sympathy and maybe even an affinity for their abductors.

The SLA was a left wing violent radical militia movement of mostly black militants. Patty told the country she had changed her name to 'Tanya' and that she had a new boyfriend, the SLA gang leader himself. Stephen Weed was supposed to get the message on that one. If Weed didn't develop a drinking problem at this point, we have to admire him.

Patty (right) and the SLA Doing Their Thing

A few weeks later, the big breakthrough. The FBI and California law enforcement found Patty Hearst and arrested her on September 18, 1975. The most famous woman in the country did not seem the least repentant. She smiled defiantly at the photographers as she was hauled in and out of police cars and courtrooms. These photos were all front page news.

As Patty tells her story to her lawyers, more crazy details come out. The Symbionese Lunatic Army had at first treated her like a rich, dirty-dog enemy of the people. They tied her up and kept her in a dark closet for a week. Male members of the SLA were free to open the closet door and rape her in her defenseless condition, and these sordid details were a big part of why the story gripped the country. It also helped that she was pretty. It would be one thing if the SLA had kidnapped Phyllis Diller, but Patty Hearst was a just a bit more interesting.

Patty went to trial. More headline news for weeks. The whole country debated the case. Everyone had an opinion. She had been brainwashed. It wasn't fair. She had no thoughts of robbing banks before she got kidnapped. A jury convicted Patricia Hearst of bank robbery in March 1976. She got 35 years!

A lot of people had thought the jury would find her not guilty and not responsible for her actions. Many people sided with her and campaigned for her early release. Jimmy Carter helped get Patty out of jail in 1979, and President Clinton gave her a full pardon.

The rest of the SLA was eventually tracked down and gunned down in two separate shoot-outs with the police. Good.

Stephen Weed went into an insane asylum for two years, but I hear he's doing oaky now.

This is from the book, *The USA in the Time of Jimmy Carter*: 1977-1981

IRAQ INVADES IRAN - 9.25.80

The clear enemy for the United States was Iran as Carter campaigned for re-election for President. On September 25, 1980, Iraq, under the one man rule of Sadaam Hussein, invaded Iran. After an advance deep into the western part of Iran, the invasion stalled. Iran held on and even counter-attacked.

There was never any doubt that the United States preferred the Iraqis to the Iranians in this conflict. The enemy of my enemy is my friend.

This war would last until 1988 and would result in almost one million dead, both sides, in combat, not to mention the civilian casualties.

Iraq had few objectives besides conquest. This was largely a wag-the-camel war. It was aggression per se. The Iraqi nation had little choice but to support Sadaam's dictatorship if there was a war on. It was partly to control power at home that he started this foreign war.

In concrete terms, Iraq wanted control of the Shat al Araab, the waterway leading from the Tigris-Euphrates rivers as they combine and empty into the Persian Gulf. If Iraq had won the Shat al Araab and kept it, the invasion of Kuwait 1990 probably would never have occurred, which would have meant that the 2003 invasion of Iraq probably would never have occurred either. It's to the individual imagination to guess how different the course of the last 35 years or so would have been in the Gulf Region if Sadaam had managed to hang on to the Shat al-Araab in the 1980's war with Iran.

From the time the US defeated Iraq in 1990-91, the left has been violently critical of how "we were the ones who built up and supported Sadaam in the first place!" The sentiment was never expressed without an exclamation point, which is essentially the point. It meant: how dare you ask Americans to go fight a war against Sadaam now.

Even if these charges were true, and they are partly true, there was no outcry against the U.S. supporting Iraq throughout this Iran-Iraq war. Even the average hippie in a Vermont ice cream store was rooting for Iraq, or at the very least was not outraged because the US was sending some technological information help and giving some political support to Sadaam and his nation. It seemed like the logical thing to do at the time and the Carter administration started it. The Carter team leaned towards Iraq in this one, right away. Why not? Reagan and Bush get all the heat for supporting Sadaam, but Carter made the call at crunch time and Carter chose Iraq.

Losing Iran and Iraq in simul-crash would leave Kuwait was America's only friend in the oil jugular of the Persian Gulf. Kuwait wasn't much of a friend and had no military force worth mentioning. Courting Iraq under the circumstances was the only foreign policy choice for Carter, Reagan and Bush until August 1, 1990, when Iraq dragged the USA into the Gulf region and changed the picture in South Asia permanently.

This is from the book, *The USA in the Time of Ronald Reagan*: 1981-1989

BONZO GOES TO BITBURG - MAY 1985

Why did a famous rock band release a song in 1985 called *Bonzo Goes to Bitburg*? Answer: To mock President Reagan for visiting a German military cemetery (and for being in a bad old movie.)

A president visits a cemetery and the world holds its breath for weeks. These are stories that only count for much in times of peace. With the ongoing insurrection in Iraq, with Americans dying in combat every week, a similar incident today would not create such a large controversy. But it was a slow news year, and in 1985, the visit of Reagan to Bitburg dominated the news for weeks.

The problem was that some Nazi SS corpses were in Bitburg, and it seemed to some that Reagan was out of line for visiting.

It was intended as a ceremonial stop to accentuate the positive state of German-American relations. It wasn't supposed to be such a big deal. Instead the Bitburg business was a big blow-up.

The President was planning on visiting Dachau concentration camp. His trip to Europe was for an Economic Summit planned for the first week in May 1985, but along the way there were ceremonies to attend.

Then Reagan decided that a trip to Dachau was too negative. He did not want to taunt the German people over their past. He wanted to emphasize the positive relations between West Germany and the USA over the past 40 years.

On April 11, 1985, spokesman Speakes released the news of the trip to Bitburg, scheduled for May 5. The administration did not know that a few Nazis were buried in Bitburg. Reagan thought that he was visiting a cemetery where some American GI's were buried, along with the regular German soldiers.

It should be noted that Chancellor Kohl had assured the Americans that no Nazi SS were buried in Bitburg. A few days later, another top German official reiterated the false fact. No SS were buried at Bitburg.

When the press found out that some Nazis were buried there and that the American president was going to lay a wreath, people at home and around the world, called on Reagan to cancel the trip. The Jewish community was bitter on Bitburg. It wanted to smash Reagan to bits. The extreme American left called Reagan a Nazi for going to Bitburg. That's a Bitburg much. When it was learned that no Americans were buried there, the pressure increased against Ronald's going.

America and Reagan were condemned as if an actual war crime had been committed. The USA was the best friend that Israel and the Jews had in the world. The United States supported Israel through all its acts of violence in the Middle East. America has condemned some Israeli actions, but never wavered in its support. The United States was there for Israel in 1948, in 1967, and in 1973, and was willing to risk a nuclear war with Russia in order to defend Israel's right to exist. If the Soviet Union had intervened in the 1973 Arab-Israeli War, the United States would quite possibly have gone to war to defend Israel. Millions of Americans would have died to save Israel. The United States provided four billion dollars' worth of aid to Israel every year in Reagan's time. That was a gift, not a loan. And this is the thanks Uncle Sam gets? Yitzhak Rabin said that Reagan "will never be forgiven."

Calling Reagan an insensitive Nazi, and accusing him of an unforgivable offense for putting a wreath on a graveyard where some SS troops were buried nearby, was ten times as wrong as the wrong he may have committed.

The heat storm just kept building as the trip to Bitburg loomed. I remember it very well. It was all over the TV and newspapers like some sensational murder trial about to open. The United States Senate passed a resolution telling Reagan he must cancel the visit. The vote? 82 to 0! Even right wing religious jerk leader Jerry Falwell, usually a dependable friend, called on Reagan to cancel the trip, and admit that he was wrong to have scheduled it in the first place.

The Communist newspapers wrote that the United States was allying itself to Nazis, past and present. We shouldn't be surprised, they said, since the USA had already shown that its national policy these days was sponsorship of 'state terrorism.'

The Soviet Union should remember a few things about its own role in World War II. Hitler could never have started World War II in the first place without the evil Nazi-Soviet pact of August 1939 when Nazi Germany and the USSR *became actual allies*. They have a nerve to call the USA out for collaboration with fascists because one guy drops a wreath on a grave-sight as a gesture of forgiveness and conciliation. There were pogroms in Russia when Hitler was in diapers.

.

The real blame lay with Kohl for telling the Reagan team early on that there were no Nazi troops buried at Kolomenshoe Cemetery, in Bitburg. Reagan and his close advisors asserted later that if they had known there were SS Nazis in the Bitburg ground there they never would have agreed to go. But once the publicity for the trip began to grow, it was too late. By the time Reagan and the State Department learned the truth, the publicity for the trip would have made cancellation as big of a problem as going there.

Caving in to pressure was not a trait of Ron Reagan. If people had asked him to cancel the trip gently and courteously, it might have worked. But when they pointed their finger at him and called him names and stridently demanded he cancel this evil trip he was planning, it aroused his stubborn temper.

There were a few voices of support.

90 year-old General Matt Ridgeway, one of the famed heroes of WWII, called Reagan to offer support, and not mere words. Matt said he would go to Bitburg with Reagan and stand beside him at the ceremony. Ridgeway would shake hands with a Luftwaffe officer over the graves. Reagan took him up on the offer.

Kissinger told Reagan that canceling the trip would do a lot of damage to US reputation in the field of foreign policy, while proving nothing. A General Chain of the USAF chipped in with this rather pertinent piece of info: Chain had served at the US Air Force base at Bitburg and he said that every Memorial Day for years there was a ceremony at Bitburg at which officers of Germany, France and the USA laid wreaths over the graves of Bitburg, and not a word of protest had ever arisen over it, locally, or anywhere else.

Reagan refused to back down and was determined to go to Bitburg. A trip to Bergen-Belsen was included in the itinerary for the same day. It would have looked bad to refuse to go visit a concentration camp for a memorial service, and then go to Bitburg.

When reporters said he was insensitive about the Holocaust, Reagan told the story of how when he worked on war information movies, he illegally made personal copies of the footage of the camps being liberated by the American troops. This story was twisted into an outrageous lie. The story made the rounds that Reagan had claimed that he had been there and had shot the film himself. Reagan had made no such boast, but I remember when that story was being tossed around. It made no sense that Reagan would make up such a lie since it could be so easily disproved, but it showed the length that people would go to try and throw dirt on him.

German Chancellor Helmut Kohl convinced Reagan that canceling the visit would force the resignation of his government. Reagan believed him. In addition Reagan on principle wanted to stand by his friend.

On May 5, 1985, Reagan visited Bitburg. Just before he arrived, some reporters planted fresh roses on the SS graves and tried to take pictures of it, but Reagan's advance team picked up the flowers before the scums could take the photos.

The left screamed in anger, worldwide, but on the scene at Bitburg there was only a very small protest element. The visit went on without incident, unless you want to count Kohl wiping tears from his eyes during the ceremonies.

Helmut Kohl was grateful to Reagan for his profile in courage. The visit damaged Reagan politically, but it helped German-American relations considerably.

This is from the book, *The USA in the Time of George H.W. Bush*: 1989-1993

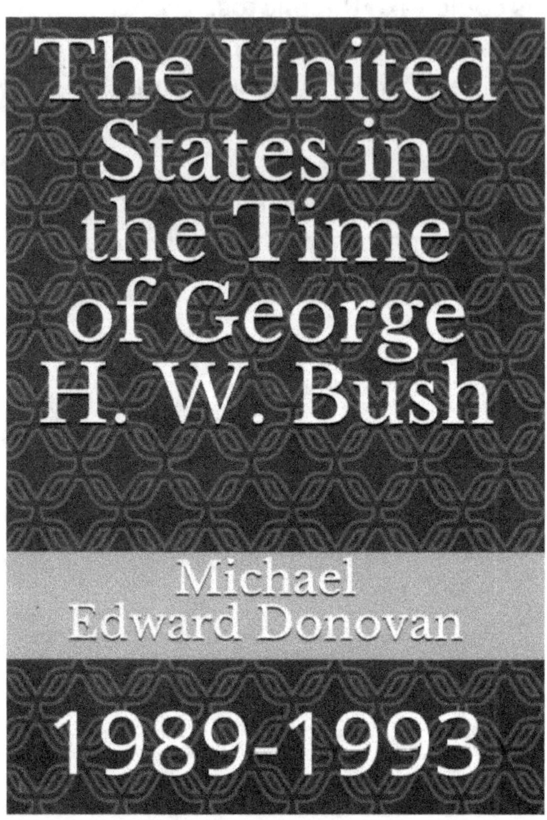

IRAQ CONQUERS KUWAIT - 8.1.90

On August 1, 1990, Washington was shocked to hear that the Iraqi army had crossed over into Kuwait, and was heading on for the capital, Kuwait City. This was no incursion. This was a full-fledged invasion. The Bush administration was in no position to stop the invasion militarily. Kuwait was tiny and distant and the USA had no base of operations in the Middle East. This was a handicap for the Bush team in responding to the attack. US military force in that theatre was afloat in international waters or scattered in small bases in small countries on the periphery of the Gulf, but not in it.

This lack of a local base, the greatest handicap in handling the Kuwaiti crisis of 1990, would in the end be the greatest result. By liberating Kuwait from the Iraqis, the USA created a permanent base of operations in the Middle East, something it never had before. Not only was this new base in the Middle East, it was in the Persian Gulf, and Kuwait was at the very crossroads of international oil supply and transport.

Kuwait was also on the doorstep of the arch-nemesis of the 70's and 80's, Iran; and was within striking distance of troublemaker Syria. American-owned Kuwait constituted an exclamation point on the old Carter doctrine warning Russia to stay out of the Gulf.

This is from the book, *The USA in the Time of Bill Clinton*: 1993-2001

LIVINGSTON RESIGNS

In late 1998, the heir apparent to the job of Speaker of the House was Republican, Bob Livingston. Bob however, was forced to resign as an indirect result of the Clinton sex scandals.

Publisher Larry Flint, of *Hustler* magazine, hated Republicans. He believed that Ken Starr was a witch hunt. Larry thought that Starr wasn't out for the truth, just for political capital. Flint also thought they were no good hypocrites because Republicans had just as many skeletons in their closet as Bill Clinton.

So Captain Flint offered a $1 million reward to anyone who could produce scandalous evidence leading to the downfall of a prominent Republican. It took a few weeks, and there weren't as many hits as expected, but one source came through, and got the dough. *Hustler* had the goods on Bob Livingston, and when he knew that an article outing his infidelity was coming out, he jumped the gun for damage control.

Republican Bob Livingston stood on the House floor and made a not that unusual speech about the Clinton scandals and how the President should resign for what he has done. Livingston was getting some scattered boos from the Dems. Bob then said that he would not ask the President to do anything that he would not do in a similar situation. Congressman Livingston then said that he was guilty of an extramarital affair and announced his resignation right then and there and walked off the podium!

I happened to be watching CNN that day. I can't describe the sound of the reaction in the audience. It was as unique as the moment called for it to be. It was something.

Turned out Livingston did not formally leave office until May of 1999, but he did resign and never made Speaker. *Hustler* changed history. Livingston was 'Out like Flint.'

Clinton was often asked if he would ever consider resigning. He always paused and gave a dramatic "Never, ever." Way to think of the country first. No matter how it could hurt the country you are so power hungry you would "never, ever" resign. Thanks a lot, Mr. Selfish. Of course he was probably just saying it to help win the battle at the moment. In any case, you know your Presidency is in trouble when the only power standing tall and scoring any points for you is *Hustler Magazine*.

This is from the book, *W: 2001-2009*

FALLING MAN

The *New York Times* published a chilling photograph on September 12 which became known as the "Falling Man." It was a businessman upside down falling to his death from 1,300 feet with the silver WTC as backdrop. He looked calm. He was never identified. He had a nice shirt and tie. The tie was pointing straight up.

More than 60 people chose to jump to their deaths rather than face the smoke and the flames. It took nine seconds of breathless terror for them to die. That's the math at the fall rate of 125 feet a second. One firefighter described bodies hitting the pavement and exploding. Now you see it, now you don't. Severed heads and limbs were part of the landscape for the rescue workers.

The *NY Times* came under heavy criticism for publishing the picture. The networks were willing to run footage of people jumping/falling to their death up until about 7 p.m. and then it stopped forever. I video-recorded the whole day, from noon 9/11, to noon 9/12. Once it stopped it stopped forever, and it wasn't even on the 20 WTC documentaries I've seen over the years. But all afternoon on day one, it was fine. The whole idea behind not showing the footage is to try to settle things down, and not incite. The video is considered too emotional.

The media should show it because most of these victims would want their lives avenged. They would <u>want</u> Americans to get upset and riled up when they saw what those demons did.

Too bad we couldn't have taken a poll of the departed 2,700 New Yorkers. There would be a few Christ-like angels who would ask us to forgive, and would say, "We need to reach out and try to understand our Arab brothers and sisters so they will not be compelled to do something like this again. And don't show that dreadful video of me falling."

There would also be the other 95% who would say, "If you love me, pay them back. If you want to honor my memory, pay them back! And don't sugarcoat what they did in the name of taste. Show the video."

It is perfectly all right to show the buildings collapsing and nearly 3,000 people dying at that moment. Just don't get in too close where we can see individuals dying, then all of a sudden, it's in bad taste.

Count me a sinner. Count me in that 95%. If it was video of me falling 110 stories to my death in a terrorist attack I would want my last 9 seconds to be the on the opening credits of a new right-wing TV series called *Kill the Bastards!* And put the clip on the closing credits too, plus in slo-mo as a bumper going to and from commercials. For music you can have the sound of Jihad music, then a machine gun, and the music goes into sour notes and then stops.

This is from the book, *The USA in the time of Barak Obama:* 2009-2017

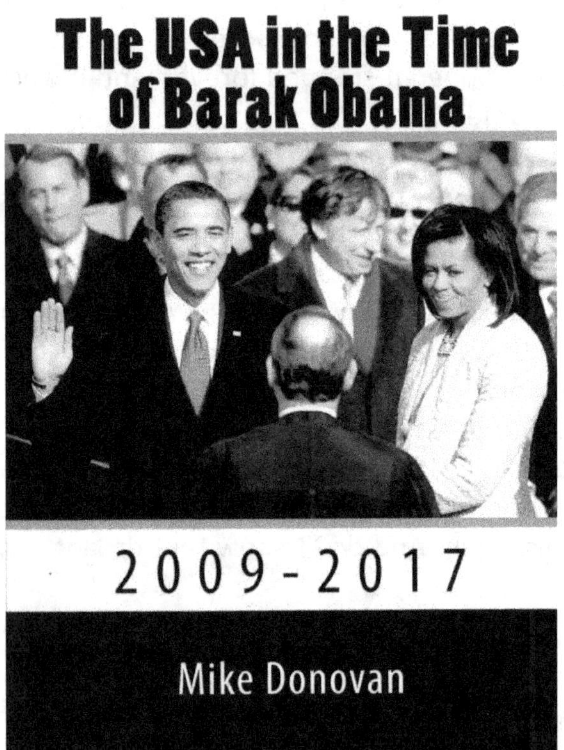

LANCE ARMSTRONG IS NO LONGER MY HERO - 1.13

My favorite athlete of all time has let me down. The top story for days is about the greatest US bicycle champ of all time, Lance Armstrong. Turns out he did all that great stuff on performance-enhancing drugs.

Armstrong strongly denies it, but it looks bad for my idol. Apparently, in the past, he got away with intimidating officials and other cyclists about prosecution and testifying.

Lance appeared on Oprah Winfrey, and what he said was on the news for days. On January 27, the entire first half of *60 Minutes* was all about Armstrong.

I'm devastated as an American, as a sports fan, and as a fan of the man, Lance Armstrong.

I'm only kidding. I could care less about bicycling as a sport, and never gave two cents about Lance Armstrong.

I think the AMB, the continued START talks, the war in Afghanistan, or a real sport like the NHL, is a lot more important than Lance Armstrong and whether he was on steroids when he won the most boring sport on earth, riding a bike. I'd rather watch nothing.

But it was a huge story and I have to report it. Lance was juiced.

This is from the book, Yes, But Tell Us How You Really Feel

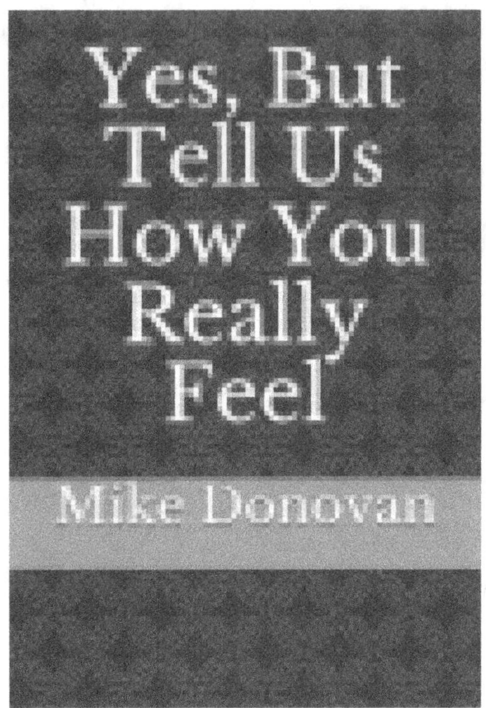

FEBRUARY 13, 2017

National Security Advisor Mike Flynn is in trouble over revelations that he was making phone calls to the Russians about U.S. policy before Obama left office. It is a breach of several laws and many people are saying that Flynn should step down.

Meanwhile Trump keeps bringing up this lie about him being the victim of mass voter fraud. He's singling out New Hampshire where thousands of outside the state voters were supposedly bused in to vote Hillary. Politicians, journalists and citizens from all over New

Hampshire are uniting to say there is zero evidence to support this and we all had our eyes wide open that day. (He lost NH by a close vote).

I'm with journalist Andrew Sullivan who believes it is time for the media to start questioning the mental health of Donald Trump. I've felt that way since I watched him misbehave like a six year old during the 2015 Republican debates.

Estimates or the cost of the wall with Mexico are in the 100 billion dollar range.

This is from the book, *Oil, Russia, the Middle East, and Desert Storm*

1918 - THE STRUGGLE FOR MOSUL

In 2017, the struggle for the Mosul, Iraq, was a dominant story in the news. The Iraqi Army battled ISIL for control of the city (ISIL stands for the Islamic State of Iraq and the Levant, or 'I'm still in love.')

Mosul is in Northern Iraq. In 1918, Iraq did not exist, but the oil of Mosul did. The Turks were still in control of Mosul, which was 180 miles to the north of the Kut-Baghdad battle lines, now controlled by the British, but opposed with some surprising heart by the TTF, the Turkish Tigris Force, under General Hakki.

The Battle of Sharqat put an end to the TTF. 12,000 Turks surrendered on October 30. Word was all about of a cease fire, but it wasn't confirmed, when the British sent two cavalry brigades to race north and take Mosul before the armistice stops the war. They were racing against peace to get to the oil. The Turks had a solid force in Mosul prepared to resist. A 1918 Battle of Mosul was shaping up when word reached all parties that the war was over as far as Mesopotamia is concerned. The greedy British cavalry stopped just south of Mosul.

Now what? The Turks were adamant about not having to give up Mosul. They reminded the Brits that it was in the terms and conditions of the cease-fire that the losers didn't have to relinquish lands that had never been conquered. The British called a few lawyers in London and soon announced that clause 17 of the Mudros Armistice clearly stipulated that Allied troops could occupy some outposts beyond what it already owned if there was a security emergency to consider. The British would therefore march on Mosul. Turkey complained that there was no security emergency, and that this is bogus. The British said 'too bad, but we'll be kind enough to give *your garrison force* time to leave so that they will not have to be taken prisoner.' The Turks said, "We are a fighting machine, not a police garrison, and your offer is insulting."

In the end, after some more diplomatic wrangling, the Turks evacuated Mosul. They split because the British wanted them to, and because the Turks had lost the war. They left Mosul-town kicking and screaming, but they left. Mosul became part of Iraq, a new nation drawn on a victor's map in 1920 with little thought as to what was going into it. The man with the red pencil who created Iraq was Winston Churchill. His baby, Iraq was an anti-homogenous collection of races, religions, regions, and political allegiances, with no natural geographical boundaries. Good work, Win. Mess-o-potamia is in about chaotic now as it was when General Hakki was throwing in the towel at Sharqat on October 30, 1918.

It's a debated subject whether this campaign was worth the effort or worth trying at all. Most of the oil could have been secured if the Indo-Brits had simply carved out a strong sphere around the Persian

Gulf alone. The march up into Iraq was perhaps as much to relieve the pressure on other Ottoman fronts (esp. the Caucasus and Palestine) as it was to secure the lands of Babylon for the Entente. The entire Mesopotamia campaign was partly or maybe even mostly political.

When all the oil fires had cleared, 28,000 British and Empire troops had died for BP. Another 80,000 were shell shocked for Shell.

This is from the book, *The Heritage of American Slavery*

PRUDENCE CRANDALL - 1831

The official heroine of Connecticut is Prudence Crandall.

Prudence tried to open up a school in Canturbury in 1831. The key word here is tried. PC was a respected educator, out of Providence, who was hired to set up a school in Canturbury, and she did so without integration in mind.

Then an African-American girl named Sarah Harris very politely asked Prudence if she could attend classes at the Canturbury school. Prudence said, "Sure, why not?"

The white folk of Canterbury soon told Crandall why not. They boycotted the new school by refusing to supply it with food, pencils, lumber, lanterns, or pupils. They tried to intimidate Prudy Crandall, but they didn't know who were messing with. Prudy was not the type to "stay home and bake cookies."

Prudence proudly told the racists that "Thou hast not seen anything yet." She enrolled 20 black girls in the school; and since there weren't any whites there anymore anyway, declared it henceforth to be a school for aspiring African-American female educators, a teachers grammar school so that young black women could in turn educate their sisters! Wow!

Some clergymen from nearby communities supported Prudy and the new school.

White mobs broke into the school. Prudence marked time up on the second floor while the jackals tore the school to pieces. Prudence was not harmed, but the school was wrecked beyond repair, never to reopen again.

This is one of the most disgusting stories in American History.

There is a Prudence Campbell Museum in Canterbury where a pink eraser that says 'Prudence Campbell' on it costs more than I was willing to pay. Not even for such a great cause.

This is from *A History of Russia*

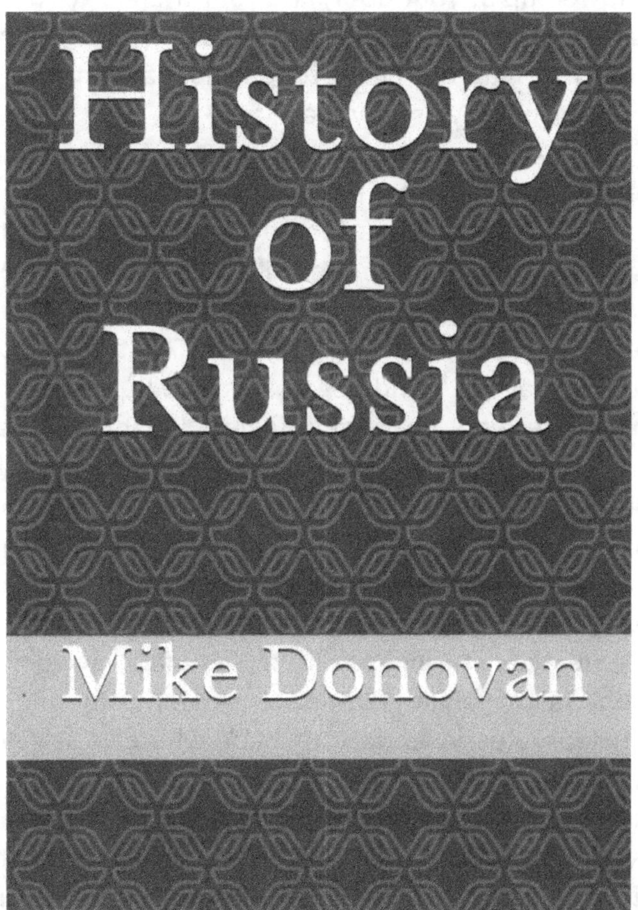

IVAN GROZNY - THE FORMIDABLE - 1547-1584

'Ivan the Terrible' was Stalin before Stalin. Ivan ruled Russia by terror. Crowned Tsar at the vicious age of 17, Ivan liked to amuse himself by torturing animals. Those who were dumb enough to ask him to stop were asked to join them. "PETA has no power here", he told them. Rather than try to change and infiltrate the established systems of authority in Russia, Ivan created a parallel government and police force, The Oprichnina. This organization was about 400 years ahead of its time. It is the template on which future bodies, like the SS and the KGB were modeled. Rather than change the system, he created a new one and intimidated the old one with it! When the Oprichnina showed up at your door, kiss your friends good-bye.

He bridged the path from one era of Russian History to the next, much the same way Ivan the First brought Russia from the Valdimir-Sudzal era the Princes of Muscovy era.

Ivan the Terrible started out as the Prince of Moscow. He was regent at the age of 3 and grew up watching a bloody feud between the Belskys and Shuisky families for power. His father was already dead when, at age 7, his mother was killed in this battle for power. Teen-aged Ivan heard that the Shuiskys were responsible for the foul deed and he had a Shuisky prince whacked. That felt good, so he made himself the Tsar at 17 and began a war on Russian nobility that was as fierce as the wars he waged against Poland, Lithuania, and Turkey.

Ivan went to war in the direction of the Baltic, just for the sake of expansion. He attacked Livonia in 1558, and drove into Poland-Lithuania. This war lasted two decades. Most of the rest of Europe wanted to keep Russia out of the heart of Europe; and soon the Russians were up against a big coalition. Denmark, Sweden, Poland, Lithuania were all against Russia. The Holy Roman Emperor contributed troops. Russia ended up back where it started in this one. No gain on the play.

In the south, things went better. Wars against the Khanates of Kazan and Astrakhan pushed Great Russia down the length of the Volga, opening up new lands for Russian settlers to move into, and they happily did.

The Tartars were being driven towards the door, but made plenty of noise on the way out. They raided and destroyed Moscow in 1571, and waged a running war against Russia for some time, but now they were on the outside fighting to get back in.

There was a negative side to victory in the south. Central Russia lost too many people to the gold rush. Estates that depended on people began to fail. Recruits were needed for the endless northwest war (which Ivan gave priority to) and there were no longer enough

Russian men to go around. The new lands of the Volga Steppe were a step up. Great Russia was sparsely populated enough for its size to begin with; now all the people were racing south like Sooners. This de-population problem contributed to the chaos and inefficiency of Russian administration at the end of Ivan's terrible reign. There weren't enough bureaucrats to go around.

I call him 'Ivan the Formidable' because the Russian word that this name is based on can be just as easily be translated to 'strong and formidable.' Even though Ivan was indeed 'terrible', that wasn't what the nickname was about. English 'terrible' could mean an incompetent person who is also a knave.

Ivan, like Peter did not have a great relationship with his son. Ivan killed his son, and messed up the succession to the throne in a way that hurt Russia.

Ivan Grozny was a very smart man with a super-memory and an indefatigable worker. When he was a young Tsar, Ivan arranged a Miss Russia beauty contest. The Oprichnina helped to bring all prettiest young women in Russia to Moscow. Ivan was the sole judge. Like I say, Ivan was a very smart man.

Ivan picked Anastasia Romanov as the winner. He crowned her Empress of Russia. He married her. Anastasia was a strong willed woman. He didn't choose a Lewinsky. Anastasia was an influential adviser, along with Father Sylvester and Metro Mecarius and Al Adashev. They made up Ivan's 'Big Four' brains' trust.

Ivan was as bi-polar as it gets. He would go on bloody benders where he killed many people unjustly, just as easily as he killed genuine miscreants. Then he would feel guilty about it. I mean really guilty. Ivan would go into church alone, lock up the doors, and cry and bang his head to the floor screaming to God for mercy for all his terrible sins. He would spend entire days begging God for mercy while people listened in from outside the doors. Then he would go out and commit all the same sins! Then he would go back to church and cry and plead forgiveness. On and on it went until he died. I hope you will agree that I backed up my bold opening sentence. I hope this makes your bi-polar problem seem small.

One man who stood up to Ivan IV was the monk, Phillip of Moscow. Ivan arrived at church service one day and Phillip refused to bless him. It was because of the massacres. Father Phil read his boss the riot act, which is usually a mistake. The Terrible was very angry, and had Monk Phillip arrested. On December 23, 1569, a mechanic entered his jail cell, and put an end to the life of a brave man. Today, he is known as Saint Phillip.

Ivan reacted to Phillip's criticism by sacking Novgorod, the land of the free speech.

This is from the book, *Who's Who in the Civil War*

MCCLERNAND - (1811 - 1900)

John A. McClernand had it out with his boss, but it was the wrong boss to have it out with in the Civil War. General McClernand had it out with Ulysses Grant during the Vicksburg Campaign and ended up sacked in June 1863, just two weeks before the fall of the city.

McClernand had served in Congress before the war and was one of the fighting politicians whose skills-set came up short in battle.

Admiral Porter, General Sherman and General Grant on three separate occasions made written reports that concluded that

McClernand was not fit for high command. They did not say that he was not officer material; just that he was not good enough to be a general. Grant was especially unhappy with McClernand's lack of leadership at the Battle of Champion's Hill and it was shortly thereafter that the long-bearded JAM got the pink slip.

McClernand was especially bitter towards Grant because John Alexander was a serious potential candidate for president in 1864. This battlefield demotion knocked him out and he knew it. So McClernand was going around Washington in the middle of 1863 telling people he had the dirt on Grant. He spread stories about how much Grant drank and hinted that he had a book coming out about it soon. This new book was going of blow the lid off the whole sham, and the world will know that we have a stumblebum drunk running the war.

But McClernand was the one who was obviously drunk, drunk with stupidity. Those stories about Grant's drinking had already made the rounds in 1862, with the help of jealous Halleck, and they had already been proven false. Besides, Lincoln was on public record that if Grants drinking produced victories like the ones he had delivered so far, then "I'll ship a case of whiskey to every general in the Union Army." McClellan was trumping with a lie that would have made no difference if it had been believed.

Lincoln did give him a limited command later in the war, to restore his dignity and avoid political problems for everybody. The two had known each other in their younger years back in Sangamon.

This is from the book, *Books* [book reviews from my non-fiction library]

MARXISM-LENINISM ON WAR AND ARMY On War, (Multiple authors) - c) 1972 - Progress Publishers, Moscow

In case of fire, throw this in. This book makes for a good chug-a-lug game. Every time you read the word "reactionary" you have to take a slug of whisky. You won't make it past three pages.

Progress Publishers made some fine physical books. This little hardcover has a nice weight and a finely textured bright grey exterior, with title letters in colored relief. The Communist propaganda pages almost never show any signs of acid breakdown. The windbag Marxism-Leninism on War and Army is still bright and sturdy 46 years later. It's hard to imagine being a young adult Russian forced to read this material and try and make any fair-minded sense of it, or use it to some positive benefit. [cover is a young Washington Irving meeting President Washington.]

This is From the Book, *The Vietnam War: 1945-1975*

LAOS 1961-62

In 1961, the United States was much closer to intervening in Laos than in Vietnam. South Vietnam under Diem actually seemed stable now, but Laos was the domino about to fall.

Laos

If Laos went Communist it would become a long dagger pointing down into Indo. We see it from the present as a dagger that was about to turn east and stab South Vietnam in the back; but in 1961, SEATO saw the threat as turning west and attacking Thailand and then Burma. Laos and the Ho Chi Minh Trail was a huge arrow pointing south but it could turn west or east, or split up into two armies. SEATO and the USA thought that South Vietnam was a sideshow compared to the real Communist plan to attack Thailand and then Burma. SEATO got plenty of active military help from Thailand and Burma, provided it was planted on the west side story.

When Thailand beefed up its defense, the HCMT/Laos flow of Communist aggression turned to one direction only: towards South Vietnam. America and SEATO hadn't even expected the showdown there. Kennedy said, "Don't you take Thailand, or I will show you that I am as tough as Ike." – "No problem, we'll take South Vietnam instead," replied Charlie.

The northern portion of Laos had been Pathet Lao (C) for pretty much all of the Fabulous Fifties, and it still was. Communist China had seen to that. The rest of the country was divided. There was a rightie opposition group under Prince Boun Oum and General Phouma Nosovan.

Prince Phouma led a neutralist faction of the non-Coms. Phouma was Prime Minister from 1956 to 1960. Oum overthrew him in a coup, backed by the United States. The neutralist Phouma had been too friendly with the Soviet Union for America's taste. Plus he had allowed some Commys in his government at Vientiane.

Kennedy didn't consider intervention in Nam until after Vienna, but he was in the Laos hot seat from the first day of his era. He authorized covert assistance to Laos, but not overt.

The problem with the war in Laos is that it was run by the CIA. US policy in Laos was not coordinated with all the major branches of government. To some extent, even the JCS had less to do with military operations in Laos than the CIA. The CIA had its own little army, navy, and air force in Laos, all under fake company names, and the American people basically had little idea there was really a war in Laos at all

The President usually mispronounced Laos, the country that the United States was ready to intervene to save. He usually called Laos "Lay-os." That says a lot to me about what went wrong in Southeast Asia. It reminds me of the Carter Administration when Cy Vance wrote of the Iran Hostage Crisis years later that, "The problem was that none of us at the top knew anything about Islamic fundamentalism." The President is going to intervene in a land he can't pronounce.

Ike had told JFK on 1.19.61, "If you uncork Laos, you expose the border of Thailand and invite the decline and fall of Cambodia, South Vietnam, and Burma as well. If a political settlement cannot be reached in Laos, then we must intervene."

Ike hesitated in Laos because with him it was a toss-up between full-scale intervention and no intervention at all. This is an admirable formula but also a permission-slip to not act on Laos and then leave the no-win dilemma to the next President. To top it off he gives the new guy a stern advisory that he would have to intervene. In other words he told Kennedy which decision to make regarding the decision that he had refused to make himself.

Kennedy bluntly asked the grandfather, "If the situation is so critical, why didn't you decide to do something in recent days." Ike replied that he did not feel it was right to act on Laos with a new administration coming in. Eisenhower apparently was too busy 'waging peace.'

The Communists of Laos, under the military-political group, the Pathetic Lao (actually the "Pathet Lao"), were fighting a civil war against the right-wing forces under General Phil Nosovan. The United States gave the rightist Laotians $300 mil during the Ike years. Now Kennedy was being asked to insert troops.

The Pathet Laos plainly won a jarring victory when they sealed up the Royal Laotian Army on the Plain of Jars. The Jars jam happened only a month after Kennedy took office. Jack asked the Joint Chiefs of Staff what it would take to save Laos from the Communists. The reply was 250,000 ground troops and a threat to use nukes in necessary. Kennedy said, 'Let me think about that one.'

Laos presented too many difficulties. Kennedy's allies in the Royal Laotian Army were of little help. For one thing, the Laotians were so passive and gentle a people that it was hard to motivate personnel on *either* side to fight hard. Opposing forces took breaks and went swimming in the same ponds. These were not the troops to back for the big fight.

In 1985, Nixon wrote that the Vietnam War was essentially lost when the United States did not intervene in Laos during the Kennedy years. Nixon believed that if Kennedy had extended the DMZ westward, well into Laotian territory, the Ho Chi Minh Trail could have been effectively blocked. In Richard's opinion, once the trail grew in strength and resilience in the mid-1960's the war was lost. There was no way the US and its South Vietnamese allies could defend their entire, long western border, against attacks from both Laos and Cambodia. The VC supply line ran right up into China. The back door was limitlessly stocked with goodies. It's a good argument.

Kennedy wanted to get tough in Laos, but after the Bay of Pigs, he began to back off on intervention. He told advisors that he had learned two lessons from the Cuban disaster. One was to never trust the advice of the CIA or his military again, and the other was to never commit US armed forces except in decisive force. For both these reasons Kennedy did not take Eisenhower's 1-19-61 advice and jump into the Laos fight. Kennedy asked the generals sharply, "How can I ask the American people to support a fight 9,000 miles away when they did not support an operation against a Communist threat 90 miles away." The setback at the Bay of Pigs had tied Kennedy's hands in Laos. "Without the Bay of Pigs, we would have troops in Laos right now," he told a cabinet member in the fall of 61. But he could not risk another failed intervention when the heat was still on from the last one.

On the other hand, Kennedy couldn't afford to continually look like he was retreating before Communist expansion. These were macho times and he knew he had to make a stand somewhere. He could not afford to look weak on anything, but especially not against Communism; unless of course he wanted to be a one-term president and hand the keys over to Goldwater or Lodge in 1964.

Kennedy nevertheless threatened intervention in Laos as openly as possible in 1961. He moved American divisions from Okinawa to Thailand, and airlifted a brigade to a spot right next to the Laotian border. The radio transmissions of the military movements were sent out over un-coded channels so the Commys would get the message. It was a bluff, and to some extent it worked.

Just in time came a breakthrough towards a settlement. Khrushchev became willing to entertain a neutralist solution. He didn't want a ground war in Asia, at least not one dependent on his Pathet Laotian allies. Besides, if Krushchev could prevent American military intervention in Laos through a negotiated settlement, he could always use Laos as a base of guerilla operations later against Vietnam, where Soviet eyes were genuinely focused. Besides, they could use the 'settlement' as a cover for continued aggressions. Tie goes to the Communists because they never honor their agreements, while America at least tries to.

A cease-fire agreement was reached, to the dismay of the hawks in the Pentagon who wanted victory in Laos, not a truce. By this new Geneva agreement, Laos would be 'neutralized.'

The cease-fire in Laos deteriorated, until, by the end of the Kennedy era, the neutrality was a sham favorable to the Communist cause. Of course the liberal English language histories stress only that the CIA conducted a secret war in Laos during these years, while completely omitting the Communist violations that were not even secret. The other side was blatantly violating Laotian neutrality with open armed attacks from both regular and guerilla units. The USA was trying to keep up the image of respecting the agreements while secretly assisting the conservative side through the CIA. The Communist side never had to worry about respecting treaties so they had no need to resort to covert operations.

Krushchev and Kennedy agreed to the 'neutralization and independence" of Laos, and both knew that in doing so the West was virtually conceding Communist preeminence there.

This is From the Book, *A History of Presidential Elections*

ELECTION OF 1840

History calls it the 'Log Cabin and Cider Campaign.' Historians sometimes get a little excited when they talk about it. 1840 was the first time that the race for president became big time show biz. The US presidential campaign process has been show business ever since.

The Whigs ran a blue smoke and mirrors campaign of fluff, hot air, and stage pageantry; while the Democrats ran like it was 1796.

The Whigs ran William H. Harrison, pushing the deliberate image of a man born and raised in a log cabin. In reality it was Democrat Van

Buren that had been born in a log cabin and Harrison had been born in a comfortable house. Some history books really vilify the Whigs of 1840 for doing this. It was a low trick, but I don't think it was all that low.

Billy Harrison was the first 'dark horse' to win the Presidency.

The campaign started with Clay as the Whig party favorite but Henry had too much baggage. Clay had made too many enemies along the way.

The behind the scenes party triumvirate of Horace Greeley, William Seward, and Thurlow Weed launched a 'Stop Clay' movement at the Whig Convention, which was held at Harrisburg Pennsylvania. Weed and Greeley were both newspaper editors: Greeley of the *Tribune*, Weed of the *Albany Evening Journal.* They successfully promoted the unknown Harrison instead of Clay.

To maintain max support for Harrison, the Whigs needed to appease the South and the Clay clan. So for Vice-President the Whigs chose John Tyler of Virginia.

Tyler was an ex-Democrat and an unapologetic slave-owner. He gave a conservative balance to the ticket. That lib Harrison now had a moderate wing under his Whig-wing.

The Whigs were so divided and fractioned on issues their only hope for unity was to campaign without a platform. Basically they took no stand on anything and ran Harrison the war hero on his personal appeal.

It wasn't easy for this party of merchants and wealthy landowners to claim to stand for the little man, but they pulled it off.

The Whigs mounted a vicious smear campaign against President Van Buren. They portrayed him as a rich dandy who washed his jewelry in a solid gold bathtub. It was an outrageous lie. The Whigs ran with a bunch of ridiculous exaggerations. There were posters of Van Buren in thousands of dollars worth of chic snob clothing with him saying in a caption bubble:

"Bring me my slippers Chadwick. And put ten thousand more gold dollars into the Royal Bank of England. But don't tell anyone."

Congressman Ogle (W) told the House of Representatives that he had gone from room to room at the Van Buren White House astonished with all the gaudiness:

"Everywhere was gilt eagle cornices, rosewood pianofortes, bergeres, tabourets, gilt plateaus, tambours, compotiers, silver tureens, and his toilet was sybaritic."

I don't know what at least nine of those words mean.

The Democrats hit back at Harrison; but like Dukakis in 1988, they didn't hit back soon enough or hard enough. Their mud-D slings included charges that Harrison had not performed bravely at all at the Battle of Tippecanoe in 1811. Liars. They also mocked his age, calling him 'Granny Harrison' regularly. One Democrat editor said that "Harrison burps dust and was a close friend of Christopher Columbus."

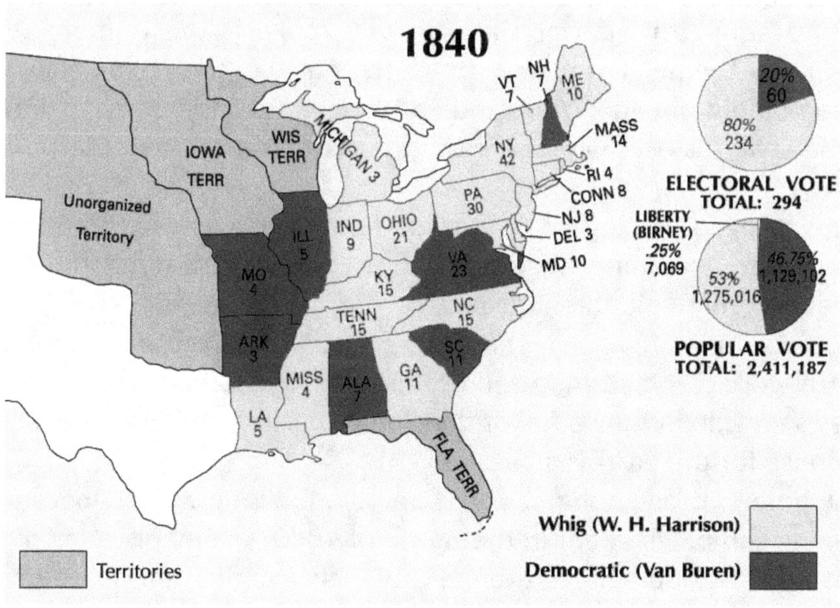

Andrew Jackson had merely opened the door to popular rule. Harrison kicked it in. That is his contribution to history, not what he did when he got to the Presidency of the United States. Whiskey and fireworks elected WHH, not policies. From the Election of 1840 on, the average American citizen would decide the elections, not the select aristocrats, even if aristocrats still were the ones who usually stood for election. The days of looking down one's political nose at the commoner were over forever.

The log cabin Whigs won both Houses of Congress in the election of 1840, as well as the throne.

How did the 1840 election campaign get to become famously known as 'Log Cabin and Cider Campaign?' I'm glad I asked. A writer for the *Baltimore American* a Clay supporter wrote disdainfully of Harrison. Give him some hard cider and put the old goat out to pasture. The exact quote was that candidate Harrison should be: *"given a barrel of hard cider and a pension of two thousand a year, and, our word for it, he will sit for the remainder of his days in a log cabin by the side of a 'sea coal' fire and study moral philosophy."*

One of the Whigs at the convention decided that it was best to take the bricks that others throw at you and build a house with it. His idea was to adopt this jab at Harrison and make it the primary Whig campaign theme. From now on, Harrison was the 'Log Cabin and Cider' candidate. The Whigs spun a story of a frontiersman of simple home-style tastes, as compared to the aristocratic snoot, Martin Van Buren.

The Whigs built log cabin parade-floats on wheels with chained raccoons (!) roaming about, and they paraded through the town squares. Whig volunteers gave away hard cider to happy voters by the thousands of gallons. They told crowds that their opponent Van Buren wore a corset and used Corinthian Oil of Cream to smell nice. They sang catchy tunes full of derision towards Van Buren and songs of praise for the earthy virtues of WHH.

One part of one song - "Van, Van, is a used up man" - became a running campaign chant in the Battle of 1840. (Many histories quote these chants and songs at length but I always find antiquated song lyrics painful to read in dry print. I mean really painful. Historians, don't ever do that.)

Historians seem to have some anger over the campaign of 1840 that I do not share. They in effect say 'shame shame' on the campaign of 1840. It was quite a long time ago, but they write emotionally of 1840. They are frowning because it was the first dirty campaign. Subconsciously I think they are just reacting more because the victim of the Log Cabin and Cider campaign was the Democratic party of Dukakis, Clinton, and Obama, the party of 90% of all history professors. If the Democrats had conducted the same low-handed deceptive campaign it would probably not give them such an emotional charge.

So the Whigs were all bark and no bite and they fooled the public. As if politics wasn't always about fighting no-holds barred. Thomas Bailey's tirade about 1840, written in 1961 is typical,

"Claptrap was king, as the electoral debauch reached an all-time intellectual low. Democracy calls for hard thinking, not hard cider. Yet an able, well-organized, and well-entrenched political party, committed to solid principles, was hooted out of office by a meaningless hoopla campaign."

Why is one as knowledgeable as Bailey so fond of the "solid principles" of the Democratic Party of 1840? It was the party of Slavery. He adds this of the Dems, "Even in defeat they were a stronger party than the Whigs." It's true, Tom. They were both solid and strong for slavery. Tom Bailey, a Stanford man is a great historian, but he has an outrageous bias in favor of the Democratic Party. The Whigs were the lesser of two evils as far as black people were concerned, but that doesn't matter to Bailey. He thinks the best team lost in 1840. He knows it.

The Whigs won by keeping it in neutral, while the Dem record killed its chances, and what's wrong with that? Rejection of the party in power is a legitimate form of political expression by the electorate. If the opposition merely has to sit and do nothing in order to see the incumbents voted out, then that is as legitimate a win as devising a complex platform to try to shake the entrenched down from their tree. So what if the Whigs built a giant log cabin in the middle of Manhattan and used it for New York State campaign headquarters? So what if the Whigs lied about Martin Van Buren perfuming his whiskers and cleaning up spilled milk with bank notes? Van Buren *was* very aristocratic.

Anyway, when all is said and done, too much credit goes to the show biz and too little to what really put Harrison in office - "it's the economy, stupid." The Panic of 1837 led to a long depression after and that's what pushed Van Buren out, not raccoons and slogans. If not for the economic hard times, Van Buren would have won anyway, and the Log Cabin and Cider campaign portraits might never have made the general history books.

It's true that Van Buren was the one born in a log cabin and Harrison certainly was one of the well to do in America. But wasn't there also some validity of the images? Van Buren was a rich and fastidious dresser. Davey Crockett said of him that when Van Buren walked into a room "I don't know if it's a diplomat or a dame." (Crockett had to make a tearful apology at a large press conference a few days later for being insensitive to transgender rights.) And Harrison had showed considerable bravery under fire at Tippecanoe. General Harrison didn't just make a few lucky decisions from the rear areas of the battlefield. A war hero *is* a man of the people. Harrison may have lived in a mansion but earned his mansion.

Harrison was also an active farmer and an experienced frontiersman. He was the rich neighbor who still got his hands dirty.

The United States in 1840 was in an economic depression, and Van Buren was caught holding the hot potato. The 1837 economic panic with a capitol P tossed that powdered Whig VB out of Washington, not campaign gimmicks by unscrupulous Whigs. A mule in a top hat could have defeated Van Buren in 1840 as long as it didn't have a D on it. Even if the Whigs had not committed campaign calumnies they still might well have won. Might've been closer but the opposition still would have probably won, regardless of its name, its platform, or its candidate. Elections are lost as surely as they are won.

The historians say that the Whigs stole the Election of 1840. Whatever. Jackson had won in 1828 because of the extension of the franchise to a lot of people with holes in their shoes, and had nothing articulate to say or read on the issues. Harrison had every right to these dumb votes too. The Whigs essentially out-Jacksoned the Jacksonians in 1840. They outflanked the Dems in the rube theatre of operations.

I say three cheers for the Whigs! And the Whigs had a better record on opposing slavery, their 'Cotton Whig' element notwithstanding.

Among the other inventions of the 1840 campaign tricksters was a giant paper ball that Whig revelers rolled from Indiana all the way to the Whig convention in Baltimore in December of 1839. It was a rolling rally. The ball was covered with Harrison propaganda. It is from this that we derive the popular slang, 'keep the ball rolling,' meaning continue foreword with something, don't let anything slow you down. (There was also a weak 1960's pop tune by that title.)

The Democrats also made their own dumb mistakes to help out the Harrison campaign. The history books often neglect to tell you that part.

Andrew Jackson blundered by giving a booster speech for his Dem pal Martin Van Buren in which he criticized the war service of Whig Harrison. AJ didn't seem to appreciate that calling attention to war records was a bad idea. Even if Jackson's criticism of Harrison's war record was on target (which it wasn't), Van Buren had no military service at all! Why spotlight that? The speech hurt the Democratic cause.

The Whigs sometimes claimed to be the real representatives of Jeffersonian democracy. By their reasoning, Andrew Jackson had betrayed Jeffersonian principles, and the Whig Party was in the contest to try and restore them. Big Whig Webster denounced the Democrats for their opposition to higher protective tariffs. The Whigs were accusing the Democrats of taking the part of the rich. The Whigs were running in essence as the true Democrats.

Some history books imply than Harrison was a man without political qualifications. How untrue. Harrison was not, like Zachary Taylor, a man with no political experience. He had been a governor and a congressman and a foreign minister. The war hero stuff was the finishing touch on a superb portfolio. Yes, the log cabin campaign was a lot of show biz, but Willy *was* a well-rounded hard-working man, an experienced political leader, and a bona fide war hero. There was something still standing after all the blue smoke had cleared.

Voter turnout in 1840 was phenomenal. One million, four hundred thousand citizens had voted in the election of 1836. 2.4 million voters turned out in 1840, an increase of 60%. That made for the highest percentage jump in voter turnout from one presidential election to the other in all of American history. What is even more noteworthy is that this giant leap was not primarily because of new rules for increased suffrage or because of population increase. The leap was primarily because a far higher proportion of eligible voters chose to show up and vote. Politics was becoming the national sport. (By the end of the century sports became the national sport. But in 1840 it was still politics.) Improvements in American education, transportation, and dedication contributed to the spike.

Harrison and Veep Tyler won the election but they couldn't carry the state of their birth. Virginia voted for Van Buren.

Because of superior campaigning, a venerable incumbent with a lifetime of distinguished service, who happened to inherit a bad economy that was not his fault, was defeated by a slick 'I'm just plain folk' sort of guy from the sticks.

Sounds like 1976 and 1992.

A distiller out of Philadelphia by the name of Charles Booze provided free whiskey in bottles shaped like log cabins. From him we get the nickname for alcoholic beverages, 'booze.' (Charlie later started a riverboat tourist agency called 'Booze Cruise.')

The Whigs ere euphoric between Election Day and Inauguration Day. Who could blame them? They had never been winners before, and now the Democratic Goliath was down and not moving. Little did they know that their choice of a virtual Democrat in the VP slot would come back to haunt them. The death of Harrison, 30 days after taking over, nullified the spectacular victory of 1840. Tyler would be expelled from the Whig party while still President and the Democrats would seem to have won the election of 1840 after all.

Long exposure to a cold rain and wind at the Inaugural may have cost Harrison his life and his presidency. But it is not 100% certain the cold weather killed him. In any case, I like to go with that. The guy should have listened to his mom who surely advised him not to go out without his warm jacket "or you'll catch pneumonia."

This is from the Book, The Stand-Up Comedy Book

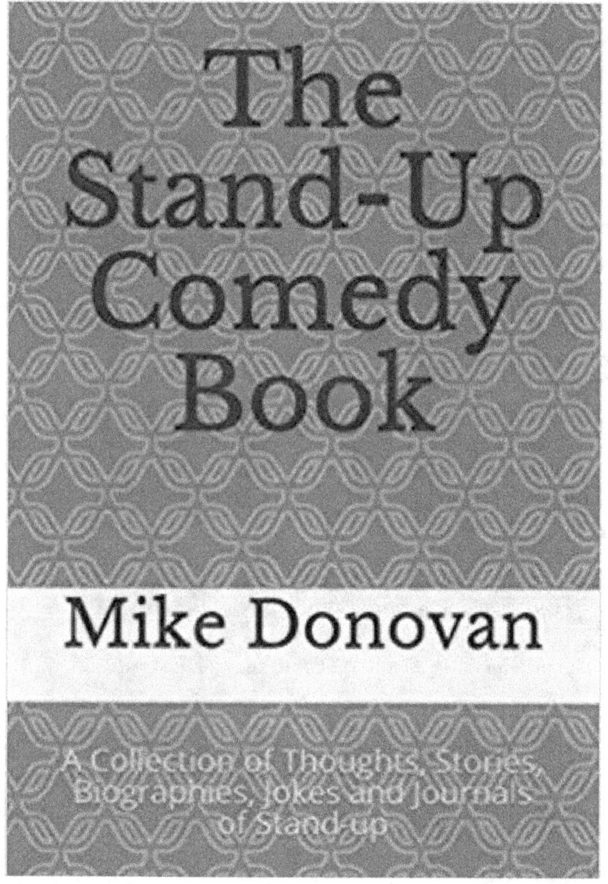

WILL ROGERS

My four favorite killer comedians of all time are/were George Carlin, Bill Cosby, Johnny Carson and Lenny Bruce.

Cosby has been kicked off Mt. Crushmore, and I have to name a fourth one, I suppose. I will not hesitate to make it Will Rogers at number 4.

The greatest comedian of all time died in a plane crash on August 15, 1935.

Will Rogers was flying shotgun with Wiley Post, one of the most famous aviators of all time, when their little plane got lost in a fog and landed in a lagoon 13 miles southwest of Point Barrow, Alaska. PBA is the most northernmost point in the United States.

"They got no income tax in Russia. That's cuz they got no income!"

Their plane made an emergency landing, due to engine trouble. It was foggy and they were a bit lost. Some Eskimos gave them directions to the little airstrip at Point Barrow. Will and Wiley thanked them and got back into action; but the plane lost power on take-off, plunged into the tundra, and killed both great men.

Wiley Post was the first person to fly around the world. The two of them loved the adventure of flying and were planning a flight across Siberia soon. The crash of August 15 ended two careers in their prime.

I get choked up thinking about this event. I love Will Rogers as if he were still alive. There is no comedian today, nor has there been one in my lifetime, whose death could really shake up a nation. This witty home-spun friendly talkin' feller was loved by millions. The death of Will Rogers upset America. What John Lennon's assassination was to my era, the death of Rogers was to the 1930's. Rogers was brilliant, real, even-handed, and very funny. He also loaned out almost all his money to plain folk friends who were hurting, and he never got paid back except in reputation.

Today's greatest comedian might meet the President at the White House Correspondents Dinner, but Will Rogers had intimate conversations with Presidents. They wanted his company, his input, and his help. No comedian today advises presidents. They just slam them or kiss up to them, depending on the party in power and the comic. Will Rogers was everybody's friend, which is what a true comedian should be, but only one, so far, has ever been that great. Will Rogers was in a class by himself.

The Comedy Central channel had a poll of the 100 greatest stand-up comedians of all time. I was surprised at how much I agreed with it, and, yes, Moms Mabley should be #3. But I knew they would make one glaring error: They wouldn't include Will Rogers.

You say he wasn't a stand-up comedian? He was. Rogers made thousands of speeches where he told sharp, relevant, insightful jokes for 5, 10 or 90 minutes. He started out in the Zigfield Follies telling jokes while spinning a lassoo. He did his comedy monologues on the radio for years and years and he spoke to countless groups live.

Rogers was also a newspaper columnist and movie star. He did so many things so well that it got lost along the way that he was doing insightful and edgy political stand-up humor while Mort Sahl and Lenny Bruce were still in diapers. Stand up didn't start in the 1950's, as the Comedy Central channel would have us believe.

Will Rogers is my idol. I read books about him when I was a teen-ager and am still star struck by his legend. He died 20 years before I was born and yet I still have trouble reading about that plane crash. I can only imagine how I would have loved him if I had lived in his time.

Will Rogers was honored with an Eskimo funeral. Three Native-Americans made it to Point Barrow to tell the tale of the crashed plane. Two white guys and 14 Eskimos went to the scene in two longboats. The plane was upside down in about three feet of water. They pulled the bodies out and placed them reverently in the longboats. The 15 miles back to Point Barrow was a solemn and still march, the natives singing the songs they traditionally sang for their own departed. I'm sure the spirits of both guests of honor would have been honored by that funeral service.

This is from the book, *Before the Presidency,* Early Bios of the Presidents of the USA

GERALD FORD

Little Jerry Ford was born on Bastille Day, July 14, 1913, in Omaha, Nebraska. He was the only president born in that boring state. But Ford is no Nebraska man. He is Mr. Michigan, perhaps the most successful man ever to come from that great state, with the possible exception of Henry Ford (no relation).

Ford is not his original name. Originally it was Cadillac. No, actually, he was born Leslie Lynch King Jr.; but his parents divorced before he was old enough to say their names. Mom rapidly moved to Grand Rapids where she wed a Mr. Ford. Gerald Ford adopted Leslie and renamed him Gerald Ford Junior. Junior liked the change. He did not want to be King.

Gerald Jr. excelled in football, baseball, and track at Grand Rapids South High School. He graduated with honors in 1931. It may be worth noting, in light of his mister nice guy image, that Ford was ejected from a South High football game for a brutal late hit on a guy long after the whistle had blown.

At the University of Michigan, Ford studied economics and politics. Ford was linebacker and center on the varsity football team, and was team MVP at center as a senior. Ford played in the East-West College All Star game, and was drafted by the Detroit Lions and the Green Bay Packers of the NFL! Some klutz. I'd like to see Chevy Chase try and get past him in a game if they were both 19. Ford would knock Chevy off his rocker.

Ford preferred law school to the gridiron, and declined the exciting football offers. I'm sure some of his friends and acquaintances told him he was crazy to turn down a chance to play in the NFL. Football meant quick glory, but short uncertain money and the risk of walking with a cane for the rest of his life. Ford knew his own mind and went for two in the bush, courageously turning down the bird in the hand. He went to Yale.

Like Bush, Bush, Taft, and Clinton, President Ford was a Yalee, class of '41.

Jerry had just begun life as an attorney in Grand Rapids when Pearl Harbor changed his plans. He enlisted in the Navy in 1942.

From June of 1943 until December 1944, Gerald Ford served on the light aircraft carrier *USS Monterey.* This ship (CVL-26) saw extensive action in the Pacific, giving air support to leapfrog operations in places like the Marianas, the Gilberts, Wake, and the Carolines. Ford was assistant navigator, athletic officer, and he commanded an anti-aircraft battery. The *Monterey* never came under Japanese attack, but Ford nearly lost his life by, of all things, slipping overboard!

All right, I fairness I should have told you that hit happened during a typhoon. This December 1943 Typhoon Cobra had sustained winds of 100 miles per hour, and sank three destroyers. The storm cost 800

Navy men their lives! Several of *Monterey*'s on-deck planes crashed into each other during the storm, igniting a major fire that severely damaged the ship.

Ford was a Lieutenant Commander when he left the Navy in 46, and remained in the reserves until 1963.

Gerald Ford won election to Congress in 1948 and was re-elected continually until 1973 when he became the Vice President.

In 1962 a non-partisan magazine named Gerald Ford the 'Congressman's Congressman.'

By 1964, there was press speculation that Ford was the logical choice for Vice President, with Republican nominee for president, Barry Goldwater.

National columnist Mary McGrory was tabbing Jerry Ford as a front-runner for president in 1968.

With the resignation of Spiro Agnew, in October of 73, the VP spot had to be filled. Nixon picked Ford. After confirmation hearings, Ford was sworn in as Vice-President in December of 1973.

Ford was 61 when he was sworn in as President in August of 1974. He was President of the USA for 895 days.

(I was kidding about Nebraska. It's the most exciting place on earth.)

This is from the book, *Diary of a Baseball Fanatic 1977*

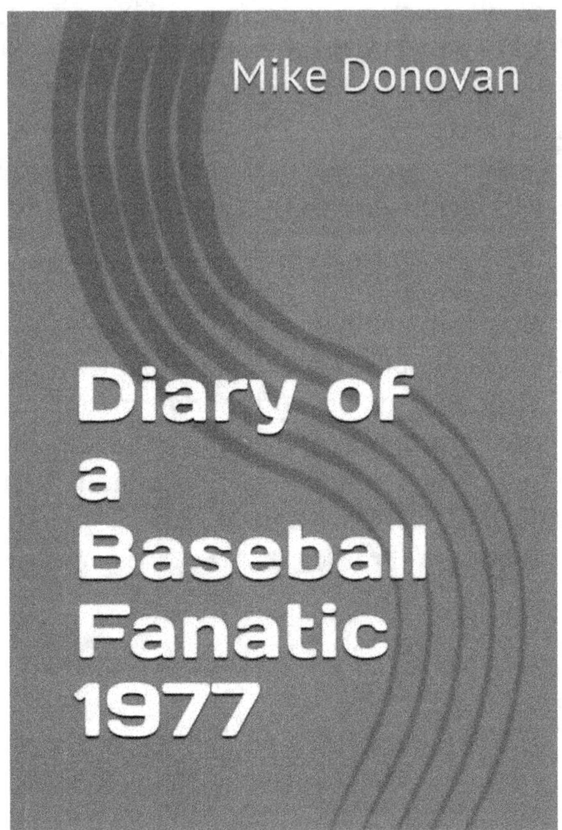

SEPTEMBER 19, 1977 [setting is Fenway Park]

Now reporter Clark Booth is back doing sports but is still doing 'on the beat' stories too, which is unusual. When he walked by I gave him a hello and his response was cursory and he averted my eyes. That's the third time I met him and the third time I got the Mr. Taciturn treatment. But it doesn't bother me, I appreciate Clarkie's work and it fit his personality to be on the run with no time for basebrains like me.

Globe writer Ray Fitzgerald followed a few minutes later. He'd met me briefly about a year ago & I didn't expect him to remember me. He didn't. Ray is more of a street guy than Booth. Fitzgerald is probably from an urban Irish neighborhood who got excited about his first big shot sweeping the floors at a newspaper at 15, and stayed with sports, his passion, for the rest of his life. Just guessing. He gave me a straight eyed hello & smile in response to my cry of "Hey Ray, what's up?"

Not much later Leigh Montville strolled by, a younger writer, moustached, also a Globetrotter. I'm one of the few people in the stands who recognize these people. Billy, who is a bona fide fanatic, had no idea who was who, even though he reads their columns at times. Daily sportswriters are basically overlooked. For years I read columns without stopping to note the name.

So I figured these guys might not mind being recognized here and there, in spite of the risk of a boring conversation with a moron fan. I wasn't going to say anything to Montville because I'm not a fan of his quote-jockey writing style. As he stepped into the aisle from the field I leaned over to Billy and told him who it was. Billy absorbed the info for a moment, gave a close thoughtful look as he passed, then shouted "Leigh Montville!" He turned and smiled politely, nodding in Billy's direction. I turned back to watch this & he took my eye. So I said, "Hey Leigh, how's it going?"

"Fine" he responded, "How's the wife & kids?" It seemed to be mocking me, as if to say, "What a game, you pretending you know me. Is that the way you want to play it, I'll expose it as a game." Maybe he was just trying to be funny but I didn't like it. I was just trying to be friendly.

It was getting close to game time and Billy and I still hadn't been booted out. What was more important, we happened to be in a section where the fill-in was generally slow. In seat hawking strategy this meant that if a ticket holding customer without an usher showed up we could slip into a couple of nearby seats without making a scene the ushers would spot. As fortune would have it the seats would be ours for two innings of the ballgame. Only in a Yankees game does a hawker concede. In other cases you just know that persistence will pay & you'll no doubt find that seat the season ticket holder didn't show up for .. provided Joe Usher isn't in a b.a. prick mood.

The electronic message board was busy as usual ith league standings, beer plugs, and the like. One message, just before game time, caused a ruffle. The Red Sox had acquired Bob Bailey on waivers from the Cincinnati Reds. My first flash was the last time I'd seen him hit. He'd fanned against Al Hrabosky in that exciting inning in May, and he'd looked slovenly doing it. Billy looked at it incredulously at first, "What?" and as he read the official proclamation a cynical defeated smile came over him. "Oh Jesus, Bob Bailey." He looked at me and I at him, our reaction the same. "Oh geez, Bob Bailey." We just kept shaking our heads and smiling the unhappy smile of a beaten fool, "How old's he, Michael, about 34?"

"At least"

"Bob Bailey" he repeated with drawling derision.

"It figures," I said, "the Yankees get Cliff Johnson and Dave Kingman … we get fucking Bob Bailey." He started chuckling and soon we both exploded in a great belly laugh.

It was a crisp, warm evening, Thurman Munson hit a solo homer into the nets which, in spite of its anti Red Sox import, was a delight to witness from such a beautiful seat. When you're that close, the crack of the bat is all there is. It's an entity not a message from a distance. It's right there in your brain.

The Sox answered in their half with 3 singles off Yankee started Ed Figueroa. The first was from Burleson leading off; the second was from Rookie Ted Cox, the rookie extending his streak to 5 hits in his first 5 at bats in the major leagues. The 3rd, the rbi single in this crucial game, came from the only man I ever idolized, Mr. Yastrzemski. For the record (and it might well be a record) Cox came up again in the 3rd and hit a spinning opposite field bloop off the end of his bat which fell to the soft turf between the onrushing Willie Randolph and the oncoming Reggie Jackson. It meant 6 for 6 in the major leagues. When Cox came to bat in the 5th the crowd showed it appreciation of the pennant race contribution with a standing ovation. Well I'll be. The kid deserved it. Naturally it went to his head. He didn't get another hit.

In the top of the 3rd something incredible happened. An usher came down with the Real McCoys and it was time to leave. What was incredible was that he was cordial, and almost nice about it. "Sorry boys," he said cheerfully. Billy and I put on our cat smiles we always wear when the jig is up. "Well" said Bill "looks like the end of the line." We agreed to split up in hopes of finding single seats, which a bushel more likely than the infinitesimal chance of finding two together. Being absorbed in this very intense game I decided not to look, for the present. Instead I went to the first base side, climbed an aisle 70% up, and sat on the cement step, pinned to the left so as to leave room for people to pass. You see, nearly every step had someone like me on it. I just picked the empty "seat." One rule about this, and 2 disadvantages: the rule is you can't sit on the steps in the lower half of the aisle. Reason: the ushers hang out at the bottom, and will not hesitate to take 2 or 3 steps up to get you out. If you're up high they'll pretend they don't see you. The two disadvantages: 1) now and then a young usher with his legs still fit & trim will climb up and scatter everyone, barking the orders like a drill sergeant, "All right, you can't sit here!" The sitters will ignore him first to test him. Now and then the weak ones will go away. "I said you can't sit here!" The rule is to wait 5 minutes and come back. Everyone does. No usher ever comes back twice in three innings. 2) The other disadvantage is that the concrete is not marble smooth and is often decorated with messy mustard packets, ice cream wrappers and abc gum.

Why not standing room? It's mobbed up there. Every friend of everyone that has anything to do with the ballclub loves to get into a Yankees game. Sitting low with the elevated patrons at my side my eyes glazed over the whole picture. The good guys vs. the bad guys. It was cold reality that the Yankees lead would still be almost insurmountable even with victory. But if they were to do it, to eliminate us, let it not be here. It would be humiliating and disgraceful for the felling blow to come here, in our living room, in defiance of our territorial rights. Sure, I'd allowed myself to think a few times that maybe it would be best if they took the two and ended it, so the end would not be slow and painful. But I wasn't thinking that way now as I bit my knuckles on pitch after pitch.

Crowds can get caught up in themselves, gloating over their power, but this was not the case. Emotion seemed to transcend the particulars. It was pride and affection. There seemed to be a credo in the air: certain things were out, like criticism of a home player or harassment of the enemy. That was behind us for today. There will always be time for that on talk shows, in bars and at future games. No, today, the crowd had a unity, a singularity of mind. Beat the Yankees.

Fisk came to bat with two on and the pitches built up to a delightful tension. Then he hit it and hit it hard. Everyone knew it would at least make the wall. I lost it in the overhanging roof from being way up in the aisle. But the crowd let out an extension of the already a roar, which told us: home run.

The scene of the celebration at home was perhaps our last moment of dignity in a humiliating season, or at least I wondered if it might be.

Even though Dave King Kong Kingman smashed the longest home run (the crowd just literally gasped as it vanished into the night sky) pinch hitting in the 8th to make it 4-3, I think most of us weren't worried. It was a feeling. It was ours. Sure enough in the last of the 8th Yaz rifled a shot into the centerfield bleachers making it 5-3. Fisk hit a triple to the deepest part of the park in right center where it's 420 feet with a 17 foot wall. Scott singled Fisk home.

After the game I went to the place where Billy said he'd parked his car and sure enough there it was, followed shortly by he. Billy never parks in the lots and gets soaked. He knows the area well enough to nail free parking spots in residential areas within 5 minutes walking distance. 30 minutes after game's end, traffic was still game related heavy. We regaled each other with comments on the victory. It was warm. The windows were open. Two very typical college girls saw our baseball hats as we sat awaiting a green light. "Who won the game?" one asked. For a Sox Yankees game, everyone wants to know. I suspected they might be interested because they were import New York students who, other than NY-Boston games which got the dormitory riled up, could care less about baseball.

"Why, who do you want to win?"

"The Yankees."

"The Yankees won 8-0."

"All right," they said, practically in unison. I'd said it pleasantly, as though I too was happy. Certainly my San Francisco, and Billy's

Cincinnati cap were ambiguous enough as indicators of our sentiments. Then the knife in a cold heartless voice:

"No, the Red Sox won 6-3." Billy and I laughed a sinister string of guffaws. Let's just say it's our way of slapping the sadists who come to the grandstands for our execution. Of course they snapped their heads away angrily, understandably stung by the subterfuge. Then Billy, who'd had a few beers at the game, shouted something I won't repeat.

"Billy what's ya say that for?"

"I dunno, I figured they deserved it."

Now a bat-man story. About an hour before the game I had gone to the underground area of concession stands, souvenir stands, and men's rooms. On the way up the ramp to daylight I was drawn to a sight at the back wall near an exit to the street. There was a kid of about 10, and he was swinging a man's baseball bat. To his left stood an angry short man. He swing a couple of times and then returned the bat to the old man. The scene was clear: little kid sees bat; finds out it belongs to player; asks for swing; gets swing, says bye. Naturally I walked up to him:

"Is that one of the player's?"

"Mickey Rivers," he answered semi-friendly. He was thin, wore thick glasses and dressed well. It appeared that he did not at all mind the indirect connection to the celebrity.

"Can I swing it?"

He was holding it with the barrel on the floor with his hand on the knob. He pushed his hand forward, directing the knob to me. I took it and took a couple of writs flicks. Man it felt light! My abbreviated preparation stage was followed with respectful quickness by two fast swings. It was absolutely incredible how light the bat felt, especially for such a large one. No wonder skinny major leaguers still hit home runs! I was so jealous: the finest wood, covered with sticky pine tar that made your grip feel oh so potent. I couldn't help but wonder how I could buy a bat like that. I hated to give it back when I did.

"How'd ya get it?"

"Oh I know Mickey" he said with calculated casual.

"Wow. Is he a nice guy?"

"Sure, he's a real nice guy."

"So how do you know him?" When you look like a typical noisy fan you can get away with considerable aplomb.

"I run a restaurant and he comes and visits me. I know all the ballplayers."

"Really? Like Who?"

"Oh I know Yastrzemski, Fisk, all of them, Pinella .."

"Is Yaz a nice guy?" I interrupted.

"Yaz is a very nice guy, sort of private. He's a family man."

"Yeah, that's what I always hear? So, you get any troublemakers?"

"Reggie Smith used to be a troublemaker. Hey, what do you want me to tell you?"

"I'm just wondering."

"No, they're all pretty much nice guys."

"You know Thurman Munson?"

"Yep, he comes down a lot?"

"Is he a nice guy too?"

"Look, you think he's a rotten guy right? He's just a competitor, just like Fisk. If he played in Boston you'd think he was terrific."

"So he's a nice guy."

"Sure he's a nice guy. Waddaya want to tell ya?"

Last week, doing that job in the department store I'd ranted to this guy about what an ass hole Thurman Munson is. He'd pressed me on my right to say that. Weakly I mentioned a couple of incidents with reporters. He pressed me on right to say it and the conversation had ended with me in the corner clinging to the belief. It has made me think. Now this old man made me think some more. A lot more. I'd be ashamed to relate that other conversation in this book because I had no right to say that.

The Yankees are the enemy still, in a sporting sense. In a personal sense they are men, men I've never met. This night may have had a profound effect on my thinking, and all thanks the Mickey Rivers' bat.

This is from the book, Beantown!, The Story of Boston, Massachusetts

A SOUTHIE IS BORN - MARCH 6, 1804

Dorchester Neck was part of Dorchester. In 1799, only 11 families lived in the place now known as South Boston. Back then it was officially titled Dorchester Neck. It was isolated from Boston by muddy flats and a shallow channel. It was a long way around by land to the thin Boston Neck.

Boston leaders began to look to Roxbury for new land to develop streets on, but some private investors looked instead across the water to Dorchester Neck.

A wealthy Tewskbury native named Joey Woodward started buying land on the Neck, and he convinced Harrison Gray Otis and three other natty investors to do the same. They bought up most of the Neck before anyone else got wise to their scoop.

Southie!

These five had clout, and they convinced the Boston government to annex Dorchester Neck and make it a part of BEANTOWN!

Dottie protested but Boston said "too bad" and renamed Dorchester Neck 'South Boston' on March 6, 1804. The property in this new place called South Boston skyrocketed. The investors quickly per$uaded Boston officials to build a bridge to Southie.

On October 5, 1805, the 1,580 foot South Boston Bridge opened up. For the first time 'Southie' (as Woodward of Tewksbury, the founding father, had nicknamed it) hooked up with downtown by foot.

A theatrical military battle was acted out for the pre-game ceremony. In victory, the Southies crossed directly into downtown Boston for the first time. When they broke the banner and stood on Dover Street, their leader shouted the immortal words: "Pissa!"

The SB Bridge did not quadruple the profits of the rich men who bought the land and pushed the bridge into being. But they made a little, and the bridge became a thing of beauty, increasing the quality of life in Boston. It offered delightful views in all directions, and became the place to walk along and show off your fancy clothes on Sundays. On summer nights, so many young couples met there - in secret and in love - that it got the nickname: 'The Bridge of Sighs.'

The old route runs close to what is now West 4th Street and West Berkeley. The Southie side was West 4th, where I once ran from the cops and the Shawmut side was Dover Street (now West Berkeley.)

This is from the book, *The Motion Pictures*

LAWRENCE OF ARABIA - 1962 - Peter O'Toole, Omar Sharif, Claude Rains, Alec Guinness, Jose Ferrer (1998 review)

Lawrence of Insomnia. That's the nickname we have for this movie in my house. Every time my wife and I watch it, we fall asleep. I don't know what it is, but if the sleeping pills won't do it, just pop this tape in and snore away.

We rented Lawrence and never finished it. Twice we tried, and fell asleep. Then we rented again and watched it in four installments; and for the first three, we fell asleep again.

This is very long, slow, and lush. I'm not saying I didn't like it; it's just that any movie with this much power over alertness can't be all good. It's a big Academy Award winner and always gets four star reviews. Not here.

It is the story of the British Arabist named T. E. Lawrence, and his assistance in inciting the Arabs (in World War One) to revolt against their Ottoman overlords, the Turks.

The history lesson that is this movie could be covered in three minutes instead of the 222 it required to tell this story. Larry's trips across the desert each take about 15 movie minutes.

The revolt in the desert was an important part of Allied strategy to win the First World War, but little of that fascinating kaleidoscope is really covered here. It's more just a hero worship deal, not my favorite thing. I'm inclined to be skeptical of super-humans. I haven't met one yet except in the movies.

The music is supposed to be an important element in the greatness of this motion picture. I disliked like the music. It's overbearing and <u>way too loud</u>. First the dialogue is so quiet you can't make it out. There is no background music and the actors virtually whisper. My bedroom TV does not have an audio remote volume control, so I have to get out of bed and turn it up so we can try and figure out what they're saying. After a bit of this, the music suddenly comes on like a foghorn for about 10 minutes. Now I have to get back up and turn it down so we don't wake the neighbors. On and on this goes.

I love history and I love Middle Eastern history, but this movie as a history lesson was a letdown. Okay, they took Aqaba. It's a good movie but way too long.

Two ** stars

This is from the Book, *The Second World War*: From Poland to Tokyo Bay [abridgement of the WWII yearbooks – 8 x 9 size coffee table book – 430,000 wds]

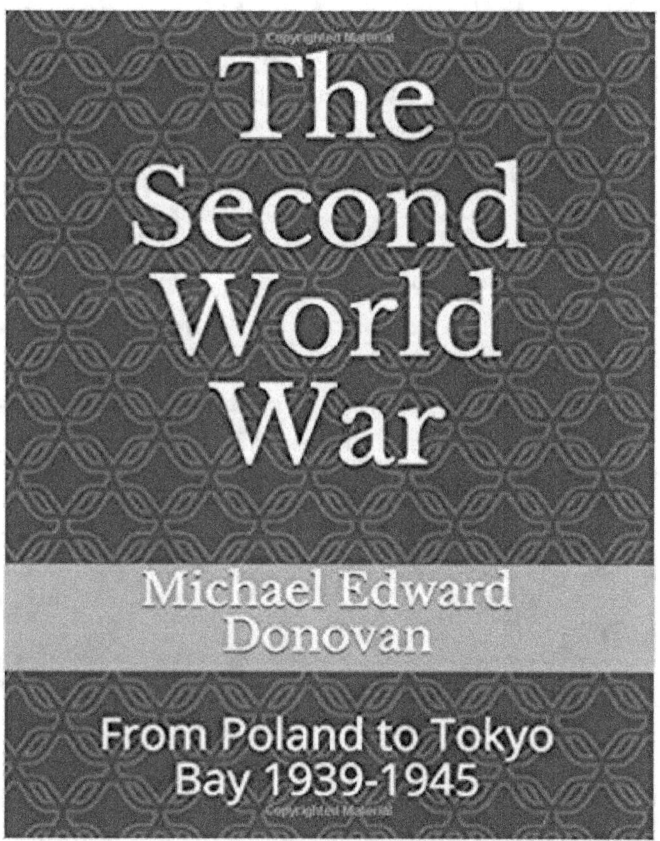

NEW GEORGIA CAMPAIGN - 1943

There were six large islands in the New Georgia group. 15,000 tough Japanese troops defended them under the command of Ishiki Iokataka and Nobumo Sasakabi (I made those names up. The real name of the commander on New Georgia was Minoru Ota.)

The main island of New Georgia ("Newgie") was located 175 northwest of Guadalcanal and 112 miles southeast of the next American objective, Bougainville. By now the U.S. Army was more involved. The Army had watched the Navy and Marines win at Guadalcanal, and now that the Marines had proven that it could be done and how to do it, the Army wanted a piece of the fighting pie. More Army units were involved in New Georgia than Marine, quite the switch from Guadalcanal where the Marooned Corps did all the fighting.

U.S. troops landed at five locations (June 30 and July 1) on or near New Georgia. The most successful and most important was the one on Rendova, because it was close to Munda airfied.

Other landings took lace at Viru and Wickham; and at Oniavisi Beach. The landing Segi Point at the Southern tip of New Georgia just across from Vangunu included the rescue of a brave Australian coastwatcher who had killed more than 100 Japanese soldiers that had tried to capture him. Don't mess with the best.

The guys hit the beach running out of their famous LCI's and LST's. They made the gallows humor joke that LST stands for Large Slow Target. (LST stands for landing ship, tank, and LCI stands for landing craft, infantry.)

The campaign for NG dragged on from mid June to mid-August before mission accomplished could be declared. The Japanese were outclassed in heavy weapons (like machine guns) but not, as usual, in tenacity. New Georgia was a ferocious fight, with the usual suicidal attacks, flame-throwers, bayonet charges, ambush fake-surrenders, sealed up caves, and the burying and burning of brave men.

The New Georgia campaign was one of the least successful strategic afforts of the USA in WWII. For the amount of effort expended, the rewards made little sense.

This was the first, last, and only true attempt at "Island-Hopping", and it left FDR, King, and Hopkins hopping mad. The failed effort to roll up the Solomons with ease led to the replacement strategic concept of "Leapfrogging." Instead of hopping from island to island, which let the Japanese slow down the Allied advance to the best of their ability; why not bypass Japanese strongholds? Let the garrisons just sit there. Let entire divisions rot while the war passes them by on the way to Tokyo. The bypassed braves would wilt on the vine, and feel utterly uselsss.

By the end of 1943 it had been tried by accident in the Alaska Theatre.

In the Aleutians, the Navy was planning on invading Attu and Kiska but had only enough material to take one. By taking the advanced one, the Navy forced the Japanese to evacuate the rear one, and so, by accident, the concept of leap-frog was born. The rear garrison's departure was excitedly noted and the lesson lit up the board.

After the really difficult fight to tame New Georgia Island, the USA decided to try the Kiska leapfrog over the big perfectly round volcanic island of Kolombangara. Leave those suicidal nuts to starve out in the hot sun while the USN express rolls towards Kavieng with an eye on the Bonins.

This is what led to the August invasion of the Island of Vella Lavella.

This is From Mike Donovan's *History of the USA 1789-1961* [coffee table sized abridgement of many books]

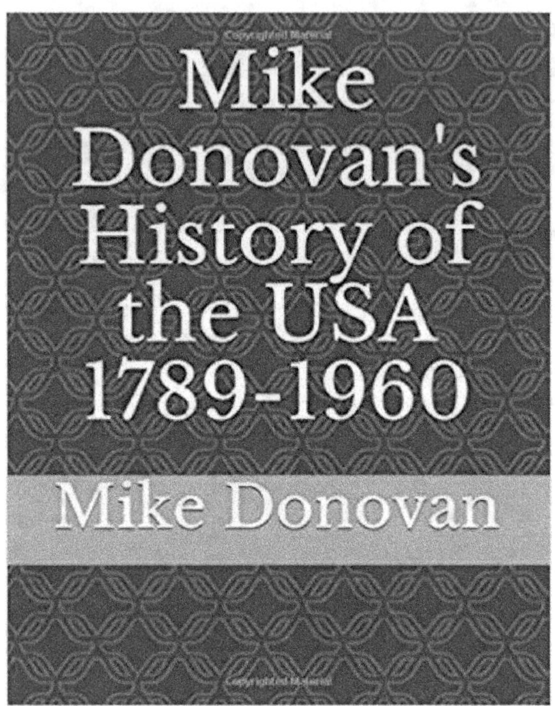

JACKSON IS AGAINST FORCED BUS

The fight over the Bank of the United States dominated Jackson's second term. He didn't want the BUS forced on him. He hated it.

The U.S. Government coined very little money and printed no paper money at all. State banks printed virtually all paper currency, and these bills were not uniform. These state notes were issued by private banks redeemable in hard coin (gold) at a later date. There was more paper out there than hard coin to back it up, but this was no cause for panic, not at the moment.

The USA had all its money locked up in the specially chartered Bank of the United States in Philadelphia (which was re-chartered in 1816 as the Second Bank of the United States.) But Andrew Jackson hated all banks, partly because he had lost a lot of money in a speculation earlier in life. He also resented the BUS location in snobby Philadelphia, not earthy Washington D.C.

Jackson was determined to put an end to the Bank of the United States, whose charter was due to expire in 1836.

Supporters of the Bank, led by its president, the wealthy Nicholas Biddle, were equally determined to keep it alive, and to humiliate Jackson in the process. In early 1832 they proposed to renew the bank's charter, years before the deadline. They thought that by forcing 'Waxaw Andy' to make a decision, they would hurt him politically in the upcoming election, either way he went. But Jackson had fought men in duels with pistols. Andrew was not afraid of political setbacks. Losing an election isn't that big of a deal when you are widower with a bullet in your torso. He would call em as he saw em.

Jackson defiantly vetoed the bill for the bank's re-charter and did it in the middle of an election year. Then he raised the stakes and began withdrawing all of the United States money from the BUS and depositing it in various state banks (or "pet banks" as they came to be called; banks that favored Jackson's Democratic Party.) Suddenly it no longer mattered whether the Bank of the United States was renewed or not, since it had no government money in it. The BUS stayed barely afloat without U.S. dollars and disappeared right on time in 1836.

Jackson's dispersal of U.S. funds into lesser banks encouraged excessive lending, created confusing and excessive paper currencies, and cost the USA some of its economic confidence. The next president would pay the price for Jackson's unsophisticated paranoia about banks.

Congress in December of 1833 officially censured President Jackson for removing the federal deposits from the Bank of the United States. It's ironic that the United States later put him on such a key piece of currency as the 20 dollar bill. Jackson did everything he could to ruin the U.S. currency system.

The AJ censure was much later rescinded by a new vote. This reversal of a solemn censure was cited in 1999 as an example of the ineffectiveness of censure. The Democrats were pleading for the censure option as the proper answer to the moral misconduct of President Clinton.

This is from the book, Mike Donovan's History of the USA 1961-2016

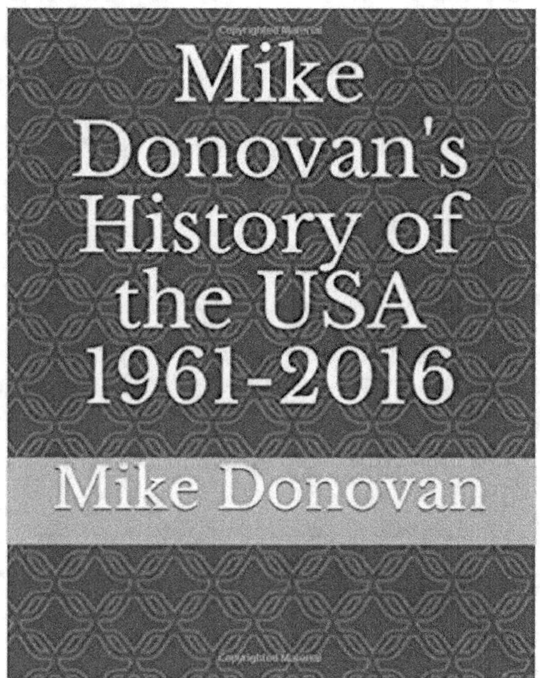

THE CHINESE EMBASSY BOMBING

On May 7, 1999, NATO jet fighters (meaning mostly US) struck the Chinese embassy in Belgrade with two deadly missiles, killing three Chinese citizens.

It was part of the ongoing Kosovo War. The United States tried to apologize for the incident, explaining that outdated computer maps were the cause. China reacted without a second thought: Total outrage and condemnation. Protests, supposedly 'unauthorized' erupted all over China. Violent demonstrations shook the streets of Shanghai, Shenyang, Guangzhou, Beijing, Buffalo, and Chengdu. One US consulate went down in flames like an open miker at a saloon gig.

An angry mob of students surrounded the American Embassy in Beijing. They were throwing rocks through the American windows for a couple of hours, but other than that, it was well-controlled. The American Ambassador feared for the safety of his family.

It is illogical to think the United States would attack like that, and deliberately damage US-Chinese relations. Why would anyone order US pilots to miss real military targets and hit the Chinese Embassy 'accidentally on purpose'? What could the United States gain from this?

There are about 70 reasons why the USA wouldn't do that. Here's reason #48 - The Pentagon isn't going to risk one of the pilots going to the press some day and saying what he had been ordered to do.

Leftywood agreed with China. Big mouth no homework movie stars charged that the air strike was deliberate.

The left critics can't, however, unite on <u>why</u> US-NATO did this bad thing. Some say it was because the embassy was being used to relay military information by radio to the enemy, while others say it was because the American military thought that Serbian villain, Slobodan Milosovich was in the building: the strike was therefore a virtual assassination attempt. It would be easier to buy their argument if they could agree on it.

One Chinese writer, in a 2005 issue of *Foreign Affairs,* says that the United States bombed the Chinese Embassy as a warning to the China to always be aware of the strength and fearlessness of US military power. That's a really stupid thing to say.

This is from *The Mike Donovan Story!* [a children's book]

"I am prepared to use deadly force if you do not obey my lawful commands." - Mike Donovan in Boston Police vehicle 1964

This is from the book, Germans of World War II

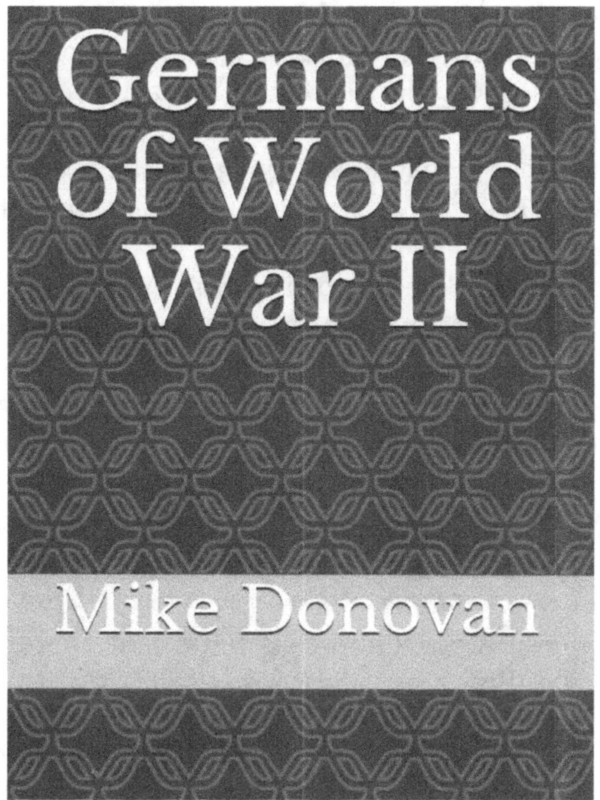

RAUBAL (1908-1931)

Geli Raubal was Hitler's niece. They had something of an affair. Then she started seeing Hitler's younger and better looking chauffeur, Emil Maurice. Hitler forbade her to see him ever again. They quarreled over this for several days. One night a gunshot rang out in Hitler's apartment. Geli Raubal, the love of his life, had committed suicide.

Hitler grieved greatly. He didn't leave his room for days. He canceled speeches. He told his intimates that he was thinking of killing himself. How could he go on? Eventually he moved on, and hooked up with Eva Braun. But he always had a soft spot for Geli Raubal.

This is the conventional version of what happened and almost all the historians buy it. I don't. Hitler shot his niece, or had one of his henchmen do it. Is there any reader out there insane enough to think he wasn't easily capable of this? The man with the worst ego in history has been confronted with a defiant response to his ultimatum. Geli has told Hitler that she can date his driver if she wants to and Hitler can't do a thing about it. She was going to humiliate him in public by dating his young chauffeur. "You are not the boss of me!" Geli allegedly shouted at one point while the maids listened near the door.

What would you expect Hitler to do in that situation?

Geli was found dead in Hitler's apartment with the door locked. No suicide note. One bullet wound to the chest. Who commits suicide by shooting themselves in the chest with a pistol? It's rare. The maids reported hearing a muffled sound, which they were not sure was a pistol shot. Sure enough, the pistol had been wrapped in cloth to muffle the sound? Who commits suicide this way: in the chest, with a heavy cloth to muffle the sound?   I'm sure there are some historians who believe that Hitler murdered Geli. I just haven't found any. A few of them mention that some people have suggested that Hitler murdered her, but they cite evidence proving this a ridiculous thought.

The Nazis manipulated the story for a decade and now the lie is part of history.

Many of the top Nazis just took it for granted that Hitler murdered Geli Raubal. They let it go and moved on, but they snickered whenever people talked about her supposed suicide. They knew the truth and they just hoped that if they ever ended up killing a prostitute or something like that, the same system would work to help them evade punishment.

Otto and Gregor Strasser believed that Hitler murdered his niece and that may be one reason the S-Brothers had to die. Greg was murdered during the Night of the Long Knives in 1934, and Otto fled to northeast Canada. Otto wrote some articles about Hitler murdering Geli. It was in the middle of the war, and no one paid much attention to the writings of an ex-Nazi hiding with the Newfies.

He spelled it all out that of course Hitler murdered her. Otto Strasser wrote to the Catholic Priest in Germany who gave the eulogy at her funeral. He wrote back to Strasser that yes, Geli had not committed suicide:

"Herr Strasser,
"People who commit suicide are not allowed to be buried in a Catholic Cemetery. That is all you need to know."
>*Father Tolenberg,*
>*Dusseldorf*

When General Paulus surrendered at Stalingrad in early 1943, Hitler screamed and shouted for two days from his Werewolf CP at Vinnista that Paulus was not a real man.

"A real man is supposed to shoot himself! Why did he allow himself to be captured alive! Paulus has betrayed me! He has betrayed himself as a soldier! He has betrayed Germany!"

During these tirades against Paulus, Hitler brought up Geli's name repeatedly:
"If this pretty delicate girl had the guts to kill herself, why can't General Paulus? A few harsh words, a petty quarrel, and she answers with the ultimate deed. This general loses the war and he dares to not shoot himself?"
This seems to support that it really was a suicide; but then he says:
"One terrible argument and she has to storm off back to the apartment and kill herself. Now my big war hero Paulus is the one acting like a woman!"
But the accounts of Geli's suicide had her arguing with Hitler *at home* until Hitler stormed off. Later that night she allegedly shot herself. Hitler drops a dishonest detail that they were out somewhere and had a quarrel, and then she stormed off, and shot herself in his apartment. But the house staff all heard them arguing inside the apartment.
I suppose it is not important that a dictator who murdered 20 million people murdered one more. But if Hitler did shoot nieces to pieces, it was once of the worst of all his crimes. He shouldn't get

away with that one. I've seen cases on the news where a serial killer is convicted of eight counts of murder, but on three counts the jury can't find enough evidence to convict. The families of those three counts are crying and upset in court, even though the maggot is going away for life either way. That's about the way I feel about Geli. If she was murdered, Hitler should be convicted of doing it, and Geli acquitted of the crime of suicide.

I charge Hitler on the dock of history with the murder of Geli Raubal.

At the very least it is unfair to Raubal's memory to call it a suicide if it even only might be true. She had the womanhood to stand up to the worst bully of all time and paid for it with her life. History has taken a brave and confident girl and turned her into a neurotic teeny-bopper who couldn't take the heat.

As for the weapon, it was Hitler's pistol. Geli Raubal committed suicide by shooting herself one time in the chest with Hitler's pistol. She made sure she muffled the noise, and did not leave a suicide note. Hitler apparently went out on the town without his pistol most of the time, even though there were always a few hundred thousand people who were out to kill him on any given day. He also left his pistol within easy access for his niece, that lady he was having red-face arguments with every day. And it was apparently lying around the place, fully loaded.

Let's face it. Geli had to die because Hitler was never going to make a real pass at her, and he wouldn't allow her to have anyone else.

This is from the book, Americans of World War II:

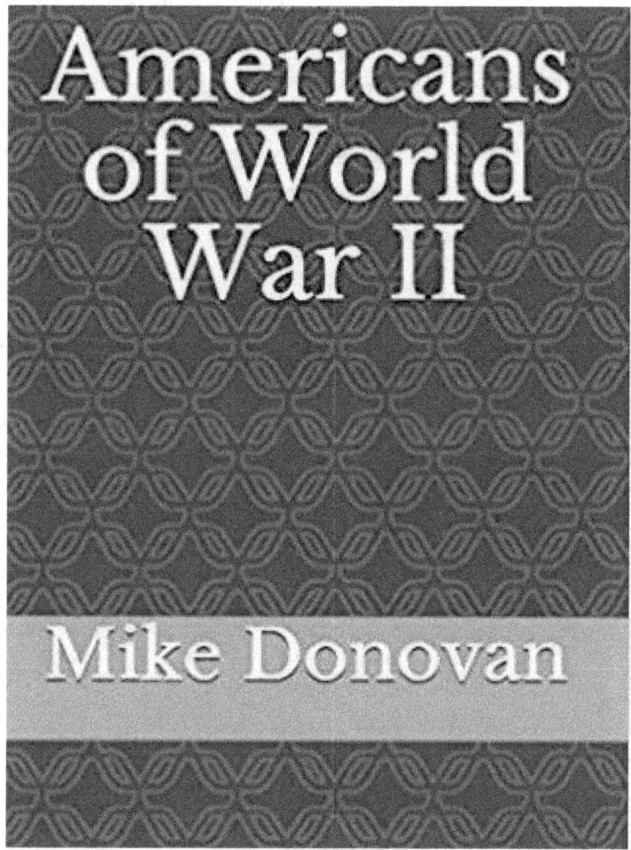

SPRUANCE (1886-1969)

Admiral Raymond A. Spruance was one of the top aircraft carrier commanders of the Pacific War. He is the hero of the Battles of Midway and the Philippine Sea. The second one involved more ships, but the first one was the more important.

In June of 1942, the Japanese tried to invade Midway Island and engage the US Navy in a decisive naval gunfight while doing it. The US sank four Japanese fleet carriers ('fleet' means a really big one that you can base an entire fleet around) and lost one fleet flattop in return. History says that at Midway, the balance of power shifted from Japan to America. I do not agree. The balance of power suddenly became even. The run of conquest was over for Japan. But that did not mean that the USA had Japan on the run and the balance of power had shifted over to the United States. Midway happened in June 1942. It took another 16 months to merely expel Japan from the Solomons and most of New Guinea. It took the USA 3 and half years to win back what Japan had run up in a five month shopping spree. Nevertheless, in stopping the Japanese pursuit of fulfilling the boundaries of the Greater East Asia Co-Prosperity Sphere (actually, they were slightly exceeding them) Midway was the greatest US naval victory ever.

Spruance was an introvert, and he didn't smoke or drink. He was modest, and did not write a war memoir. He easily could have. He said that people get the wrong impression from his serious face. "They think I'm in deep thought, but no, not really. My mind is a blank most of the time."

Anyone who can say a thing like that is all right in my book.

This is from The Sports Book

SEPTEMBER 15, 1989 - SCD

The new Sports Collectors Digest came out today. The front cover logo says "The Hobby's Oldest & Largest Publication." It is the baseball card collector's bible, the one we love to read.

They publish quite a few sportswriters. Today, they ran a "Designated Editor" piece. The guest editor was me. It is the first time I have been published as a sportswriter. I usually procrastinate forever when it comes to contacting publishers and editors, but this matter drove me to it. I was surprised and thrilled when they called me and told me they were going to run it. I was also very pleased and surprised that they didn't cut anything out, not even a phrase.

I didn't pick the headline.

It's printed on page 228.

They illustrated the piece with photos of the baseball cards of Mickey Mantle, Willie Mays, Ken Griffey Jr., Dwight Smith, and Bo Jackson.

SCD 9.15.89

Designated Editor

BEWARE THE RACIST ELEMENT

By Mike Donovan

More new books are coming out these days about the card hobby and the card collecting business. As one who has been addicted to this hobby for a year and a half, I find it fun to see that my local bookstore seems to be getting more card books every week.

Two months ago, however, I browsed through one book only to find myself sad and angry. It seems that one book that introduces newcomers to the card hobby has an entire chapter dedicated to explaining that it is important to buy white players instead of black players. The subject is given a chapter all to itself called "White or Black?" The author claims it is sad but true that the collector should be careful on this matter.

I left the bookstore outraged by this racist filth. I thought about writing a letter to the author or a letter to the SCD on this matter, but as a few days passed I calmed down hoping that no one in their right mind actually takes this idea seriously.

Today I was in a card store talking to the dealer about Brewer rookie Greg Vaughn whom the dealer knew little about. Trying to make good conversation and be a good tipster, I told him how Vaughn has hit for average and power all through the minors and how he recently hit his first major league home run and how he's going to be one of the best hot 1990 cards to look for. Over in a corner a young man interrupted in a slow serious tone, "Is he white?"

A bit thrown by having a good conversation ruined, I stammered, "Yeah, I guess so," but the young man soon was under a deserved attack. "You know," I said, "I really don't know if he's white or black. So you think at really matters, eh?"

"Of course it does," he said.

For the next 10 minutes the dealer could only stand by and watch the sparks as I began to let the man know my own feelings on this so-called trend. By the time it was over he stood accused of not only being completely wrong, but of being someone who is promoting out-and-out racism. In the end he insisted that he was right and I was wrong, yet a text of the argument would show that he had not scored a single debating point.

"Look at Gooden," he exclaimed. "He's much better than Clemens and Clemens is worth much more." Of course, if you can read statistics you know that these two are approximate equals and if you know prices you know that both of their rookie cards are in the 1984 Fleer update and both go from between 60 and 80 dollars.

"Look at Wally Joiner!" he exclaimed. "The guy's done nothing, and rookie card is worth what, eight dollars?"

"Wally Joiner is one of the most consistent hitters in baseball," I responded. "Majors - AND minors - he has consistently hit 10-30 home runs and consistently hit .300. He's never hit below .280 in his life and he's still young. His card is worth what it should be.

"The fact of the matter is," I continued. "Is that there is no truth to this whatsoever. It's a myth that someone started and now you're buying into it. It has no basis in fact. Give me a few more examples. I can completely defeat any argument you have."

"No way!"

"Oh really! Well who are the hottest cards this year? Mitchell and Bo Jackson? What color are they? And what color is the guy with the $11 Upper Deck card?"

"That doesn't prove anything."

"You're wrong," I said. "It proves plenty. You're promoting racism, do you realize that?"

"Look, I'm not saying it's right. I'm not promoting racism, I'm just saying ..."

"Of course you're promoting racism! Whether it's true or not, by <u>believing</u> this is true, you help make it so. If it isn't true, you and people like you are making it true. If it is true, you're making it even more true. If enough people start believing this, it could actually become a fact but only because people started believing it."

I eventually stormed out of the store.

It has never even entered my mind to buy white over black or black over white. I am Caucasian and so are my three friends in the cad hobby. In two years we have averaged 20 hours a week of collective phone calls and get together conversations about baseball cards. Who's hot, who's not, who to buy who to sell, who's injured, etc. Not once has the subject of white even come up. The subject has not even come up in order to dismiss it. There has never even been a moment when one of us asked, "What do you think about the white-black thing, do you think there's anything to that?" while the other replies, "No, that's not only racist, that's crazy."

Now I find this waste material in a book introducing the newcomer to the hobby and I am subjected to the same manure verbally in a card store while I'm trying to have a fun conversation about Greg Vaughn.

The book in question cites as "proof" the case of Willie Mays versus Mickey Mantle. They see Mantle worth three times as much as Mays and decide that this is proof. Proof that skin color greatly affects the value of a card and that newcomers to the hobby (like children we are trying to teach values to) should be smart enough to keep this in mind when investing their allowance money.

There is one player whose price value is affected by skin color. Jackie Robinson cards are worth <u>more</u> than they would be if he had been white. As for the case of Mantle and Mays, let's put this myth to rest once and for all.

There are four good sound logical reasons, consistent with trends in the card market, why Mantle is worth three times as much as Mays. We can all agree that as for statistics they are roughly equal, awesome ballplayers. If one had to be picked as better than the other, Mays would be the correct choice but roughly they are equals. Yet Mickey is the card collector's choice.

The first reason is a minor one but seeing how Pete Rose cards are cold, it is not inadmissible. Willie Mays was involved in a gambling situation after he retired and was barred from employment in baseball by the commissioner. Willie's actions were relatively tame and his name is cleared today but the scandal hurts to a minor extent.

The second reason is relatively minor, but counts too. Mickey Mantle hit the longest home runs. He hit them so far

(racism, page 230)

and so long that millions of kids looked up to him as a god. Willie hit his share too – Mays hit almost a hundred more home runs than Mantle. But Mantle hit them farther. And Mantle hit the longest home run ever measured in a major league game, 574 feet at Griffith Stadium in Washington, D.C. Individual feats of awe count in card value. If Clemens' rookie card is worth $80 and Gooden's is worth $75, don't you think that's because of Roger's record 20-strikeout game? After fanning 20, no baseball fan could ever look at Roger Clemens again without a sense of awe, and no fan could look at Mantle like an ordinary mortal once he laid claim to the longest home run ever hit.   Today, Bo Jackson's statistics are hardly overwhelming. But his card is on fire because Bo hits memorable home runs and makes memorable throws. He is hitting less than .260.

The last two reasons are major ones.

#3. Willie Mays left New York for more than a decade. He left in the 50's and returned in the 70's. What would happen to Mattingly's rookie card if he spent the next 12 years in San Francisco? It's a long time to project but I hope you get the basic point. New York is the hottest place a card can be. Randy Myers is worth five times more than Dan Plesac. Both are the same age and have the same careers. I really shouldn't waste time trying to convince you that New York makes a card go hot and leaving it makes it go cold. That's just common knowledge. Leaving New York hurts. Leaving anyplace hurts. Moving from team to team hurts. Card value does not live by statistics alone. Most great cards are of a player who spent his career in one place. It is important that a player be loved somewhere. Moving from team to team prevents this from happening. Al Kaline in Detroit, Yaz in Boston, Dale Murphy in Atlanta – these players are loved in these places and their card strength is based on this as much as on their stats. In the case of Mays, who has the right to call him theirs? In New York they loved him but then they knew he was no longer one of theirs. In San Francisco they loved him as best they could but they knew they had been handed something that by all rights belonged to New York. Willie Mays is not forever a New York Giant or a San Francisco Giant. Willie Mays is Willie Mays. On the other hand, Mickey Mantle is, was, and always will be Mickey Mantle of the New York Yankees.

The last reason I will put to you in questions. How long has television been around? How long has the World Series been televised nationally? Is it true that just about everyone watches the World Series, even people who don't follow baseball? Does being in the World Series help make nobodies famous and the famous even more famous? How many World Series did Willie Mays play in? Now, how many World Series did Mickey Mantle play in? Does being famous help the value of a card? Has your mother ever heard of Lonnie Smith? Has she ever heard of Bo Jackson? Which of the two has the better stats? Which of the two has a hot card? And as for stats, what famous Yankee dominates the all time slugging stats for the World Series including most total home runs? I rest my case.

The idea of buying any color skin cards over another is a disgrace. In fact, it is a whole series of disgraces. If a racial price differential exists (it does not exist), then it is a disgrace. If it did exist, it is a disgrace for anyone to "advise" another to beware of it, thus advancing the plague one more person. If this does not exist (it does not exist), then it is a disgrace that people are now spreading a filthy racist lie and believing it. If people keep believing this is so it will someday become so. Another disgrace. And the biggest disgrace of all is to think that anyone would ever put a pig theory like this in actual practice, putting a price tag on skin color. I tremble with revulsion!

What in the name of God is the image we are trying to present of ourselves to outsiders? Do we wish to alienate blacks from entering this rewarding hobby? What is a black child to think if his first lesson in card collection is "buy white?"

There is some truth to the black athletes' complaint that blacks must perform better than whites to get noticed and signed. But this situation is not prominent at the major league level and the issue here is whether skin color affects price value. Listen, this is up to us.

We determine the race factor, if any, in the card business. If we say that blacks are worth less, we are creating the very racist element we think we are merely making a note of.

End of SCD article:

This is from *The Rise and Fall of the USSR*

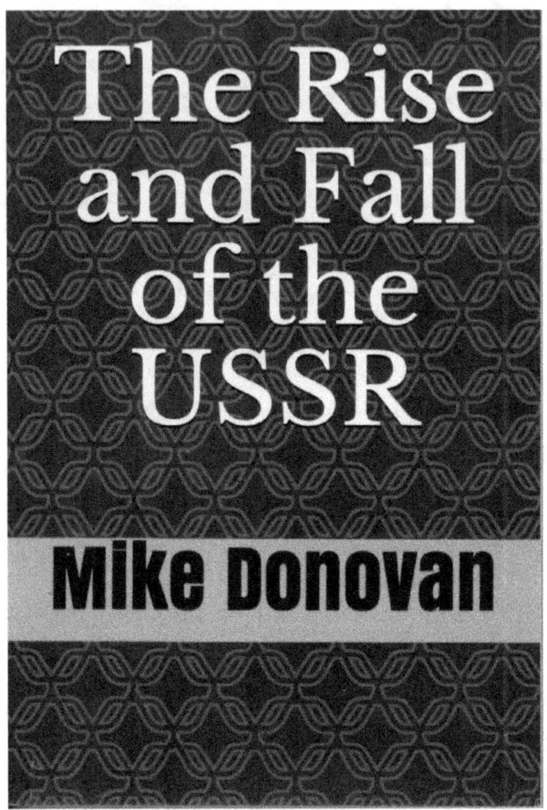

INVASION

On December 20, Soviet helicopters landed all over Afghanistan. On Christmas Eve, the invasion began.

It shocked the world. Afghanistan was now under complete Soviet occupation, not mere control or influence.

It was a very Merry Christmas for Peter the Great and Ivan the Terrible. Pan-Slavism is hereby revived!

It stunned Carter and all the peaceniks who thought that the United States was the cause of all the bad things on the planet. There was no leftist rationalization available for this one. For the first time since World War II, the Russians had invaded a country that had never been a part of the Communist bloc, and hadn't been liberated by the Red Army.

Carter, Brown, Vance, and Brzezinski had to act, but they were tied down in Iran, planning a possible military intervention there. They could hardly intervene in Afghanistan and Iran at the same time. The Russians probably factored that in when they made their move. There was a risk of nuclear war if the US responded directly in Afghanistan; and there were 4,000 US citizens in Afghanistan.

The Russian invasion put cold water on US plans against Iran. Carter wanted the world community to condemn the Russian invasion and to focus on it. If the Americans now intervened in Iran it would look like 'both sides do the same thing.' Condemning Russian military aggression in Afghanistan tied one political hand behind Sam's back in Iran.

Afghanistan, while definitely still independent, had been within the Soviet sphere of influence for some years. It was paying protection to the Mafia. The USSR took care of Afghanistan with economic aid, and Afghanistan agreed that what little foreign policy it had would be conducted favorably to Russian interests.

But Afghanistan made the mistake of thinking it could change its mind and leave the Soviet sphere of influence. You can't leave the Soviet mob (unless you're Egypt strong.)

Jimmy Carter's only answer to the Russian invasion of Afghanistan was to have the USA boycott the 1980 Summer Olympics being held in Moscow.

In fairness, the invasion did, in the big picture, turn Carter from dove to hawk. Every man has his limits, and Afghanistan, coming so close after Teheran, pushed Carter to his. He was like Gary Cooper playing the Amish man who got bullied once too often, and finally started taking bow and arrow lessons with ill intent. From now on, Carter would support increased military spending, and the modernization of strategic weapons, like the MX Missile and the B-1 bomber. If Carter had won re-election, he would have faced the world in his second administration with a much stronger military capability. But he lost, so it was Reagan who inherited and enhanced the Carter post-Afghanistan military buildup.

As for the Soviet Union, it was riding the tiger in Afghanistan. The occupation would cost Russia people 50,000 casualties. Afghanistan was Russia's Vietnam War, minus the protestors of course.

The Russians boycotted the 1984 Olympic Games in Los Angeles in retaliation for Carter's withdrawal from 80. I don't follow the Olympics so that didn't bother me a bit.

I am looking at a clip of Carter at a press conference on January 20, 1980, answering a question about the Olympics. The words if you put them in print are not particularly harsh, but to see the anger he is deliberately trying to convey in face and voice is to see the real diplomatic note. He is angry for his country and he is very stressed out. He is earning his pay. This was the cross a president has to bear. Jimmy's toothy smile of the 1976 campaign is history as he speaks in a controlled rage:

"I can't say at this moment which other nations will not go to the summer Olympics in Moscow. Ours will not go."

Many athletes and their families ripped Carter for turning the Olympics into a political tool, and costing many individuals their one chance in life for glory and achievement. They want Wheaties endorsements for their kids and Carter is ruining everything with his stupid diplomatic gestures.

The Soviet invasion was unique. It did not involve a classic across-the-border assault by several infantry divisions. Rather it was an airlift invasion centered on Kabul. The front began near the center of Afghanistan, at the airport of the capitol city, and expanded from there.

The Soviet's soon overwhelmed the militarily weak country. The occupation force started with 30,000 troops and eventually reached a peak of 100,000.

The Afghanistan resistance, the Mujahadeen, was never out of the fight. They were terrorists and saboteurs. The USA and many other countries supported them with weapons. In time, the Russians were put on the defensive.

In the immediate aftermath of the invasion, Carter felt strongly that the Soviet military occupation changed the Cold War map in

Asia to a degree that threatened the security of the USA. In addition, it was an affront to his competitive nature. They had made a big move on his watch, an 'in-your-face' invasion of a nation that had never been part of the Russian or Soviet empires. Unlike Cuba, Korea and Vietnam, this Muscovite thrust was made with Russian troops. The full Carter team agreed that the Russian military position in Afghanistan was a direct threat to Pakistan and Iran, and had ominous overtones for the historic Russian quest for access to the warm water and the oil of the Persian Gulf.

The result was a bellicose warning to the Soviet Union in Carter's State of the Union Message to Congress in January of 1980. It was the turning point of his Presidency. He became for one speech an honorary Reaganite, but don't tell him that. Had he taken this attitude much earlier, he would not have been defeated for re-election.

Here he is explaining to the world, via Congress, that he had reached his limits and was no longer going to lose sleep over the fact that the world might come to an end on his watch:

"Any attempt by any outside force to gain control of the Persian Gulf region will be regarded as an assault on the vital interests of the United States of America, and such an assault will be repelled by any means necessary, including military force."

Carter dramatically stressed the phrase "military force" and Congress erupted into an exceptionally dramatic, long, loud standing-ovation. If a Reagan had made such a statement it would have been a snore, but coming from the pacifist, the deacon, the born-again, it was a thrilling moment in American history. John the Baptist puts on his gun belt and says, "Let me at em!"

The press dubbed this new stance the "Carter Doctrine." Some said that James Earl was bluffing because the USA was not physically capable of stopping a Russian invasion of Iran. But he was not bluffing. He was openly playing with nuclear matches and giving Leonid fair warning. His 1982 Oval Office memoir has this chilling passage on the matter:

"The fact was that mine was a carefully considered statement, which would have been backed by concerted action, not necessarily confined to any small invaded area or to tactics or terrain of the Soviets choosing. We simply could not afford to let them extend their domination to adjacent areas around the Persian Gulf."

This was Kennedy's Cuban missile Crisis brinkmanship speech, but spelled out a little less bluntly. Not only was Carter declaring the Persian Gulf off limits to unfriendly powers, he was extending the forbidden zone to the 'Persian Gulf region.' This 1980 Carter Doctrine should be remembered when considering the 1990 Iraqi invasion of Kuwait and the decisions made by George H. W. Bush to reverse it. Carter had set the policy. All Presidents afterwards adhered to it faithfully.

Some of the same Congressmen, who gave Carter a standing ovation for this declared policy in January of 1980, slammed George H.W. Bush for enforcing it in January of 1991.

Cyrus Vance is clear in his memoir about the perceived Soviet menace to the Persian Gulf, a threat it is hard for Americans to imagine today in the post Cold War era:

"Afghanistan and the continuing disorder in Iran were threatening the Persian Gulf security system. There was a danger of a vacuum into which Soviet power would spread toward the Indian Ocean and the Persian Gulf."

So it was normal in 1979 to consider the Persian Gulf an area where a primary US objective was to keep the Soviets out.

This perception of the Gulf region held true throughout the Reagan years. During all this time, Iraq was a close ally of the Soviet Union. The United States tried to court Iraq during these years for two easily understandable reasons.

One: The clear enemy was Iran and Iranian fundamentalism. Iraq was the USA's accidental ally on both counts, hence the support for Iraq during its war with Iran.

America was secondly trying to wine and dine Iraq out of the Soviet orbit. Iraq was not Communist, and was not fundamentalist Islamic either. There was a perceived hope that the alliance between Iraq and the USSR might be temporary, and subject to fair competition. So the Carter, Reagan, and early Bush 1 years saw the United States "coddling Sadaam," and with troubled conscience supporting Iraq in its war with Iran.

Iraq was not merely close to the Persian Gulf, it was a Persian Gulf state. If the Soviet Union became too dominant in Iraq it could invade the Gulf using Iraq as its hit-man, with limited political responsibility.

Is it possible that this is exactly what happened in 1990?

How could Iraq, a long known close ally of the Soviet Union, a nation with 20,000 Soviet military advisors inside its armed forces, invade Kuwait in 1990 and leave no suspicion in the west that it was doing the dirty work of the USSR in its historic quest for control or at least shared control of the oil resources of the Gulf?

Simple answer: the disinformation campaign of Perestroika and Glasnost. The west was so dazzled by the political changes *within* the USSR that it became blind to the age-old ambitions of the Russia outside the USSR. Nothing had changed in the close ties between Iraq and the USSR but when Iraq invaded Kuwait no one said a word about possible Soviet complicity. If the same invasion had been launched in 1987 the Reagan team would have screamed about Soviet involvement.

It's geo-ironic that Afghanistan was far removed, across mountainous territory, from the Persian Gulf but when the Russians invaded, there was a clear and direct response by the United States. But when Iraq, an ally of the Soviet Union, actually took over the Persian Gulf, no one put two and two together and pointed to the historic national security issues dating back to the very recent Carter years when he warned the Soviets to stay out of the Persian Gulf or else. The Soviets played a double-game in the 1990-1991 Gulf War. They hoped America would not intervene, and when it did, they faked a smile and said they were glad it did.

The oil of the Persian Gulf was a prize worth the effort of a disinformation campaign. If Iraq could take over in the Gulf, and no one pointed any fingers at Moscow, they'd have pulled off one of the great coups of all time. All those decades of threats and warnings from the United States to stay out; and then Russia's closest client takes it over and the Kremlin does not get blamed a bit because of the media hysteria over Glasnost and Perestroika. Then they consolidate a new oil axis of Baghdad, Moscow, Kuwait City and command the world's economy. They wouldn't even need to control Saudi Arabia to dominate the oil market of the world. Relations between Moscow and Baghdad were anything but strained on the eve of the invasion of Kuwait in the summer of 1990.

This is from *The Ice Age to Last Week*: A History of the World

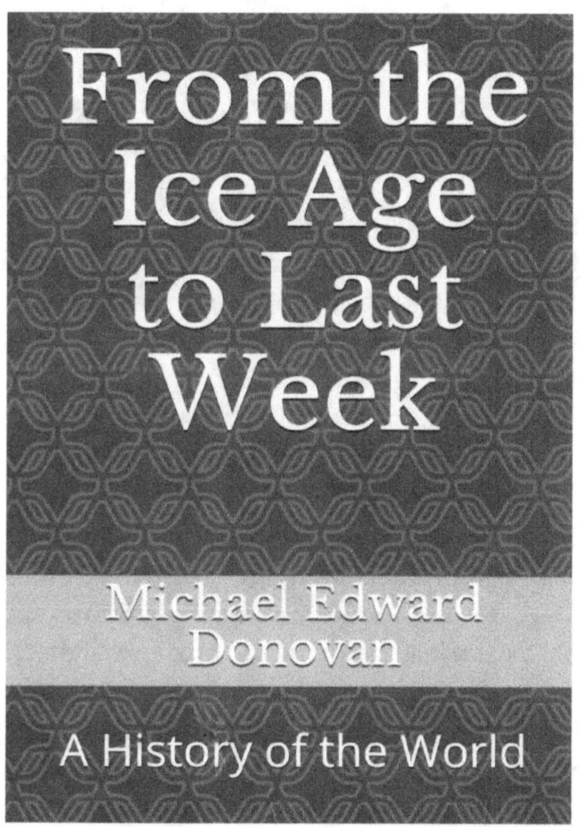

MIDDLE ACT

The Middle Kingdom, which began just before 2,000 b.c., was a time of renewed Egyptian unity dond power.

Two strong rulers, Amenemhet I, and Amenemhet III, were in charge from 2000 to 1788 b.c., and the Double-A's put Egypt back on the right track. A-3 took over in 1849 b.c.

Amenemhet built several route canals. He did not built a canal deep and great enough to allow ships to sail from the Mediterranean

Sea to the Red Sea; but he did built one that linked the Red Sea with the Nile, which meant that ships could make it in two steps from Red to the Med. Not bad, considering that the Suez Canal would not be built for another 3,500 years. Amenemhet 3 also built a canal up at the Nile's First Cataract, and took control of Nubia.

The canals helped trade and increased "revenue" (there was no money in Egypt - grain and other commodities were used for barter.) Amenemhet III said to his wife, "what should I do with all this damn revenue?" She replied that "I think you just answered your own question." And so Amenemhet III began construction of a great Nile dam over the Fayum marshlands. This increased control over flooding by creating a great man-made reservoir.

The nobles and the priests competed for power, with each other and with the Pharaohs, and by 1600 b.c. the Middle Kingdom weakened and became vulnerable.

Egypt was well protected, geographically, except for that avenue of the invaders: the Isthmus of Suez. An Egypt that was civilized yet weak was a prize and a temptation for tough nomads from Asia, great and small.

The first invaders - of far too many down the road - were the Hyksos. These easties conquered Egypt, destroyed temples and slaughtered the conquered; sometime around 1600 b.c. However, there are alternate historical opinions. Some feel that the Hyksos migrated almost peacefully into Egypt during the crumbling time of the Middle Kingdom, and when Egypt became strong again, there they were and they took over the joint. So why do Egyptian scholars tell the apocryphal story about the Hyksos doing a Nanking on half of Egypt when they probably did not do that? To save pride. It would be a humiliation to admit that a great civilization had been taken down without a fight by a bunch of wandering immigrants.

The Hyksos did not assimilate, and the Egyptians regrouped and drove the bums out (1560 b.c.) Go back where you came from, Hyksos! Egypt found strength and unity again, until about 1100 b.c. This third run was called The New Kingdom. Pharaohs of the New Kingdom ruled from Thebes.

One thing the Hyksos had going for them was the horse-drawn chariot. The Egyptians had never thought that one up, and developed their own chariot-driven army based on the hyped up

Hyksos example. Egyptians had used donkeys for their earlier chariots.

The chariot army expanded the Egyptian Empire, and it came to include foreign peoples from eastern and central Africa. Egypt learned the hard way that it is sometimes easier to conquer than to administer. The New Kingdom even extended north into Palestine and Syria.

This is from *The World War II Reader*

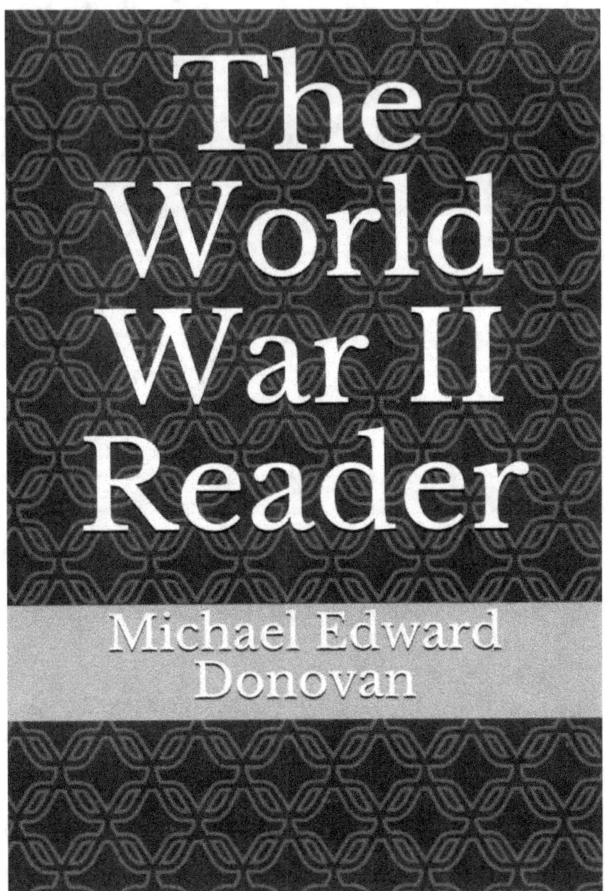

DAY OF THE JACKAL - APRIL 1943

That is the title of a 1960's movie about a fictional plot to assassinate de Gaulle in Paris. But there actually was a very real attempt to assassinate de Gaulle in 1943, and it happened in England. Who tried to kill de Gaulle at Hendon Airport? No one knows for sure. It's a mystery.

In early 1943 FDR wrote to Churchill that,

"I am fed up with de Gaulle. There is no working with him. I am absolutely convinced that he has been and is now injuring our war effort and that he is a very dangerous threat to us."

Wo! Those are strong words. "A very dangerous threat to us." Think about that. The President of the United States saying that to the leader of Great Britain. You would almost think FDR might be willing to look the other way if his own OSS under Wild Bill Donovan tried to whack de Gaulle.

De Gaulle was at Hendon Airport just north of London on April 21 1943 about to take off in a Wellington bomber for Scotland. It was 10:03 a.m. and the Wellington roared down the precariously short runway. Hendon field had no margin for error for a bomber the size of a Wellington. Only skilled pilots were even trusted to take off from there in a four-engine bomber. Peter Loat was the skilled pilot.

Loat roared down the runway when he realized something was wrong with the rear gear. He stopped the Wellington in the nick of time, avoiding a fatal smash up by
just a few feet. Only an alert and skilled pilot could have saved de Gaulle in that situation.

It turned out someone had sabotaged de Gaulle's plane. They had sprayed the steering lines with English tea (or maybe it was acid.) In any case the corrosion ate right through the lines and rendered the rear steering helpless.

When it was proven that this was an assassination attempt, the historians jumped on it and said it was obviously the work of the Nazis. But there is no record of any German secret agent activity in this part of England at this time. After the war, all German sources come up with nothing and the Germans insist they had nothing to do with it. They clearly had nothing to do with it.

So who did? Did the Allies actually try to whack de Gaulle. And they did it with enough dis-connect for plausible deniability if caught. Maybe.

Charles de Gaulle never stepped on a plane in England again, at least not for the rest of the war. He from that April 1943 day forward insisted on traveling by train.

This is from *The Korean War*

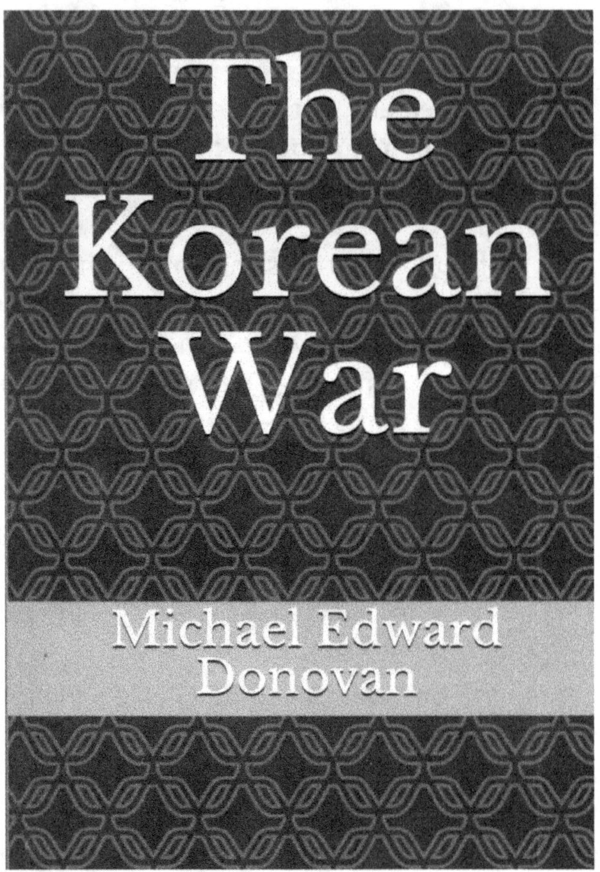

US WAR AIMS IN KOREA - JULY 1951 TO JUNE 1953

After the second communist spring offensive of 1951 stalled, the situation in Korea froze. Sort of. The Chinese (North Koreans after mid-1951 were a minority in their own divisions) launched many serious attacks against the American line in the stalemate months. The UN/US usually fell back a few miles and then gradually fought to retake lost ground. These campaigns were serious and the UN took more than 70,000 casualties in the stalemate campaign. The US/UN was capable of attacking the line too, but Mark Clark and the rest of the JCS did not feel it was worth attacking the North Korean line if their team was not planning to actually try and win the war. As long as they were being asked to fight with one hand tied behind their back and the other in a sling, it was not worth spilling any more UN/US blood for a bogus offensive operation going nowhere. When the North attacked the line, the Communist soldiers knew they could keep going if they had a breakthrough. The UN/US troops didn't have that option. They were stuck in a Vietnam Syndrome before the term was invented.

So what exactly was the UN and the US fighting for in the last two years of 70,000 stalemate casualties? The left in America today and the North Korean press in 1952 would say that this question is easy: it was to achieve global US hegemony.

Wrong, bruddah. The sole goal of the last two years of the war in Korea was the protection of 90,000 people who had never been to America. The last half of the Korean War was fought to protect the 90,000 North Korean and Chinese PW's who refused to go back to the world they had known under communism. They begged and pleaded to not go back, and asked for asylum in the countries they had fought to conquer. Thousands proclaimed that they would rather kill themselves than go back to live under communism. And they often fought to the death with these communists behind PW barracks doors.

Once the negotiations began at Panmunjom, this became the number one sticking point, the one point the communists insisted on, or else the war had to continue. If at any point in these negotiations the United States had simply said, "No problem, if that's what it takes to end this war and bring our boys back home, then these 90,000 must return to North Korea" then the war would have begun to wound down within a matter of days.

The USA fought the last part of the Korean war to protect 90,000 men it had never met before except on the battlefield. USUN took about one casualty for every enemy PW it was trying to protect.

Is there any other war in history where a country was fighting and spilling its own blood in order to protect the rights of its own enemies, its own Prisoners of War to choose where they want to llve? The testimonies of these 90,000 Asian enemies, and the lives they lived when they were finally released to freedom, are a fine salute to the US flag.

The is from *The First World War*

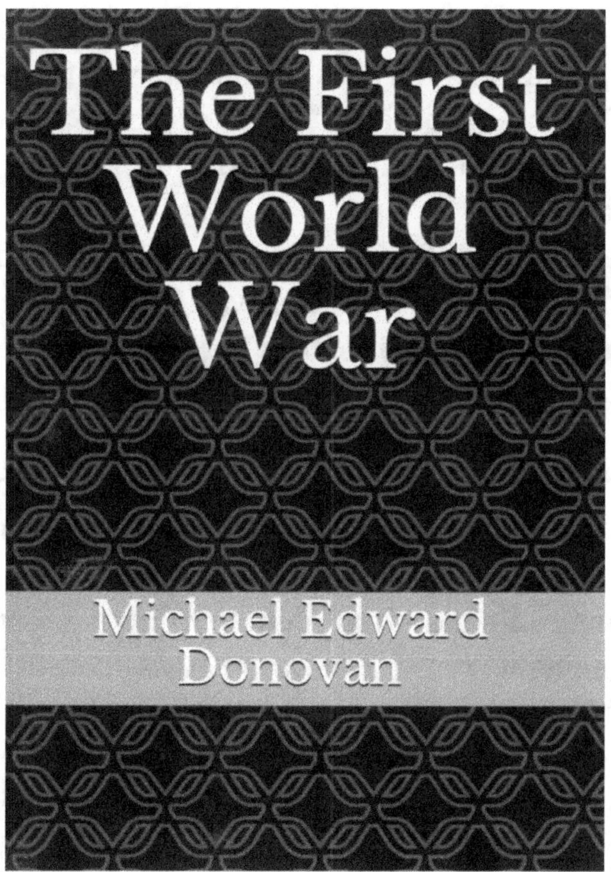

WHISKEY INFERNO - INNES & GRIEVES - APRIL 2

By the spring of 1916, German Zeppelins had bombed London several times. Way up north in Scotland very few people feared air attack, and no precautions had been imposed against such a possibility.

On the night of April 2, 1916, two Zeppelins hovered over the sky in Edinburgh. Citizens looked to the sky, speculating what it could be. They found out when German bombs began landing on the streets of Edinburgh. The German crew had to drop each bomb by hand (what a job) and they put down their full loads on a shocked city.

The Zeppelins had initially wanted to bomb some British warships in the eastern harbors, but anti-aircraft fire drove them off. So they floated away to bomb Leith and Edinburgh. Each Zeppelin carried about 20 bombs, half of them incendiaries.

Most of the bombs did relatively minor damage, but one scored a lucky hit on the booze-warehouse of Innes & Grieve. I didn't know that booze was so flammable until I read about this. I knew that it was inflammatory, but not that it was so flammable. The warehouse lit up like a Roman candle and the fire spread. Several blocks of Edinburgh were destroyed by the whiskey inferno! The whole town was lit!

At least ten people died that night and for the rest of this war and the next one, Edinburgh was careful about enforcing night blackouts, and mandating child evacuations.

Tragically, Innes and Grieve had insurance for everything except air raids. This was a new thing and no one had insurance against air raids. The insurance companies refused to pay off. The employees didn't even have enough whiskey left to drown their sorrows.

At least two web sites list the death toll in Edinburgh on 4.2.16 1916 at 1,262 killed, but I'm pretty sure that's the death toll for all the Zeppelin raids on the UK in WWI.

This is from *Journals to 1978*

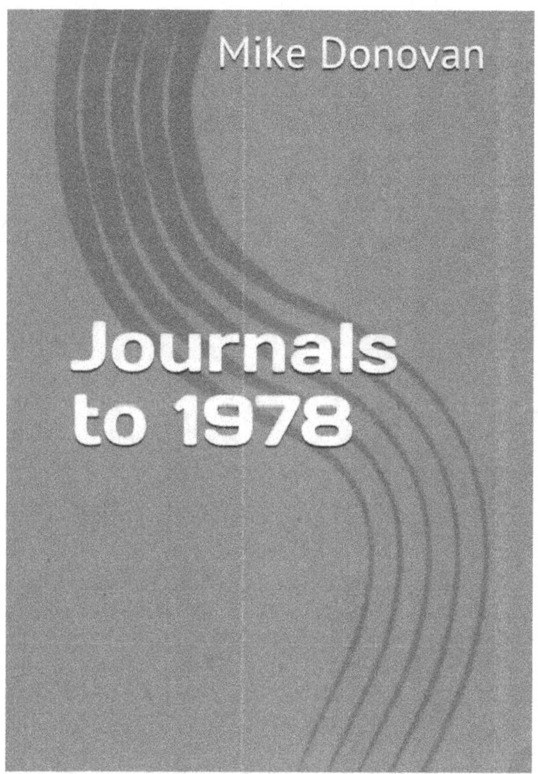

July 26/27 1978 Wed/Thurs exactly 300 am / Just in from Andrew Square Ho Jo's. And to think I almost didn't go tonight.

I had a chance to meet one of the most fascinating, most incredible, the most highly energized, naturally funny, extroverted people in my entire life, Lenny Clark. He is undoubtedly going to be famous some day. Undoubtedly. I know it. Lenny Clark is going to be famous some day.

I had no idea he would be funny. I only knew him as the guy who gave me a compliment of the night not too long ago. A man who seemed like Paul (Hey what's up) and I did not expect to be nearly (ha!) as funny as he was. If anything he seemed insecure.

Watching him d standup tonight was a joy. He was rough at times but his attitude, his spontaneity. The Comedy Connection is actually loaded with brilliant talented comedians. It is awesome how many Bostonians will be famous someday. Morey was great ... Well let's review.

This is from Journals of 1979

February 5, 1979 442 am/ The cure for inertia is 13 hours sleep and Bic Clics suck. Just lit my last Gold Label "oh yes". Yesterday was Sunday, the day before that, Saturday, & Friday before that.

Friday I was broke & decided to stay home & work. But the mind knew it could not sit for so long. I went to Billy Stewart's and went to the Rat with him & John. Largest event was the star tripper. Took a cold walk around Fenway, & while I was at it, stopped in and hung out at King's Row for all of five minutes. Had small conversation with handsome Dunkin Donuts worker & talked comedy without spilling the beans about myself; felt good.

Saturday, which was, well, almost yesterday, was a strange one. My mind awoke before my body got me up at 9 o'clock after sleeping at 3. At 11 am I took a nap for just a couple of hours, my mind felt eager to work, but a little stale. I'd planned on working hard on new material for FOYBL set.

I awoke at the absurd hour of 615. Sue called as designated, shortly thereafter & I had to have her meet me at the club cause my hair was filthy and I had no time.

It was a wonderful night at the club. It will easily go into my all time top 10 shows, possibly top 3! Some super ad libs. Especially important because they were not at all self conscious & were not designed to work, I was just being cocky and carefree, as I've been striving to be. It's been a major change of late. I just got fed up with being intimidated.

"That was a lot of work for a shitty laugh."

"Then it was the Popes funeral." Winged it into facial and body mannerisms that got not only laughs, but swelled into inklings of applause!

Even deadpan mentioning of Cubs and Expos got laughs, & by the time I got to Harry I had them eating parakeet seed out of my hand!

The Job Application took on dimensions of power I'd never known existed within it! There were extras too, I just threw in, not worrying about the risk, & they got big laughs. "Ever been convicted of a crime – yes, I murdered my fellow employees." The line was supposed to be family but the magic took over, and it compelled me to say "I murdered my interviewer" laugh "Okay, you're hired, no problem." Laugh. Laughs are coming out of the walls.

It's obvious that I should script up handwriting & tomorrow. There were some good laughs though. I think I just wanted to establish my beachhead on the subject before another comic does and makes me feel uneasy about breaking it out. Ditto on future unveilings like Lost in Space & Family Affair.

One other glorious ad lib got an 8 laugh.

'No really you have to be a little irritated to be a comedian.' (woman in audience makes comment, unintelligible but audible – to her partner, not to me, but unusually loud) 'like I'm irritated with you.' Ha ha snap body.

It was that kind of night. The plaudits I had after, I anticipated. As opposed to a lot of "very good" or "hey I liked your act" it was a lot of grinning "excellents".

Sue was with me and it was nice. We got high with Jim Morris, or me and Jim did with Sharon also getting a hit. They all know Sue now. It makes me a little self-conscious, I mean I hope they like her.

Sharon and Nancy had the car pinned in. Nancy had made an idiot pitch about how I was so young, & Sue & Jim & I played pinball at the H-Deli. To Sunnyhurst for Gold Seals and a fun ride up & back.

Sunday I got up early again, 9 o'clock. I read a little and wrote a solid page on October 2. Then it all started to creep in. 250 budget. Still early. Movie tonight Park. Doesn't start till 7. [illegible wd] just short on dough. But I don't feel like writing or reading all of a sudden. Sleep yes. Patrick plays piano, dogs and planes and noisy children. On and on. I know it's time to get out of the house. What about Connection? What if Mary Ann's there? My hair is dirty & I've got a new pimple I hate. I've got a slight knawing toothache. Inertia faded into negative inertia, a radiant negative inertia. Finally I slept 13 hours with some vy bizarre dreams including a fight with Hoolie & a dream of an island and a journey and cliffs & rocks.

Thank GOD it's Monday. Only Sunday can do that to me. I've still got 250. Actually I have tentative plans to go to Matt Talbott's tonight to see how comedy night is going. It was in the Phoenix.

This is from Journals of the 1980's

New Year's Day Sunday 2:16 pm 1984 Brigham's Brighton/ One more trip around the sun. Worked at Charles last night for first show only. A bitter post Christmas decision. Also took work on my birthday. I'm staying straight today. And in the long run I intend to make some money. Staying straight. It's going to be fun. Key. When you get upset, go <u>read</u> something grim. Don't go get high. Hey, you're not quitting forever, just 31 days. Key. The seasons to make the Park or Cranberry League are getting shorter.

The most significant thing I accomplished in 1983 was an understanding of Russian History from ancient times to 1700. This year I must make it from 1700 to 1920. It is a big order, and mostly because there are so many other great books to read and I buy more and more. It's <u>so</u> <u>hard</u> to stick with one topic. By normal inclination I'd read Russian History 2 or 3 times a month, 10 hrs a month. As it stands I seriously must have averaged 1 1/2 hours a day or about 500 hours of Russian History study this year. I'd like to double that in 84 and go for a thousand. I might have to be straight a bit.

Betamax, twin cassette deck & new hockey skates can only make the problem of time more difficult. But it's hard to regret such problems. I might even try some skating today! At the very least, I'll try some righty tossing.

It's going to be fun to read "Paths That Led to War" again. Going to be fun to see my bank account reflecting my sobriety.

New Year's Eve party at Christen's last night.

Free Lance sample from Boston Herald – November 2000

Electoral College still works

It may happen for the first time since Benjamin Harrison. They're still counting the votes.

The person who loses the popular vote may win the presidency of the United States.

There will be a hue and cry for the abolition of the Electoral College.

We're hearing it already.

AS YOU WERE SAYING . . .
Michael Donovan

It's stupid and outdated!

It's unfair!

It's undemocratic!

Well, it may be argued that it is all of those things, but it still an exceedingly wise part of the Constitution as drafted by the Founders.

When the Founding Fathers gathered in Philadelphia in the summer of 1787 there arose a great controversy as to the representation of the people in the new government. The smaller states demanded an equal vote with larger states. The larger states (in population) demanded an overwhelming vote relative to their overwhelming population.

This was the greatest issue dividing the nation makers.

The compromise was reached with the upper chamber, the Senate, giving all states large and small two votes each, while the lower chamber, the House, gave each state a voting block proportionate to its population. The Electoral College is a reflection of this Great Compromise. To abandon the Electoral College is to abandon the compromise.

The Electoral College gives small states more clout. Many of these states, although small in population, are great in size and importance. Alaska, for example, is a small state. But it is also a great treasure chest of natural resources.

Without this system, the larger states and their local issues would be disproportionately catered to and the smaller states would find their concerns disproportionately ignored.

Why should a presidential candidate fight for votes in Alaska or Wyoming when he could just roll up the Northeast and win it with the popular vote alone?

The Electoral College creates respect for our original concept of federalism — it really is the United *States* of America. Unlike other nations, which are merely divided into large governing districts, our states have considerable autonomy and in some matters independence. The Electoral College represents this directly. We hold 50 separate state elections for president and pool the results.

James Madison, the father of our Constitution, was a political wizard. Few people have ever lived who had studied world government as much or as well. The other 54 men who helped shape the document included brilliant political minds like Ben Franklin and Alexander Hamilton. I would personally stack up their knowledge of government organization and its fairness against any ranting radio talk show host shouting that the Electoral College is an unfair joke. They had considerable time during the long American Revolution to study the issues of fair government and then had more time to see the need for it under the ineffective Articles of Confederation.

Their plan for the Electoral College was a wise one. The farmer in a small state feeds thousands of people. Just because his state is not populous does not mean that it is not important.

If the Electoral College is unfair then so is every decision arrived at in the U.S. Senate — a body in no way representative of the population or of the popular vote.

But I have yet to hear a single man-in-the-street interviewee or television analyst suggest that our Senate is a farce or an anachronism.

We are not a pure democracy. We are a constitutional republic which every four years holds a presidential election.

And every four years we prove the Electoral College is worth keeping.

Michael Donovan lives in Brookline. As You Were Saying is a regular feature of the Boston Herald. We invite our readers to contribute pieces of no more than 600 words. Mail contributions to the Boston Herald, P.O. Box 2096, Boston, MA 02106-2096, fax them to 617-542-1315 or e-mail to oped-@bostonherald.com. All submissions are subject to editing and become the property of the Boston Herald.

[I'm not sure I agree with it anymore!

BOOKS IN PROGRESS OR COMING SOON

Who's Who in My Life: A-Z
Noise Pollution
Quotations
Cops and Robbers
Music
Southie
TV
My Stand-Up Comedy Act: Word for Word
The Lessons of Cleveland
Stories of World History
Stories of World War II
101 Stories of American History: Volume II
Who's Who in Russian History
Who's Who in World War One
The Governors of Massachusetts
Greenland in the World Wars
Lenny Bruce
The Battles of Labor U.S.A.
The Vocabulary Story
A Short Biography of Paul Reynaud
Correspondence
Jokes and Gags
Photography
Radio
Stories of Ghosts UFO's and Reincarnation
How to Play Craps and Bet Sports Futures
A Short History of the America's Cup
Caption This
Disaster!
Wars of the World
A History of Canada

For Queenie

www.ingramcontent.com/pod-product-compliance
Lightning Source LLC
Chambersburg PA
CBHW070649250726
48662CB00001B/34